THE TOP 20%:

WHY 80% OF SMALL BUSINESSES FAIL
AT SALES & MARKETING
AND HOW YOU CAN SUCCEED.

D0887068

From the author of THE SUCCESSFUL SALES MANAGER

Lawyers

Accountants

Doctors

Dentists

Real Estate
& Insurance
Agents

Business
Owners

Salespeople

Technicians

Developers

Craftsmen

and more...

THE TOP
20%

in the Modern Digital Age

Why 80% of small businesses
fail at SALES AND MARKETING
and how you can succeed.

DUSTIN W. RUGE

THUNDERBIRD

PUBLISHING

The Top 20%: Why 80% of Small Businesses Fail at Sales & Marketing and How You Can Succeed.

ISBN: 978-0-9905046-4-1 (Paperback)
ISBN: 978-0-9905046-5-8 (E-book)

Library of Congress Control Number: 2015951521

Printed in the United States of America

Copyeditor: Courtney Wilhelm Vincento

Cover Design and Interior Formatting:
OneVoiceCan.com

The Successful Sales Manager:
Scottsdale, Arizona

PRAISE

• • •

As a founding partner of ClearChoice Dental Implant Centers, America's largest provider of Dental Implant treatment and the founder of the first LASIK Centers in all North America, it's amazing to find someone like Dustin that has such an understanding of professional advertising. Having been successful in the professional marketing and advertising business for more than 25 years, it was refreshing to read this book and still learn so many new ideas that you can immediately and cost effectively implement to grow your business. Hats off to Dustin!

— Larry Deutsch, Founder and President, Patient Marketing Specialists

Anyone who's ever wanted to become a top-notch small business owner can confidently benefit from the down-to-earth knowledge in this book.

— Michael LeBoeuf, Best-Selling Author of *How to Win Customers and Keep Them for Life*

Dustin has a unique insider's view of sales and service. In this business climate it comes down to clients perception and ultimately how they feel about their transactions. Service is everything and certainly the key to good business. Dustin's understanding and how he teaches us how to perform better will significantly help you increase your bottom line. A must read!

— Harlan Schillinger, VP & Director of Marketing, Network Affiliates Inc.

"Outstanding! A must-read for anyone who wants a successful career as a business professional."

— Christopher Levinson, Administrator Of Vititoe Law Group/Consumer Advocate.

"The Top 20% cuts straight to the heart of sales and marketing for attorneys and every other professional service provider. I've personally trained over 15,000 attorneys and I've never read a book that so concisely captures in a step-by-step manner precisely what a professional service provider needs to do to market and double their revenues! The straightforward and practical tips in chapter 5 on closing the sale is easily worth hundreds of thousands in new revenue to any lawyer or professional who applies them. This book is going on my 'must read list' for all my new clients!"

— Stephen Fairley, CEO, The Rainmaker Institute

"*Seldom does anyone capture the essential facets of entrepreneurial success! The 80% can gain the knowledge to launch their dream...and the 20% can use this book to excel!*"

— Mark T. Wehner, CEO/Founder, REEsults Coaching

TABLE OF CONTENTS

• • •

Chapter 5
Closing the Sale: Where It All Pays You 177

Chapter 6
Marketing Success: How to Make It Rain 209

FOREWORD

• • •

When I was a young child I had a tendency to dream big and loved to compete and win—which ultimately led me into sales. I have now been in sales and sales management for most of my professional life as both an employee and a business owner. My work has led me down roads I never would have dreamed of at the beginning of my career. As a result, I have become a frequent speaker at professional conferences across the nation, became an author of a bestselling book on sales management, and have worked with people whose lives are better both personally and professionally as a result of our work.

Over the past seven years, I have been working almost exclusively with and speaking throughout the nation to professionals in helping them to improve their sales and marketing skills. In my experience I have found that of all of the industries I have worked with over the past few decades, none were more in need of help in their sales and marketing efforts than professionals and small-business people.

I will never forget one of my first experiences in working with an attorney who many attorneys in the same city considered to be one of "the best" in his field. Upon meeting him, I could immediately tell he was professional in appearance, articulate, and highly accredited in his legal work—as witnessed by his landmark case wins and the many accolades and awards that adorned his walls.

What stood out the most to me with this attorney was what he was lacking the most; namely, clients and cases. How could somebody who has so mastered his profession, who has successfully helped so many clients, be in such need of new business to support his practice?

What made this even more perplexing was another attorney I worked with in the same city who had the exact opposite situation. This other attorney had never stepped foot in a courtroom, and as best as I could tell, had never written a pleading in his entire career. Yet he was one of the top business generators for his area of law with one of the highest case value averages in one of the largest cities in the United States—which is no small feat by any means. Moreover, his credentials and experience couldn't hold a candle to most other attorneys—including the aforementioned attorney who is now in need of business.

So how is it that these two professionals of such dramatically different backgrounds, experience, and credentials could be producing such diametrically different business results? Moreover, are consumers and the market best served when access to and awareness of the best professionals are commonly limited to how good the professional is at selling and marketing him or herself compared to others? What makes this story even more troubling is that it is commonly seen in nearly all professions—not just in law.

This need is what compelled me to focus my work on closing this sales and marketing gap for ALL professionals, so that in the end each professional will be far more heavily judged by their professional value than their ability to sell and market it. For most professionals this work is only beginning, and the gap is still wide, so there is a great deal of work still to be done.

This book is dedicated to every professional whose goal is to not only survive but thrive and find the highest levels of success in both their practice as well as their business to support it. Welcome to your journey to becoming part of the top 20 percent.

INTRODUCTION: CONGRATULATIONS, YOU ARE NOW A PROFESSIONAL

. . .

Congratulations, you have decided to become a professional and/or a small-business owner! You are now one of millions of other professionals who call themselves lawyers, doctors, dentists, developers, therapists, counselors, accountants, plumbers, technicians, salespeople, business owners, insurance agents, real estate agents, etc., and have decided to specialize in what they provide.

Many choose to become professionals to master their trades, provide superior levels of services, produce the highest level of results, and live a better life. Some professionals decide to offer their trade through other businesses while many decide to follow their dreams and go out on their own. What most of these options have in common is the need for professionals to sell and market their services and themselves to others. The problem for most professionals is that, despite their expertise, the vast majority (nearly 80 percent of new entrepreneurs) will fail to succeed in as little as eighteen months.[1]

Why?

Most professionals today learn to master their trade yet fail in the ability to successfully sell and market themselves and their services to others. Without awareness, without effective marketing, and without sales of your services, no matter how masterful you can perform it compared to others, you are doomed to fail. Remember: Your profession and success is YOUR business, no matter who you work for, whether that be yourself or an employer.

Additionally, don't think that just because you may work as a professional in a business run by others it eliminates the need for you to master your own sales and marketing skills; the reality is quite the opposite. For example, the quickest way to become a partner in a law firm is to not only be a competent attorney but to bring in a lot of new clients and cases; the more you bring into the firm relative to other attorneys, the more valuable you become. The opposite is also true—for this rainmaking value or the lack thereof not only helps to chart your value and trajectory in a larger organization but also expands or limits your options to take your skills elsewhere if so desired. In short, it is a simple concept of supply and demand. **Good sales and marketing professionals are in short supply and high demand and therefore are commonly able to command better jobs, better pay, faster promotions, and more options in their career.**

This brings us to those professionals who are successful and are part of the top 20 percent who survive and thrive. How have these professionals become both experts in their field and successfully sell and market their services at the same time? How have they mastered the art of balance and discipline between both their business and professional activities by growing their business by better selling and marketing their services to others? These are the top 20 percent of professionals who have succeeded and made it, and this book is dedicated to helping you do the same.

UNDERSTANDING PARETO'S LAW

Many professionals will take pause when told that their dream of succeeding as a professional is against the odds. This is where the initial excitement people feel of becoming something special becomes very concerning, statistical, and real. Despite the odds, the top 20 percent will still find a way to pull it off and succeed. Ironically this imbalance of success permeates nearly every practical aspect of our professional business lives and was initially introduced to us in theory over a century ago.

In 1906, an Italian economist named Vilfredo Pareto made an observation that 80 percent of the land in Italy was owned by only 20 percent of the population. This imbalance of distribution was later applied to many aspects of our lives and business and become known as Pareto's Law.[2] In many businesses today, we commonly see Pareto's Law in practice when 80 percent of a business can come from only 20 percent of customers, when 20 percent of businesses account for 80 percent of an industry's revenues, and when 80 percent of professionals will eventually fail while only 20 percent will thrive.

In a professional's world, the imbalance can run even deeper. For example, it is not uncommon for failing professionals to be receiving 80 of their revenues from only 20 percent of their customers. What potentially happens to your business if you are so heavily reliant on so few customers to produce so much income for your business? What happens if they leave your business? Smart investment managers would never tell you to put all your investment eggs in one basket, so why would you do the same thing with your business?

It is also not uncommon to see a professional spending 80 percent of their time working *in* their business while spending only 20 percent of their time working *on* their business. The biggest mistake most professionals make is failing to understand that going out on your own is, in effect, creating two or more jobs from the one you just left. If you are skilled at your trade and feel you can practice more effectively on your own, how skilled are you at also running a business and working for yourself as a result? Since most professionals lack the skills to run a business, they end up being consumed and prioritized by what they know the best (their trade) while strategically ignoring the most important aspect of their survival: running and growing their own business.

Finally, it is also not uncommon to see failing professionals who will only allocate 20 percent of their time and resources to customers who can help generate 80 percent more customers for their business, and instead will focus 80 percent of their time and resources trying to help bad customers who will only ever account for 20 percent of the revenues for their business. Instead of these failing professionals being in control of their businesses, they let their bad customers take control of it for them.

The examples of imbalance are many and the previous examples are only a few. You can certainly dig deep into any business and find more imbalances in nearly every aspect of a professional's business. Ironically all of these lead to the ultimate imbalance of them all: an 80 percent small-business failure rate.

THE PROFESSIONAL'S DREAM BECOMES REALITY: THE PROFESSIONAL MEETS THE BUSINESSMAN

The various business professions today are numerous and unique, but the stories are nearly all the same: "I have mastered a skill and now want to provide it to the world." Nothing is more exciting than the thought of going out on your own and making it big. It is the American dream and the foundation of a free-market economy.

It is also the natural foundation for innovation. It is a well-known fact that the larger an organization, the poorer the foundation for innovation and vice versa. There are many differences between large and small organizations, but the chasms between the two are commonly defined best through the lenses of innovation and agility. But don't just take my word for it. Let history speak for itself: Since the Fortune 500 was established in 1955, only 13 percent of the original designees remain.

Why?

Why is it that what typically leads larger organizations to initially become effective ultimately ends up becoming the source of their own demise? Steve Jobs said it best when he stated that, "The [big] company does a great job, innovates, and becomes a monopoly or close to it in some field, and then the quality of the product becomes less important." In business the number one ingredient to quality is consistency. So when quality fails, service is diminished, and all you are left to compete with is on price.

As a professional, you need to be aware of this dilemma and use it to your advantage. The source of this problem for larger organizations is largely systemic in making. Large organizations drive earnings through increased sales and cost controls. **In most organizations today, it is far easier to control costs than it is to innovate and grow to achieve a bottom-line result.** These short-term cost solutions are often led by accountants who create a short-term financial win often at the expense of long-term innovation and growth.

So therein lies the quintessential paradox of large organizations: Most continue to drive the short-term profitability for their shareholders at the expense of their long-term viability and growth. This problem is fundamentally no different than politicians who promise unsustainable future government funding, pensions, and benefits to their supporters for their own personal short-term gains while kicking the liability can down the road for somebody else to deal with. This is far easier for politicians since governments rarely fail as opposed to companies, which frequently do. In both cases, the pathology of these problems, often decades moved from their sources, become largely unaccountable and, in the end, anachronistic.

This problem, in part or in whole, is why many professionals become frustrated and leave these larger organizations for a better way, better compensation, and better control of their work. As a result, many professionals will venture out on their own to a dream of a better alternative.

Sound familiar?

This is where the fairy tale ends for most professionals and reality sets in. Now that you have removed yourself from the corporate torture chamber, a whole new level of responsibility is thrust upon you. Before, you were a professional who could largely focus in on your trade. Now the organization that previously supported you, the one you may have despised in part or in whole, is gone.

You are now free to practice your profession, but at a far different cost—in resources and time. You may now be dealing with new responsibilities such as payroll, overhead, insurance, hiring, benefits, expenses, accounting and accounts receivables, human resources, technology, vendors, business taxes and compliance, and of course, sales and marketing.

This is where many professionals start to realize that instead of working for somebody else who can assist them in any and all of these functions they are now working for themselves, who may have little or no time, experience, or resources to help support them. Think about it; who wants to work for a boss like that? But as professionals, this is what many of us end up doing—intentionally or not.

In Michael Gerber's groundbreaking, bestselling book, *The E Myth*, he speaks to this problem and how small-business owners need to learn how to work on their business in addition to *in* it. As a professional, your comfort zone and expertise is to work *in* your business, since that is your professional expertise and where you excel. But as a business owner of your practice, you now have new responsibilities, which, like it or not, are now **MORE IMPORTANT to the success of your business than how well you perform your professional work in it.** Why? Because unless you have enough target customers to service at a profitable return while having enough time to work on your business while you work in it, you will never be part of the top 20 percent.

This is where the dream of becoming a professional meets the reality of becoming a professional who is now also a business owner. And the lifeblood of any business comes from customers you will first need to successfully sell and market to in order to succeed.

YOUR CUSTOMERS HAVE MILLIONS OF CHOICES—WHY DO THEY NEED YOU?

Now that you have decided to become a professional, let me nail this point home: You have A LOT of competition! At the time of the writing of this book, there are around 1.28 million attorneys; 650,000 CPAs; 190,000 dentists; 422,000 real estate agents; 420,000 plumbers; 440,000 insurance agents; 300,000 massage therapists; 141,000 web developers; and 28 million small businesses in the United States alone. The vast majority of these professionals actively market their services and sell their services to the same people you do. So how can you successfully compete with that?

In order to help stand out from your competition, you have to start by defining your target market and what "unique value" you plan to provide to it. Many major economists agree that as a business, **you can only compete and succeed long-term based on price or service—but not both.** Adding to this mix is the fact that as our economy matures, many of the products and services provided are becoming increasingly commoditized—meaning consumers are having a harder time differentiating services based on anything other than price.

Most successful professionals do not start out their practices to compete based on price, nor do most have the experience, resources, and capital necessary to scale to a level were price can become a viable competitive option. This means that **most professionals are left to compete based on service.** So here are a few questions you need to ask yourself as you define how you are going to compete and win against your competition:

- Who are my target customers?
- Are there enough target customers to sell to and support my business goals?
- What is the unique value proposition I will provide to my customers?
- How will I uniquely define my brand in the marketplace?

- What services will I provide that will support my unique value proposition?
- How will I plan to continue to provide a higher level of value than my competition over time?

These are just a few questions you need to formulate answers for as you move forward in the planning and execution of your business and becoming part of the top 20 percent. We will cover many of these as you move forward in this book, but it is a good idea to start thinking about how you plan to set yourself apart from your competition now, because there is a lot of it ahead of you and if you don't succeed at this, your competition will.

THE IMPORTANCE OF BUILDING YOUR SECOND INCOME STREAM: EQUITY VALUE

The destiny of any business is to eventually be transitioned and hopefully sold; whether it be by you or others in the months, years, and even generations ahead. Much like the inevitability of death and taxes, so too will be a business transition. Unfortunately for 80 percent of business owners today, the transition will be to shut down over a period of five years or less. But not for the top 20 percent.

The problems most professionals deal with today when it comes to transitioning a business is being able to properly position their business for the most advantageous transition; namely **selling the business at a profit**. In order to accomplish this, a business must develop real and transferable value that somebody is willing to pay for in order to want to purchase your business at a profit to you. In this case, the equity value to you as a business owner/seller would be the total amount of pre-tax income you would receive from the sale of the business minus any outstanding debts/loans to the business. The enterprise value may be the total purchase price of your business but the equity value would be the enterprise value (purchase price) minus any outstanding debts to the company that still need to be paid. The added benefit of this equity income you can receive upon the sale of your business is how in most instances it can be taxed at a much more favorable tax rate than the ordinary income and profits you had previously received from the business.

For example, most people will buy a home with a thirty-year mortgage. When you sell the home, your enterprise value is the purchase price of the home and your equity value is the enterprise value minus your remaining mortgage balance. Ideally you want this equity balance to be positive in order to make a profit—which is what you want to have happen for your business as well.

The main thing to remember about **equity value** to a business owner is that it is the **most valuable asset you can develop** beyond yourself. The problem with most professionals today is they don't understand how to ideally create this equity value over time. They end up creating a business that doesn't have any real value beyond their own work or, worse yet, has negative value by returning less to the owner than what was invested in total time and money. In this instance, the real money that was created was based on the ongoing income and profits from the business alone—so when you sell your business, you will have nothing to show for it beyond what you had previously earned from your work in the business. In short, you will always and only be working for money (as income) instead of your money working for you (as equity). The analogy here would be getting to the end of your thirty-year mortgage and then selling your house for nothing; and who wants to do that? But that is exactly what most business owners end up doing with their businesses.

In the following chapters, we are going to be discussing how you can help create a sales and marketing system that is scalable, repeatable, measureable, and successful—all of which can help you increase the equity value of your business over time. Many **small businesses today are valued and sold based on multiples of revenues and earnings**, and the more of each you can create through successful sales and marketing planning and execution, the more equity value you can create for your business and the better chance you or others have of one day selling your business for a lot of money. **The average small business today will be valued between two to six times EBIT** (earnings before interest and taxes), with a number of additional variables ranging from asset values, future growth projections, uniqueness of your value proposition, competitive threats, etc.

CHAPTER 1

SALES PLANNING: THE ROADMAP TO SALES SUCCESS

· · ·

Selling is both a discipline and an art form. Some say certain people are "born" to be a salesperson while others say that it is learned—and both may be right. In my experience, some people have certain natural tendencies and abilities that easily translate into sales success while others simply don't. But that ability alone does not translate into a successful salesperson. As in any profession, sales must be learned and mastered.

Like it or not, most professionals have to become effective salespeople as well. Unless you have the luxury of hiring people to sell for you, this is yet another hat you must wear as a business owner in order to be successful. When I hire salespeople I look for a number of key characteristics in a top-performing salesperson.

These include:

Drive

Without drive, all of the other sales skills you may have are a moot point. People with drive are commonly motivated, highly competitive, and optimistic about winning; they typically don't like to fail and don't give up easily. People who sell have to create their own success and drive is what wills and motivates them to make that happen, despite the odds. As a professional, you should already have passion for your work and be highly engaged and ready to succeed. If you are not, then you should seriously consider if your profession is right for you and/or whether you need to hire sales resources to take on this responsibility for you. Either way, look first for drive. If it is not there, pass and move on until you find it either in yourself or others you hire. Unfortunately, drive is not something you can teach, so you or your salespeople either have it or you don't.

Consistent Performance

One of the most effective ways to determine if somebody is a great salesperson is to look at their past sales performance. Great salespeople typically produce consistently great results no matter where they work. If you are in a position to hire salespeople to help you and your business grow, make sure you start with people who have a track record of consistent sales success. Although past performance does not guarantee future results, it is a great indicator of what they are capable of and allows you to mitigate your risk in hiring them.

Strong Prospecting Skills and Initiative

Most professionals need new business, therefore they have to be able to prospect for it. Absent good prospecting skills, professionals will have no new clients to sell and provide services to, no matter how good you are in your professional capacities. We cover some key prospecting strategies later in the book to help you.

Strong Communication, Persuasion, and Relationship-Building Skills

Can a professional who is selling discover and articulate value to their prospective customers? Can they connect with the customer and help create and uncover a need and sell to it? A great salesperson will typically have a strong grasp of the knowledge and wisdom that is needed to become a great communicator. In the end, people buy from people, and most people want to buy from people they like and can build credibility and trust with. Successful sales professionals also have a uniquely strong understanding of their customers' needs and/or businesses and always strive to find new ways to help educate, challenge, and provide new ways of thinking to their customers. Remember, you have A LOT of competition for your services, and you have to be able to find ways to interest your customers in your services and be able to articulate it in a way that is unique, compelling, and motivating.

Confidence and Organizational Skills

People with great sales skills are often unfazed and even emboldened in the face of rejections due to a high level of confidence. We know from studies that 44 percent of salespeople will give up on a sale after only one "no."[1] These 44 percent are not great salespeople. Nearly half of all leads generated in most businesses today are qualified but not yet ready to buy on your time. Confidence not only allows you to sell to and close prospective customers who are ready now, but more important allows you to discipline yourself to do the same with those who are not. This leads to the importance of good organizational skills. How are people who sell supposed to manage ALL of their opportunities, follow-ups, etc., without good organizational skills? Great salespeople are able to organize all of their processes, from prospecting, note-taking, selling, closing, to marketing. The more organized you are, the more successful at sales and marketing you can become. Being organized also means good follow-up, which is the key to any sales process. In most cases, a lack of follow-up skills comes down to either a lack of drive and/or the ability to effectively organize your sales processes.

Strong Sales Skills

There are no college degrees for sales today, so most people who sell have to learn sales somehow, somewhere, and from somebody. The fact that you are reading this book indicates a desire to improve your sales skills, which we will cover in more detail later in this book. For those who wish to further their sales skills, I provide a number of additional sales books I recommend to other professionals toward the end of this book as well.

Once you have identified the sales skills that will help you become successful, you then need to put a plan in place to make it all successfully, consistently, and habitually happen. Golfer Ben Hogan once said, "Golf is a game of luck. The more I practice the luckier I get." Like golf, a sale is not a game of luck, it is a game of action and results. The best actions start with a plan that is successful, repeatable, and developed through practice. Recent studies show that only 65 percent of businesses have a defined sales process, which means that 35 percent (many of which are professionals and small businesses) are winging it when it comes to sales.[2]

Successful sales professionals also create their own luck through constant practice and repeatable performance. They know that it is much more effective to develop a repeatable system, even if they are part of a larger organization that has a defined process, that will make them more efficient each time that they sell. They will often memorize and/or document their system and use it over and over again, especially if they ever want others to achieve similar results in their practice.

The sales plan you create for your business should be simple, understandable, and executable. Any plan should clearly define each and every step that is necessary to achieve the desired sales objective, ranging from planning to prospecting to closing. A well-written plan is also a critical component of your business if you ever plan to scale and add additional resources. As with any successful business the rule is simple: Your people run your processes and your processes run your business—sales is no exception.

THE SIMPLE SALES EQUATION

Success and failure in sales all come down to a very simple yet powerful equation:

ACTIVITY x EFFECTIVENESS = RESULTS. In order to succeed in sales, you need to have a firm grasp of this equation and use it as a lens in which you measure your progress. Let's briefly look at each component of this equation:

Activity

Activity is nothing more than the things you and your supporting resources do to help you in your everyday sales work. Activity is typically measured by the quantity of your actions, such as the total number of phone calls, appointments, sales closed, etc., in a finite period of time. Higher levels of activity typically come from salespeople who are highly engaged in their work, well-motivated, and work a sales activity plan. For most professionals, engagement is frequently highest during the early stages of a new organization and typically wanes over time when they become overwhelmed with all of the responsibilities that increase for a business owner while the time in their day does not.

Effectiveness

Effectiveness is how impactful your actions become, and is measured by the quality of your work. Most seasoned salespeople will tell you that with experience comes higher levels of effectiveness, which is often reflected in higher close rates, average order sizes, call conversions, and new engagements. If you are new to selling your work to others, you initial levels of effectiveness may be low. Conversely, if this is a role you are familiar with in your previous work, then your levels of effectiveness should be higher.

RESULTS

Results are nothing more than what you end up producing as a result of your activities and effectiveness. Results are commonly measured in sales, meetings, close rates, etc.

THE SIMPLE SALES EQUATION

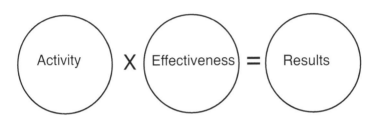

Marketing	How many new high quality sales leads are you able to produce and at what Cost-Per-Lead (CPL)?	Enough sales leads generated to convert and support defined sales objectives and achieve the highest Return-On-Investment (ROI)
Prospecting	How many new sales leads are you able to move into your defined sales process?	Higher lead conversion rates
Customer Qualification	How well do you identify each customer's unique goals and gaps to sell to?	Higher lead qualification rates

Presentation /Positioning	How well do you present and convey a high value exchange to each sales prospect?	Higher prospect conversions and average order values
Sales Objections/ Delays	Ability to overcome objections and move a sale out of a "Stall"	Faster sales velocity and average sales cycle time
Closing	Total opportunities closed	Higher closing ratios
Asking for Referrals	Habitually and successfully ask for referrals from the "Right" people at the "Right" times	Higher customer referral business based on referral lead source
Generating Repeat Business	Successfully "Stay in Front" of former and current customers	Higher customer retention rates, reorders, and life-time customer value to the business

In sales, you cannot have activity without effectiveness and vice versa—anything times zero always results in a zero. For example, without activity, there would be no sales since you would have nobody to sell to—no matter how effective you are. Conversely, you may be able to fill your day with sales activities and meetings, but if you lack the effectiveness to sell and close during those meetings, you will have no results.

This equation is also helpful based on the tenure of the people selling your services as well. Most professionals and/or salespeople just starting out are typically highly engaged due to a high level of excitement over their new roles, which means they are well motivated to operate at a level of high activity. However, since they are newer and learning, their effectiveness levels may be lower and therefore they need a higher level of activity (calls, meetings, etc.) to compensate for their lower level of effectiveness (close ratios, call conversions, etc.).

For more tenured professionals who sell their services, it is not uncommon to see higher levels of sales effectiveness due to experience yet lower levels of activity. Many will intuitively act upon this sales equation by intentionally lowering their levels of activity and compensating for this through a higher level of effectiveness in their activities. For example, a new salesperson may have a close ratio of 20 percent, meaning he/she needs five meetings to close every one sale. An experienced salesperson, through increased sales effectiveness, may have developed a 50 percent close ratio, meaning he/she will only need two meetings to close a sale versus five for the newer salesperson.

Top professionals selling their services will commonly excel in both activity and effectiveness, knowing that the two are intertwined and paramount to their success. They also know that even though higher effectiveness can be a substitute for lower activity, both must be constantly improved upon at all times to achieve the maximum results. But this is where many professionals fail in selling, for they do not understanding how this is best accomplished.

The most fundamental mistake many professionals make is in the understanding of capacity in both their activity and effectiveness. **Unlike activity, sales effectiveness is unique since it is limitless in application**. With action, you and your supporting resources have a finite level of capacity—commonly measured in time. Most professionals only have around 1,750–2,350 working hours in any year. Effectiveness, on the other hand, is potentially limitless and infinite, which is why it is commonly the deciding factor between the failing 80 percent and the top 20 percent of professionals in selling and results.

Due to its unlimited scalability, sales effectiveness is something every professional needs to learn through experience, training, and self-learning. The fact that you are reading this book is a good indication of the direction you are taking here. The bottom line is that you are a professional who sells without a degree in selling, therefore you need to constantly learn and get better—especially at the one thing that is unlimited in your sales work: your sales effectiveness.

START EACH DAY WITH A SALES PLAN AND GOAL

If there is one common thread among nearly all highly successful people in sales and in life, it is a path to success defined by a goal. Top-performing people in sales know what success means to them by defining that success in a goal and working tirelessly to achieve it.

Harvard University did a study of their 1979 graduates and found that ten years after their graduation, there was a significant variation in incomes between those who had goals and those who did not. In their findings, 84 percent of the graduates indicated they had no goals established, 13 percent had goals that were not in writing, and 3 percent had written goals. For the 13 percent who had goals that were not in writing, they earned on average twice as much as the 84 percent with no goals. For the 3 percent who had written goals, they earned ten times as much income as the other 97 percent combined.[3]

As a professional, the greatest advantage goals provide you is focus. The top 20 percent want to achieve great results, and the best way to accomplish this is by defining goals and staying laser-focused on them. Good sales goals should be reasonable, achievable, written, executable, and mutually agreed upon by all involved.

In developing a laser-focus on defined goals, successful professionals are not only able to focus in on what they want, but they are also able to effectively remove all of the competing priorities and obstacles that potentially stand in its way. Author Greg McKeown wrote that focus is "not just haphazardly saying no [to distractions], but purposefully, deliberately, and strategically eliminating the nonessentials. Not just once a year as part of a planning meeting, but constantly reducing, focusing, and simplifying. Not just getting rid of the obvious time wasters, but being willing to cut out really terrific opportunities as well. Few appear to have the courage to live this principle, which may be why it differentiates successful people and organizations from the very successful ones." [4]

Failing professionals treat sales-goal setting in a similar manner to how the 88 percent of us treat a New Year's Resolution—we make a declaration of objective at the start of each year and then drift back into our bad habits and results. The primary reason for this failure is a lack of personal accountability. A goal without accountability in nothing more than a dream. Most professionals today will commonly create their annual goals and then never follow up on those goals throughout the course of the year with good habits to execute on them.

When it comes to professionals, it is important to understand that inspiration and desire is what may have gotten you started in your career, but is it your habits that will keep you going and make you successful. Habits are inherently no different than business systems, since habits are systems you create for yourself. Just as you cannot run and scale a business without systems, you equally cannot grow your own productivity without good habits.

The best way to reach any annual goal is to break it down into daily activities. Without a daily focus, professionals are left with weekly, monthly, quarterly, and annual measurements that in most cases are too late to effectively measure and manage. This is why you as a professional need to take this upon yourself.

Start with the math. Most people will work around forty-six weeks a year excluding holidays, vacations, sick time, etc. This works out to around 230 working days in a year. Once you have defined your annual sales goal/s for the year, take that number and divide it by 230, which will give you your daily goal/s.

For example, let's say your goal is to close $500,000 in new sales (business) this year. If you know your average sale size/client revenue ($4,000), your average call-to-meeting success rate (10 percent), and your average sales-meeting close rate (20 percent), you can then quickly determine your daily goals based on the following equations:

Daily Sales Goal: $500,000/230 = **$2,174/day** (Annual sales target / 230 days)

Daily Sales Meetings: [($500,000 / ($4,000 X 20 percent) / 230] = **2.7 Meetings/Day** [(Annual sales target / (Ave Sale Size X Average Close Rate)/230]

Daily Sales Calls: 2.7/10 percent = **27 Sales Calls/Day** (Daily Sales Meetings / Average Call-to-Meeting Success Rate)

For those professionals with much longer sales cycles and/or very high average sales sizes, using a daily sales target may not seem practical, which is okay. The most important point to remember here is what DAILY ACTIVITIES you need to engage in to achieve your sales goals whenever the sale takes place. For example, your sales may take place once a month and therefore cannot be tracked in daily sales. But by equating your sales numbers down to a daily average, you can then derive what your daily averages are for your sales activities needed to hit your monthly goal—which is your primary focus here. If the numbers don't end up working out in your sales targets, then you need to make adjustments to your other sales activities that support it.

This simple daily activity equation can also be applied to ALL of your business-generating activities, even if they don't involve sales calls. For example, say you also generate new clients from other means of marketing such as emails, TV and radio advertising, trade shows, mailings, online advertising, etc. The goal is to make sure you can break down all the sales and marketing activities from your marketing plan into your daily activities.

YOU CANNOT MANAGE WHAT YOU CANNOT MEASURE

Far too many professionals today haven't a clue as to how their current sales and marketing efforts are supporting their business goals and providing a solid return on investment (ROI). Many wonder where that last customer really came from, but they don't truly know. What happens when your new customer says they found you on the Internet? When you have multiple Internet marketing vehicles in play, which one was it that really worked? Or how about all those recent trade shows you attended; how did they work in comparison to your other marketing strategies and which one provided the best and worst results? And how about the recent TV and radio advertising you just ran; which one provided the best results and ROI, and why?

There is only one way to accurately measure any progress in business, and that is through numbers. Measuring by how things look and feel and how they are perceived to be is the surest way to fail as a professional business owner. Running your business "by the numbers" will help remove biases and provide a basis of performance and comparison for all business decisions you make; especially when it comes to sales and marketing.

In order to run your business by the numbers, you first need to define what numbers you need to track and why. Once you start diligently and methodically tracking these numbers, you will be able to get a snapshot and trend of all these numbers over time so you can start making more informed and better decisions for your business moving forward. From the sales and marketing perspective, here are a few key measurements you should be tracking:

- Average Income per Customer
- Average Customer Acquisition Cost (CAC) by total and individual marketing sources
- Average Lead Conversion Rate (LCR) by total and individual marketing sources
- Average Cost per Lead (CPL) by total and individual marketing sources
- Average Return on Investment (ROI) by total and individual marketing sources
- Average Return on Marketing Investment (ROMI) by total and individual marketing sources

- Total marketing leads by source
- Total number of customers generated by lead source
- Total new-customer revenue generated by lead source
- Average customer revenue generated by lead source
- Product/service profit margin for each product and service
- Average net new gross profit margin by lead source
- Daily calls/contacts into your business
- Daily calls/contacts converted into a lead
- Daily calls/contacts converted into a paying customer
- Daily calls/contacts received by marketing source and/or campaign
- Average close rate per sales lead
- Average customer lifetime value per marketing source/campaign
- Sales made per day/week/month/year
- Average length of sales cycle from contact to close by day/week/month/year
- Etc . . .

You can never have enough numbers to measure your business by, but you do need to **define the most important numbers so you don't get lost in all the data.** Once you start this process, you will find that certain numbers are far more important and easier to measure than others, and those are the ones you should focus on the most.

The ideal objective is to tie all these numbers together in as few systems as possible so you can connect, analyze, and trend this data over time. Many professionals utilize Customer Relationship Management (CRM) systems to manage some or all of these data points. Popular CRM systems like Salesforce.com are widely adopted in multiple industries, and their deployment and use as a web-based system has dramatically lowered the cost of CRM-system deployment and usage over the years to where most professionals can easily afford to use such systems today.

Depending on your profession, a single standard CRM system alone may not be enough. It is not uncommon to find industry-specific versions of CRM in use today as well as additional systems to provide more robust marketing and lead-conversion capabilities. Moreover, professionals like attorneys, dentists, doctors, and CPAs commonly have their own unique data and document management limitations that can add further systems to this mix. The ideal strategy is to eventually have a single system that can tie all of your most critical sales and marketing data points together for analysis and decision making. Once that is achieved, a whole new framework of business management and growth will be at your disposal.

YOU HAVE ONLY THREE TYPES OF CUSTOMERS

Today, professionals spend far too much time selling to and dealing with the wrong customers. Many professionals inadvertently create this problem by pursuing short-sighted sales goals at the expense of longer-term sales growth and customer retention. Because of this and other factors, US companies, on average, will lose 50 percent of their customers every five years, 50 percent of their employees every four, and 50 percent of their investors in less than one year. [5]

Most professional businesses today are on one of two trajectories: They are either growing or dying. Growing businesses tend to be much more focused on innovation and providing superior customer value. Businesses that are dying tend to provide insufficient customer value and therefore cannot incrementally acquire new clients and/or retain them. Dying businesses tend to pursue short-term profit over long-term value creation, which is why determining if a company is growing or dying should not be based on short-term profits alone.

For a professional business to grow, it needs to provide superior customer value and attract customers who will help promote that value to others. In order to do this, you first need to start by determining who exactly these ideal customers are.

Create a Target Client Profile

One of many responsibilities you have as a business owner is to make sure you and your resources are as productive as possible. One of the most effective ways to start in this direction is to make sure you are selling your services to the right customers. This may sound counterintuitive to some people, but not every customer is the right customer. Yes, they may all initially be able to buy your services and therefore increase your sales, but at what cost to your business does this happen?

We know it costs, on average, seven times more to acquire a new customer than to retain one. Once a customer is acquired and the initial sale is made, what value or lack thereof does that client pose to your business and future sales? How do you know in the end that you sold to the right customer?

One of the most effective ways to answer these questions is by creating and selling to a Target Client Profile. A Target Client Profile is nothing more than a picture and description of the ideal customer for your business. If you already have an established professional business, start by profiling who you consider to be your best customers and find the commonalities among them. If your business is new, start by painting a picture of who you expect will receive the highest level of customer value from your services and how they can help you spread that value to others.

When creating your Target Client Profile, define your ideal customers' demographics and characteristics in detail. This may include details such as where they live and work; their age, gender, and occupation; their company sizes and industries; how much they typically spend on similar services; who else successfully sells to them, and how; and why they make purchasing decisions today.

Secondly, you need to define their **common problems** and what they are **trying to gain**. Remember, people make purchasing decisions based primarily on these two factors, so you must understand what they are before selling your services to them. If what you ultimately want to sell is not considered a higher-value service to your Target Client Profile, it will not matter how good it is if nobody ends up buying it.

Finally, you need to publish your Target Client Profile and make sure that you clearly understand it. You should also make sure that anybody you employ to help you is also aware of this profile, for it will have impacts on and help define all aspects of your business moving forward.

Focus on Customers Who Will Help You Sell

Most businesses sell to customers without being able to properly segment them. When you create your Target Client Profile, you help to define who your ideal customer is. The problem, however, is that nearly all professionals will continue to sell and retain customers outside of their Target Client Profile. In fact, this may have been going on for years before you ever defined your customer segmentation process. As a business owner, you must be able to properly segment your customer base so you can maximize the sales efficiency for you and any people helping you. Absent this, you will never be able to fully address your customer and sales problems.

For example, we've all had what most would consider to be "problem" customers. These people can be a drain on you, your people, your business, and your resources. Over a customer's life cycle, these people are sold to at a higher overall "cost" of doing business with them. On the opposite side of the spectrum, you will have customers who fit your Target Client Profile and you will always want more of them. The problem is that most people don't understand the value of customer segmentation and end up wasting far too much of their time with problem customers at the expense of their Target Client Profile customers.

To help address this issue, you should segment all of your customers into three simple category designations: Promoters, Buyers, and Demoters.

© TheSuccessfulSalesManager.com

Promoters

A number of years ago I attended a Salesforce.com customer event in New York City. At the time, Salesforce.com was not yet widely known or adopted in the CRM community; they were an up-and-coming company. I was considering Salesforce.com as an integration partner with a software company I owned so I thought I would attend the event and see what their customers were saying.

The roughly one-hour meeting started off with the Salesforce.com representatives asking a group of a couple hundred customers in the audience what they thought of their CRM system. What followed for the next thirty minutes had me speechless. One customer after another stood up and had nothing but glowing reviews for Salesforce.com and their CRM service. A few customers even said that Salesforce.om was charging their customers TOO LITTLE based on the value they were receiving. Now, how many businesses have had this happen to them? I was sold. This was either the greatest show ever produced outside of Hollywood or I had just sat through one of the best and most effective customer-supported sales events in my lifetime.

What this customer event illustrated, among many things, was the power of customer promoters. "Promoters" are those customers who, if you help them, will help you in return. You will typically know who these customers are when you first sell to them: If they are good to sell to, they are good to have as customers. In the Salesforce.com customer meeting the room was filled with Promoters, and what they were doing—intentionally or not—is exactly what any business wants their customers to do: help them more effectively sell their products and services to others.

In most industries, Promoters will range anywhere from 10–25 percent of your total potential customer base. Their percentages may not be large, but the multiplier effects they can have on your business can be astronomical. As a business professional, you need to understand and be able to explain to your people that these are the customers they should be giving the majority of their time and effort to. The returns to your business can be enormous, but only if you know who these people are and how best to manage them.

Buyers

The largest segment of potential customers—around 50 percent for most businesses—are people who simply buy your services and do nothing else. They don't try to help you sell to others and they typically don't complain, either. What makes this segment of customers unique is that they are typically the largest buying block in any one market, and they are not considered early adopters.

Early adopters typically represent up to 15 percent of a typical market and they like to buy early and often. Early adopters are the people who buy the newest and greatest TV so they can be one of the first to own it. They also buy the next new iPhone model to be released when what they already use will typically meet their needs.

Buyers are different from early adopters because they more often purchase to solve a problem instead of gaining something as a result. Because of this, they are more inherently skeptical than other buyers and oftentimes require proof and successful citations from others before they will buy. This is where Promoters come in.

Promoters will help you sell to Buyers. By helping Promoters, they in turn will help you sell to Buyers by providing you with valuable success stories, references, referrals, etc., that are needed to successfully sell to Buyers. The problem is that most professionals don't understand this and instead spend far too much time with the wrong customers—Demoters.

Demoters

When most professionals talk about their "bad" customers, they are usually referring to a "Demoter." A Demoter is a customer you CANNOT make happy. You can make them money and even successful, but you cannot, no matter how hard you try, make them happy. Demoters may sometimes fit within your Target Client Profile but by their very nature **they lack loyalty, are undesirable customers, and are a drain on your sales and business.**

Much like with Promoters, Demoters are typically a smaller segment of a potential customer base, ranging anywhere from 20–30 percent. You will typically know who these people are when you sell to them because they are **hard to sell to**. This should be your first indication of a potential Demoter. If they are hard to sell to, they are hard to manage as a customer.

Demoters are also takers by nature and therefore will do NOTHING to help you and your people grow your sales. If you help them, they will commonly not help you in return. The most common reward people receive by helping Demoters is keeping them quiet and not complaining. This is the heart of the problem with Demoters: They love to complain and we waste far too much of our valuable time trying to make them happy. In the end, we cannot make them happy and all the time wasted was time that would have been better spent helping our Promoters instead.

LEARN HOW TO SAY "NO" TO BAD CUSTOMERS

A few years back I worked with a well-known bankruptcy trustee lawyer on the East Coast. During my regular meetings with this attorney, he would frequently ask what more I could do to help generate even more business for his practice. When I asked him how much business he currently received his answer was always far more than he could handle, yet he still wanted more. This story may sound a bit perplexing to many people, but this attorney ran one of the most successful legal "businesses" I have ever worked with, and his secret was his command of the word "no."

This attorney gave me some great business advice that can benefit any professional, not just attorneys. When I asked him why he wanted more cases despite the fact that he was already overloaded, his response was that he learned something most attorneys have not—namely, how to say "no" to any potential client that comes his way. This ability to freely refuse new referrals and potential customers allows him to better pick and choose the most valuable clients in the least amount of time. The more potential customers he had to choose from, the greater the opportunity for success without the guilt and wasted time. This ultimately led to his creation of a highly effective lead-intake system that anybody could efficiently operate. As a result, he was able to increase his billing rates and income and free up his time to do what he loves the most: fishing.

Creating an effective "NO" strategy is not difficult but requires discipline, planning, and refinement. On a side note, I do not promote the literal use of the word "no" in communications with others. The word "no" is a pejorative word that evokes a physiological condition of rejection that is hard to overcome and can negatively impact future referrals. There are more effective and non-threatening words and phrases that can be used in place of the word "no," so apply it in the figurative and not literal use of the word.

The first step in this process is to **set a goal of generating more business than you can handle**. How much business is too much business? This is the question that most professionals ask themselves, and it is the wrong question based on the wrong goals. The goal of every customer engagement is to maximize the value exchange for both parties, which means being too busy is not always being the right kind of busy. Most professionals today only network, market, and advertise to their desired level of workload and then stop. Because of this, most professionals always fear a potential future drop in business, which increases their levels of paranoia and obligation. This commonly leads to lower billing rates, revenue, and the retention of undesirable clients and cases. All of this can be solved with one simple solution: Set your goals to increase your new-business flow. When you do, you will have more to choose from (not take), leading to an increased demand and options to raise what you charge for your services and overall business revenues.

The second step is to **create an effective customer-intake system that ANYBODY can run**. Great businesses are run by great systems that are operated by great people. People should not run your business—people running repeatable and effective systems should. Having systems in place allows you to change your personnel without changing your business—a common problem with professionals today. This also applies to how you manage the intake of leads and referrals into your business. Professionals who fail to create a repeatable system for the intake of leads most often end up having to intake leads on their own, thereby running out of time and feeling overloaded. Sound familiar? Conversely, **good business managers will create and continue to refine a lead/referral-intake process that ANYBODY can potentially operate, allowing you to maximize your resource utilization and time**. More important, your system should allow your business to accept and reject (say "NO") to undesirable leads and referrals that DO NOT meet your targeted goals.

Third, **don't suffer from Referral Syndrome**. Most professionals today suffer from referral syndrome, which comes from a sense of obligation most feel when a potential lead comes their way from ANY source. This begins most often when professionals started their businesses and took nearly any customer who came their way in order to pay the bills. As their networks and advertising grew, so too did their inquiries and referrals, yet they continued to treat them all with equal value. We all know that referrals tend to be better sources for leads and convert at a higher rate than most other marketing sources, yet most professionals still treat all leads with high value and attention. With attorneys and real estate agents, many contingency-fee referrals come with a finder's fee/royalty, so you hope that the leads you generate on our own will make up for your percentage of the payout and ultimately hope to replace them over time with your own cases and clients. The bottom line is that you are NOT obligated to take ANY referral and/or lead provided to you, nor should you expect to. It is more often our personal sense of obligation and fear of losing future business that creates this competing interest.

Fourth, **don't offer free services and/or advice to everyone**. Referral syndrome ultimately leads to professionals providing things such as free consultations, free RFP responses, free services, etc., and leads to the fear of ever being able to increase their rates and/or cost of services to their true market value. The most important resource you have as a professional is time, and it is limited, so you cannot afford to waste it on no-revenue-producing activities like providing free services to everybody. This is why I always advise attorneys who offer "free consultations" to replace it with "free case reviews." To most attorneys this denotes the same activity, but to consumers this no longer implies, through semantics alone, that you are obligated to provide them with initial legal advice. The same thought process applies to all professionals.

In summary, it is just as important for you as a professional to know what will help make you successful as WHAT WILL NOT. You are going to receive both bad customers as well as good ones, and that will NEVER change—it is the nature of marketing and advertising. So embrace this reality, create and refine a solid system to help manage and scale it, and learn when to say "no." This is exactly what nearly all of my top clients do to run a successful professional business, and so should you.

THE ONLY WAY TO LEARN IS THROUGH DAILY REFLECTION

As children, many of us either had a hamster or knew others who did. What was so unique and entertaining about the hamster was its habitual marathon running along a hamster wheel. We all would watch as the hamster, free of any real cognitive reasoning, willfully jumped onto a hamster wheel and ran and ran and ran. Why? What is it that compels a hamster to want to run on a wheel until exhausted, and where does he think he's going? More important, are you as a professional guilty of the same kind of problem?

Most professionals jump onto the proverbial hamster wheel each day, work until they are exhausted, and do it all over again—day after day, month after month, year after year. Was this your dream when you decided to become a professional? And how is what you are doing now any different than what the hamster does on his wheel? You may be getting paid, but most professionals end up working longer hours for less pay per hour with more responsibilities and more headaches. At least the hamster can get off the wheel when he wants to—most professionals cannot.

The main difference between a hamster and a professional is the professional's ability to learn. And **learning can**

only come through reflection. Many of the most successful professionals I have met in my life had an unusually strong sense of reflection. These people typically viewed unfavorable outcomes as another opportunity to learn and grow. To them, failure was only the result of the inability to learn, adjust, and move on. In short, they are able to see the hamster wheel for what it really is. Their ability to adhere to this mindset comes largely from a keen and habitual sense of reflection.

Reflection commonly takes place daily, weekly, monthly, and yearly for most successful people. They realize, intentionally or not, that reflection is needed to pull one's psyche out of the hamster wheel of their daily lives and learn and reflect from a basis of "why."

To illustrate this point, I often tell professionals to start the first step of this process by writing down their accomplishments on a whiteboard or piece of paper at the end of each day and reviewing it when the workday is done—with no further distractions. Notice what happens to you both psychologically and physically when you realize just how much you have actually accomplished in your workday; or better yet, what did you forget that you actually accomplished and now have a hard time recalling? Without daily reflection, most professionals don't realize this and often leave their days feeling like they accomplished little and with little purpose.

The next step in reflection is to start your days by writing down your goals for the coming day, executing on those goals, and then reflecting on your goals before your day is done. Goals now allow you to create focus for your reflection. One of the reasons I recommend professionals create a daily goals checklist is to give them a daily basis of defined goals and a means to reflect on them.

When you begin your reflection process, do it chronologically, as if you are rewinding your day all over again. Walk through what happened, what you learned from it, what you could do differently next time, and what you ultimately accomplished. Remember, good reflection relies on focus, focus comes from goals, goals support your purpose, and ALL are executed through good habits.

Once you begin your new journey into reflection as a professional, make sure to stop by a pet store and buy a hamster wheel. Place it on your desk and use it as a visual aid when you start your daily reflection process. This will serve as a reminder that you will never again work without clear direction, focus, purpose, and vision—all aided by your learning through reflection.

SCHEDULE STRATEGIC SALES TIME AWAY FROM YOUR TACTICAL TIME

The most successful business professionals I have worked with over the years all had one thing in common; they were just as effective working *on* their business as they were working *in* their business. This means that they were able to successfully remove themselves from their professional responsibilities and make sure that running their business had an equal or greater priority.

The amount of time these professionals allocated to managing their business typically varied from 20–50 percent of their time on average. Those who were growing and building a more scalable business typically found themselves increasing their time on business management as the organization grew by creating documented and repeatable business systems for all aspects of their business. Once these systems were tested and in place, they could easily replicate those functions by utilizing and/or hiring additional resources to help run them.

In growing businesses, most professionals take on more of the sales and marketing functions themselves over time and/or hire additional resources to run these systems for the business; the larger they grow, the more resources are needed to support their sales and marketing. No matter what resources run sales and marketing, the goal should always be the same; do not let your time and resources spent in your business take away from your time and resources working on your business.

LEARN HOW MUCH YOUR TIME IS REALLY WORTH

In order to determine what you should be doing to become part of the top 20 percent of business professionals, you need to understand a key fundamental of business: what you and others are worth. Each resource in your business, including yourself, is limited by time and/or cost. You can only work so many hours in a day, week, month, and year, and then you run out of time and the ability to create more of it on your own. This is where leverage comes in.

Rome was not built in a day and it certainly was not built alone. I frequently remind people in business that Bill Gates became a billionaire by creating a lot of millionaires, and most professionals who have built successful and sizable businesses have done the same thing—on a smaller financial scale than Microsoft, of course. The point is that in order to succeed, grow, and be happy, you will need help. Think about it: As a business owner, you are now taking on the roles and responsibilities of multiple people in addition to your own professional work. **Was that your plan when you started out—to do it all, run it all, work weekends, and then run out of time and miss your children's sporting events as a result?**

In order to solve this mess you need to start with the numbers. When it comes to professionals, here is where I typically begin. First, the most important resource you have is your time. There are 365 days in a year, which means you have 8,760 hours to work with. Of the 52 weeks you have to work with, most professionals will be down to 47 weeks after vacations, sick time, and time away from work; leaving you with **2,350 hours** to work with based on a 10-hour workday.

Now let's set a financial goal: What do you want/need to earn this year to be successful? Let's say your goal is to take home $200,000 this year before income taxes. Dividing your desired income ($200,000) by your total hours worked (2,350) gives you your cost per hour ($85). Now that you are a business owner and not just a professional in practice, you now know what your desired cost is to your business on an hourly basis ($85).

From this information, you can now start writing down all of the functions of your business; especially your sales and marketing functions, and their relative time and returns. The easiest place to start this process is by looking at your marketing plan and start time-tracking all of these functions on that plan. The easiest way to do this is to clock yourself on these tasks and/or the resources you utilize to complete them. Next, once you start tracking the return on investment (ROI) you receive over time from each marketing source, you can then answer the following questions:

- What does each sales/marketing function require on an hourly basis to complete on a daily, weekly, monthly, and/or annual basis?
- When procedurally documented, which sales/marketing functions can be completed by other people (internally or externally), and what skill sets would those people require?
- Which sales/marketing function is providing the highest return per hour?
- Which sales/marketing function is providing the lowest return per hour?
- What does each sales/marketing function cost on an hourly basis when comparing my hourly rate ($85) to the rate of an additional person or resource?
- Which sales/marketing functions are the lowest costs per hour?
- Etc.

The ultimate goal is to get as many low-cost, low-return, and time-consuming tasks off your plate as possible. If these tasks can be successfully completed by anybody who charges less than $85 per hour your first objective is to get these tasks procedurally documented and in the hands of these people as quickly as possible. The initial time needed for you to create a step-by-step procedure for any or all of these tasks can be time intensive at first but well worth it in the long run.

Once you have your sales and marketing systems in place, you will now be able to more effectively hire and manage the people and resources needed to run them on a far more consistent basis. Since your systems will now run these processes, it becomes far less important who you hire and when they may leave since the sales and marketing system you created will always remain with your business. More important, you will know the real value of each employee, including yourself, and how best to align the resources to their appropriate roles.

MANAGING A SALES PIPELINE
AND FORECAST

Most business professionals today have to balance a lot of sales opportunities and at different stages all at once, which is far more difficult to do properly without processes and technology to help support it. Moreover, the lifetime value of a customer is typically not limited to one transaction alone but rather a lifetime of future transactions with that same customer, which need to be properly managed. Because of this, businesses create sales pipelines and forecasts to answer such critical questions as:

- How many leads do we need to convert to our targeted number of sales?

- How many sales opportunities do we have, and at what sales stages to convert to our targeted number of sales?

- When do we expect sales to close and in what amounts?

- Which of my salespeople has the highest and lowest levels of prospecting, close rates, average order size, etc.?

- How much more marketing and/or sales activity do I need or not need in order to hit our sales goals?

- Which of my marketing mediums is producing the highest and lowest levels of sales activity and results?

- How long (in velocity) does each sales stage last and why?

- How many new opportunities were added to the sales pipeline over the past week?

- What opportunities are projected to close over the next week?

- Etc . . .

Now that we understand why we need better sales predictability and measurements, let's address the second issue, which has to do with the confusion many people continue to have when understanding what the difference is between a sales pipeline and a forecast. When somebody asks me to explain how to forecast sales, I will typically respond by asking them the reason for the question. Don't we, as salespeople, business owners, and professionals, all know how to forecast sales? And how did it become such a subjective process in the first place?

When I talk about forecasting, I am reminded of one of my favorite sales situations from a few years back. At the time, I had a salesman who had a few great sales months in a row and just prior to the next month, told me that he had a ton of great opportunities ready to close. Because of this he said that the next month would be his best ever; and it was. So how many of those great opportunities that were ready to close actually closed? Zero! So how did he have such a great month? Because he never once changed his daily sales habits to give greater time to his sales-forecasted opportunities over continuing to build his pipeline, despite his initial prognostication.

The sales-forecasting-versus-pipeline lessons learned from this story were many. First, sales pipeline building and management should never take a backseat to more short-term forecasted sales opportunities. Second, never let your salespeople solely define their sales forecast for your business. Third, there is a fundamental difference between a sales pipeline and a forecast, and when it comes time to prioritize, they **should be managed as being mutually exclusive**.

On average, most sales managers will spend **37 percent (over one-third!) of their time on forecasting sales**.[2] This means sales managers spend more time around a crystal ball and less time doing all the things they could be doing to help improve their sales team's performance. For most sales managers and business owners, forecasting sales and being held accountable for their predictions rank somewhere between a good root canal and getting run over by a truck.

Despite the dread that most people share of it, predicting sales for most organizations is a necessary evil. Production needs guidance for the resources needed to support sales output. Finance needs guidance in order to help fund the organization. Management needs guidance in order to properly align resources, strategy, and direction, and sales management needs guidance to help keep all these people happy and off their backs.

Forecasting anything, including sales, is problematic by nature. I remember watching an interview of an economic forecasting specialist (yes, these people really do exist) who was asked how they were able to predict the future of economic events with any level of certainty. His response to that question was, "If weather people can do such a good job of predicting the weather, why can't we be able to do the same thing for the economy?" So there you have it—you are now in good company!

Now that you know the necessity, bane, and sometimes utter futility of forecasting, there are a few guidelines you can use to help you better manage this process:

Six Steps to Better Predicting Sales

1.) Know the Difference Between a Sales Forecast and a Sales Pipeline

A sales pipeline is a view of ALL of your potential sales opportunities at any and all stages. Your sales forecast, on the other hand, is a much smaller segment of your sales pipeline with stages close to closing within a defined time frame (typically a day, week, month, or quarter). The problems we commonly face is that your salespeople, if you have them, will too often focus on their forecasted sales opportunities at the expense of their pipeline and future sales growth. Sales and business managers can further reinforce this problem by managing their salespeople to artificially focus on short-term forecasted opportunities to make a number, thereby reinforcing bad sales habits that can be hard to break. By reinforcing successful sales habits that strike a strong and consistent balance between both pipeline and forecasted opportunities, you can better grow the long-term health of a business.

2.) Make Your Salespeople Be Salespeople and Not Fortune-Tellers

A recent survey of sales managers showed that **only 23 percent of sales managers trust the forecasts of their salespeople.**[2] The responsibility of salespeople should be to sell, and the job of a sales manager should be to forecast for them. If your responsibilities are one in the same, then this may or may not be an issue depending on your structure but always remember that the motivations and downsides to having a salesperson provide a forecast may be far different than a sales manager's. If you are a sales manager, part of your responsibility is to help provide sales guidance so your organization can help support your sales. The salesperson may have other motivations, oftentimes focused on one thing—themselves.

For example, why is it that poor sales performers typically have great months forecasted right before they end up leaving a company? And why is it that new salespeople will often forecast sales results far in excess of what they will actually produce? It all comes down to individual motivations and/or a lack of experience—which is what you as a potential owner or manager are supposed to be able to figure out first.

You can read a lot into the forecasts and pipelines provided by salespeople, but make sure that the read is interpreted at your level before it may need to get any higher in your business. If somebody is out looking for a new job while working for you, don't be surprised if their pipeline suddenly drops and their forecasted sales artificially increase in the process. If you have an underperforming salesperson who has been warned about their lack of prospecting, don't be surprised when new pipeline opportunities are magically created while their prospecting habits remain unchanged. And if you have new salespeople, they may be very excited and have high sales expectations but lack experience in sales with your company; which is often reflected in their lofty forecasts, which many will fail to initially achieve.

3.) Measure Your Pipeline in Sales Steps/Stages, Not by Guessing

The worst thing you can ask a salesperson to do is provide a probability to close at all steps and in all stages in their pipeline. By doing this, you are once again asking salespeople to become fortune-tellers and preventing a true read and efficient flow from a pipeline to a forecast. Always stick to sales steps first and only involve probabilities when you reach the last step before closing.

Sales Stage	Sales Stage Defined	Sales Activity	Results/Next Steps
0	Prospect	Sales and marketing activity	Identify new lead/s
25	Lead Generation	Potential prospect contacted and/or responded to sales and marketing activity	Lead/s identified
50	Sales Prospect Qualified	Sales engagement (call or meeting) to qualify prospect	Move to product or service positioning
75	Sales Prospect Presented	Sales engagement to present and position to prospect	Product or service presented
100	Close	Attempt to close business	Action to win or lose sale
			If won: Fulfillment and CLCM If lost: Move to CLCM If delayed/Goes quiet: Move to CLCM
5	Customer Life Cycle Management (CLCM)	Monthly drip marketing (Rule of 12)	Monthly updates from business via e-mail/mailing, etc.

Most sales pipelines will mirror the various sales stages within a business. Depending on the nature of each business and industry, the pipeline stages can vary. Here is an example of a typical sales pipeline and their relative sales steps:

4.) Forecast Sales by Activity, Not by Hoping

In sales, timely and active follow-up is critical, especially since many salespeople fail miserably at it. Great salespeople control the sales process and are always moving to the next steps needed to close business. Those next steps are critical in understanding what is truly expected to come through the door when your sales forecasts are due, and therefore should define the basis of your forecasts.

5.) Measure and Learn from Your Results

We are all human and humans make mistakes. If we learn from them, the mistakes we make in the past should only help us make better decisions in the future. Because of this, it is important that you analyze and learn from past forecasting results so you can get a better read on where you stand moving forward.

6.) Do Not Substitute Insight and Action with Automation

Only 65 percent of companies recently surveyed indicated that they have a defined sales process. Of those, 15 percent use a sales process provided by their CRM vendor. In short, one out of ten companies use a CRM system–provided sales process. Yes, there are a lot of great sales management automation tools (CRM) in use today. The problem is, even the best CRM systems are still perceived by many salespeople as providing less incremental value to them personally over the time investment they have to make for it to be successful for the company. Because of this, salespeople continue to reluctantly use them and typically only at a minimum level of required interaction.

The potential benefits provided by CRM systems today are still far greater for the company than to the salesperson who has to feed them. The result we commonly see from this is bad forecasting and pipeline management; garbage in and garbage out. Because of this, if you have salespeople working for your business you should not fully rely on them directly using sales automation alone to give you a truly accurate read on your sales outlook. Moreover, in doing so this also breaks a cardinal sales-management rule that you should never allow your salespeople to directly forecast their sales. CRM systems should not be an excuse for poor sales management and they should only replace those functions that cannot be better accomplished through alternative means.

CHAPTER 2

PROSPECTING: CREATING AWARENESS AND PROSPECTS FOR YOUR BUSINESS

• • •

When it comes to sales, most salespeople have one thing in common: They love to sell yet hate to prospect. Most people who sell will tell you that their highest levels of engagement and fulfillment in their work come around the sale and the close, not when cold-calling and prospecting. No matter what people feel about prospecting, there are no sales and services to be sold without a prospect to sell to. This means that most professionals are left to eat only what they kill themselves. So why is it, then, that we see the following failures as it pertains to prospecting and selling?[1]

- **48 percent** of salespeople will **NEVER follow up** with a sales prospect
- **30 percent** of leads received today are not followed up on at all
- **44 percent** of salespeople give up after only one follow-up

- **91 percent** of customers say they would **give referrals**, yet only **11 percent** of people **will ask for them**
- The average salesperson only makes **two attempts** to reach a sales prospect
- **50–72** percent of sales typically go to the **first salesperson** who contacts a prospect

Like most aspects of business, prospecting is a numbers game, and those who properly set this expectation in their planning, execution, and attitude are those who tend to excel at this process. The bottom line is that **prospecting commonly involves a higher degree of rejection** than anything else you will do in your life. The mental fortitude and discipline to fight through these rejections and remain confident enough to sell to the few that remain is the key to the process.

Another aspect of prospecting to consider is that prospecting is NOT selling, and should not be treated the same. Many larger businesses have recently come to this realization and are beginning to bifurcate some or all of the prospecting functions away from their salespeople so each discipline can be maximized based on their respective specialization, repetition, and refinement. For most professionals, however, they will lack this luxury and have to take on many if not all of these prospecting and sales tasks on their own.

When it comes to your own prospecting, each industry will have their own twists and best practices based on a number of factors, including your target market, your resources, skills and expertise, advertising rules, guidelines and ethics, your competition, your goals, and, of course, your priorities. Before we jump into the details about various ways to improve your prospecting skills, there are a few keys areas of prospecting you should consider.

First, **know your target market and THEIR needs**. Once you have defined your target market, learn as much about them as you can and use that information to your advantage. For many professionals, this starts with obtaining a list of all of your potential prospects if possible and augmenting that information with key intelligence and information both now and over time. For example, what are your sales prospects' birthdays, wedding and work anniversaries; what do they like to eat; what do they like to do; where do they work; what profession are they in; etc. Remember, you can never have enough information about your prospects, and with new CRM and customer management automation systems, you now have no excuse for not being able to organize that information into a useful system to help support your prospecting efforts.

Second, your prospects will ONLY respond to your prospecting efforts based on three factors: **curiosity, obligation, and urgency**. Every time I review a professional's prospecting activities I start with three simple questions: **Did this action make me curious? Did I feel any sense of obligation to respond? And did it create any sense of urgency for me to want to act now in response to it?** Absent any one of these three elements, your prospecting efforts will be highly inefficient and likely doomed to fail. For example, most professionals who create mailers, emails, literature, commercials, etc., get so caught up in the creative and actionable elements of the marketing medium that they lose focus on how their target market will actually react to it. What ends up happening through this process is the creation of a whole lot of potentially good-looking billboards in a proverbial cornfield, producing nothing more than a waste of time and money. When this happens, congratulations—you can now add "starving artist" to your resume. The bottom line is when it comes to prospecting, these three simple questions based on curiosity, obligation, and urgency will help guide you toward success so you can leave everything else for the starving artists.

Third, create and follow a **REPEATABLE prospecting process**. Ask yourself: Do I have a defined elevator pitch that I can use at any time that defines the value I provide to my target market in a brief, clear, and concise manner? How about branding and messaging? Or how about a plan to con-sistently prospect in the most effective manner over the next twelve months? There is a very simple formula you can follow in any marketing effort; **frequency times reach equals results**. Most professionals can grasp the concept of reach, which is defined by the total size of the audience you can create awareness to at any one time. Where they often fail is when it comes to frequency, which is the amount of times you can repeat your reach. I continue to run into countless professionals who will run one or two TV or radio advertisements, mailers, blog posts, newsletters, speaking engagements, emails, etc., and then STOP. The key to frequency for professionals is developing a solid marketing plan that balances both reach and frequency and creates a discipline to execute on both in a repeatable manner.

Fourth, **coordinate ALL of your prospecting activities together** and utilize multiple touch points. All people react differently to various forms of stimulus and marketing efforts; one size does not fit all when it comes to marketing and prospecting. For example, some people may be more responsive to phone calls versus emails. Others may respond better to speeches than mailings, while others may ignore trade shows but watch TV. The goal is to design your marketing plan to surround and touch your target market in as many different ways as possible while producing the highest rate of return on your marketing investment. In order to accomplish this, you also need to make sure all of your various prospecting techniques are timed and deployed in a way to provide the best coverage and results. For example, absent any actionable events such as income-tax filing season, inclement weather, etc., prospecting efforts should ideally be evenly spread out over time and not clustered in defined time segments. They should also be coordinated for maximum synergies, such as sending out a mailing, emailing, or cold-calling immediately after a speech or major event. For example, when following up on new sales leads received, a **"coordinated" follow-up schedule of email and phone calls can typically result in a 16 percent increase** in the chance of reaching the lead by phone. Most prospecting efforts are far more effective when they are run in an interrelated marketing system than independently and on their own.

Fifth, **nurture your prospects, turning cold leads** into warm prospects. Most professionals hate the repetitive grind of having to personally introduce and reintroduce themselves over and over, day after day to the same people; it can get old after a while. The good news is that new marketing tools and techniques can now be leveraged to help you do this much more effectively. The other good news is that nurtured leads typically make 47 percent larger purchases than non-nurtured leads. So if you need to raise your sales effectiveness and average order size, this is a great place to begin.[2] To start with, you need to create awareness so your target market clearly knows what you do, with the goal of actively remembering you when they have a need for your services. Remember, up to 50 percent of qualified sales leads are not ready to buy when you are ready to sell your services to them, so a "no" now does not mean a "no" later.[2] In short, prospecting is not a sale, so you need to keep digging. By actively and consistently staying in front of your prospects, you create higher levels of awareness, brand identity, and trust, which leads to much more convertible sales over time. Moreover, it makes selling much more fun and less of a grind when your sales prospects already know who you are before the sales process begins.

Sixth, know that persistence pays off in the long run, so **DON'T GIVE UP**. Many professionals fail at effective prospecting because they give up way too soon while looking for more immediate results. We live in a society that is highly impetuous and increasingly impatient; two words that will not help you in marketing. When I give speeches describing marketing to professionals, I will commonly place a plant in front of them and ask somebody from the audience to come up and watch it grow. I will then ask them what is needed to make the plant grow. The most common responses I receive are water, oxygen, and light; all of which I provide them with. I then let them sit a little longer and ask them if it is growing. Most will laugh and say, "I think so." "So how can you tell?" I will ask them. You can't, but it must be growing; it has plenty of water, light, and oxygen. What this exercise illustrates to the audience is the final two ingredients you need in order to know if the plant is growing: **discipline and commitment**. These just so happen to be the same ingredients you need in your marketing efforts in order to make it grow and be successful. Most people don't want to sit through a presentation watching a plant grow, for they won't see it happen immediately despite knowing it will over time. So when you decide on your marketing plan, place a plant in your office to remind yourself where to look if you ever find yourself wanting to give up on it.

Seventh, **become an expert** in your chosen profession. Everybody loves credentials, prominent awards, and recognition. Why? Because it conveys a unique level of competency, credibility, and trust with your prospective customers, which can help lead to increased sales, revenues, and customer conversions. My career advice to anybody I work with is to pick a profession and set a goal to become regarded by others as an expert in that field. There are around 320,000,000 people in the United States at the time of this book, so how do you plan to make yourself stand out? By profession, there are currently around 1.2 million attorneys; 650,000 CPAs; 422,000 real estate agents; 440,000 insurance agents; etc., in the United States; how do you plan to make yourself stand out? Even if you are able to get everybody in the world to recognize you at first glance, **what do they really know about you and**

what your brand and promise means to them? By becoming an expert in your chosen profession, you are sending a message to the world and defining your brand and yourself as someone who is potentially unique, of higher value, and who commands respect.

Eighth, **measure your results and adjust** as needed. There is an old saying in business that "you cannot manage what you cannot measure." All of your prospecting efforts must have a form of measurement, otherwise how will you know if it's working, when it's working, and why? Since marketing requires higher levels of discipline and commitment to be successful over time, you have to define what success looks like so you know when you achieve it. The first measure of success is progress to your defined business goals. Are your prospecting efforts supporting your sales, growth, revenues, and income objectives? Next should be your return on investment (ROI) for your marketing budget. Is your ROI increasing or decreasing over time? If it is increasing, what are you doing right and what is producing the best results for you? If it is decreasing, what adjustments do you need to make to your marketing plan to make it more effective and produce better returns?

KNOW WHAT YOUR CUSTOMERS ARE REALLY WORTH

As a professional and a businessperson, do you really know how much your customers are worth to you? Many professionals may think they know, but most do not—unless they are part of the top 20 percent. When answering this question, most professionals today tend to think of what they currently charge their customers for one or more services as their value to the business and nothing else. They make no distinctions among things such as sales to existing versus new customers, what type of customers they are, the loyalty of the customer, referrals received from a customer, etc.

The consideration of worth and value in business is pretty simple: The value to a customer is the total value of your service minus the price. The value to a business is the price less the cost of doing business. The worth of a business is the total value of a business less the total cost, and **the worth of a customer is the Customer Lifetime Value (CLV) of your service minus the costs**.

Customer Lifetime Value (CLV) is the net present value of all of the earnings (both direct and indirect) you can expect to receive from a customer over the lifetime of their engagement with your business. The CLV factors in all of the value a client can provide to your company, including revenue growth, referrals received, pricing premiums, etc., minus their initial Customer Acquisition Costs (CAC), operating and main-tenance costs, and defection rates. Here is how to calculate the CLV for your business: Customer Lifetime Value (CLV) = Net Profit per Customer x (Customer Retention Rate (percentage) ÷ [(1 + Money Discount Rate (percentage) – Customer Retention Rate (percentage)].

Here is an example of a CLV calculation for a business. Assume you generated $500,000 in sales last year from 125 customers ($4,000 average order size per customer), your net profit margins per customer are 30 percent ($1,200 per customer), you have a 90 percent customer retention rate, and your cost of money is 3 percent (Money Discount Rate). Based on these numbers, your **CLV would be $2,769** ($1,200 x (30 percent ÷ [1 + 3 percent – 90 percent]). In this example, we can see that the initial profits earned per customer are less than half the total estimated earnings value of that customer over their projected lifecycle with the business.

A similar measure of the CLV is based on the customer's expected net present value of their business alone. In short, how much total business will a typical client produce for your business calculated in the Customer Lifetime Revenue (CLR)? Similar to the CLV equation, the CLR equation replaces the Net Profit per Customer and replaces it with the Average Order Size per Customer. Following the numbers used for the CLV above, the **CLR would be: $9,230** ($4,000 x (30 percent ÷ [1 + 3 percent – 90 percent]). Again this number is slightly more than twice the average order size.

Both calculations will vary based on factors such as the cost of money, your average order size, net profit margins, and your retention rate. These numbers can dramatically change just by little changes in our percentages—especially your customer retention numbers. For most businesses today, **just a one percentage point improvement in selling to existing versus new customers alone can increase the value of the average customer worth from 25 to 100 percent**. Why? Because the cost to acquire new customers is typically seven times the cost of retaining them for most businesses today. Moreover, the longer you keep a customer, the more profit you will receive from them over time. In the example above, a mere 5 percentage point improvement in the customer retention rate alone can result in the doubling of the total number of customers in as little as fourteen years. So why isn't customer retention a priority for every business today?

Customer retention is often overlooked by many businesspeople today because their primary focus is frequently short term based on more immediate sales objectives measured in generally accepted accounting principles. Most people who sell services typically have short-term sales targets measured in days, weeks, months, quarters, and years. The same is true for accountants when measuring the performance of your business. This is why you have to be careful in measuring the value of businesses based on short-term sales and revenues alone, since it can be both misleading and hide the true long-term path and value of your business based largely on customer retention and the impacts it has on the business years from now.

So now that you know what your customers are really worth to your business, what are some of the things you can do to increase their worth to your company? Here are a few places to start:

- **Focus on selling to the "right" customers.** As previously discussed, you need to create a Target Client Profile and design all of your sales and marketing efforts around those customers. This not only means to focus on them but also having the discipline to say "no" to other business that potentially moves you off this mark. Next, you need to segment your customers into three categories:

Promoters, Buyers, and Demoters, and treat them differently based on their segmentation.

- **Increase your customer-retention initiatives.** Losing customers, especially your best customers, can kill a business over time, so don't let it happen to you. We know on average that it costs around seven times more to acquire a new customer than to retain an existing one, so the more your business bleeds customers, the higher your Customer Acquisition Costs (CAC) will become—leading to lower profits. Because of this, make sure that you exceed your current customers' expectations and continue to find ways to add value to your relationship, especially with your Promoters. Also, be careful not to oversell or overcharge your existing clients; any short-term gain will not justify the long-term costs to your business of having to replace them.

- **Increase your referrals from your customers.** As we discuss later in this book, customer referrals are typically your best potential source of new business. These are leads that include immediate citations and tend to convert at a much higher rate than most other forms of marketing. Entire businesses such as Google, Quicken, and others were largely built by the referrals of others— mostly by their happy customers. As we have seen with companies such as Google, happy clients can in effect become your sales force and can propel you to even greater sales—if you provide them with enough value to properly motivate them to want to refer you to others.

Depending on the ethics surrounding your industry, don't be afraid to reward good referrals as well, either directly or indirectly. In many professional businesses today, the cost of rewarding a good referral is significantly less than the cost of acquiring new customers through direct sales and marketing efforts.

- **Measure your customer retention through Net Promoter Scores (NPS).** Far too many businesses today use false measurements in their customer-retention efforts. Many will send out lengthy customer satisfaction surveys that are both too time-consuming to complete and provide a poor measurement of retention. Research has shown that 60 to 80 percent of customers who have left a business had said in a survey just prior to leaving that they were satisfied or very satisfied.3 So don't confuse retention for satisfaction.

The Net Promoter Score is a simple one-question survey you can ask (by email, calls, mailers, etc.) of your current customers: "How likely is it that you would recommend our services to a friend or colleague?" The responses are provided on a scale from 1 to 10, with 10 being the most loyal and 1 being the least. Based on the NPS model, unhappy customers will respond with a 0 to 6, loyal customers will respond from 9 to 10, and passive customers will answer 7 to 8.4 When surveyed frequently (monthly or quarterly), the NPS scores should be reviewed on a per-customer basis with internal alerts and actions for the company to follow to address any problems—especially if the customer is classified as a Promoter or Buyer.

- **Run an effective customer defection analysis.** In business, you should always understand that whenever price exceeds perceived customer value, your customers may and will defect. Many people tend to overanalyze customer defections when it all really comes down to Occam's razor; meaning the first answer is usually the right one. Remember that in business value is a ratio of quality to price, so always analyze both when doing your defection analysis. One of the best ways to accomplish this is by following the "Rule of 5 Whys" in questioning.

The Rule of 5 Whys is based on the notion that you can get to the root of most problems by simply asking the "why" of a question five times. The 5 Whys should form the basis for how you interview defecting customers. For example, you may call a customer who canceled by asking them, "Why did you cancel with us?" He may respond by saying, "The price was too high," to which you may reply, "Why do you think the price was too high?" They might then say, "I just didn't see the results from your service," to which you might say, "Why were the results not of value to you?" He then says, "I just never really knew what was going on with my service," to which you might reply, "Why were you not in the know about your service?" He then may say, "Your company never provided me with any updates by phone," to which you respond, "Why? Didn't you get any of our weekly emails or texts?" He responds, "I don't have email or a mobile phone, so how was I supposed to get them?" The pathology of this cancelation was pretty clear: It wasn't price but a communication breakdown due to his lack of access to the business's preferred customer communication efforts. In addition to potentially addressing this client's real issues, the business can now address the systematic problem as well to help ensure this doesn't happen to other customers.

How you run a customer defection analysis is just as important as whom you run it with. If one of the corner-stones to growing a business is selling to the right customers, you need to focus your retention efforts and defection analysis on your RIGHT customers as well. Most companies today have a customer defection/cancelation rate of 10–30 percent per year. Owners and company financial managers will typically look at their defection numbers with no customer segmentation beyond their individual spending levels. The result is a short-term financial analysis based on profits and revenues alone—the surest way to start killing a business.

By understanding your Target Client Profile and how to effectively segment your customer base, you can now create a much more accurate understanding of the true long-term impact of customer defections on your sales and retention numbers. For example, let's say your customer-defection rate was 20 percent last year. When looking at a segmented list of those customers, you discover that the vast majority—more than 75 percent—were Promoters. Now what is the potential impact of losing so many Promoters, and how would that compare to the opposite of losing more than 75 percent of your Demoters instead?

When looking at this example, the short-term financial numbers alone may tell you nothing—the dollar loss could be the same to an accountant and therefore provides them with no real long-term and strategic guidance. But looking at who you lose or retain by segment is far more valuable for the longer-term health of the company and your sales outlook.

The benefit of segmentation can be applied to your customer-defection analysis as well. If you or your business conducts post-defection interviews/surveys with your former customers—which you should—how do you know WHO you are really talking to? Moreover, with larger businesses, how can you look beyond all of the numbers and know WHO you should really be talking to and WHY? Does the feedback provided by a Demoter carry the same weight as a Promoter? Of course not. The problem is, absent this type of customer segmentation, most business owners and managers look at them all on an equal plane. And guess who will complain the most and create the most concerns for the executives? The same Demoters who do nothing to help you grow your new sales and business. That is why customer-defection interviews and surveys should be primarily focused on your Promoters using a Customer Defection Segmentation List.

CUSTOMER DEFECTION SEGMENTATION LIST *(Example)*			
Date:			
Client Segment	Customer	Company	Post Defection Actions
P=Promoter B=Buyer D=Demoter			
P	Tom Burris	XYZ Industries	Interview
D	Anne Gains	ABC Law Firm	No Action
B	Peter Forrester	Better Car Dealers	Send Survey
B	Ira London	Simple Cleaning Service	Send Survey
P	Tim Foster	Top Freight	Interview
D	Jan Rhodes	Top to Bottom Company	No Action
B	Bridget Jones	Magic Airlines	Send Survey
P	Richard Smith	Best Round Golf Course	Interview
B	Todd Fleming	Better Pools	Send Survey
D	Burt Newbaur	Hats and Things	No Action
D	Lisa Guilfolye	Car Equipment Suppliers Inc.	No Action
P	T. Goldman	Better Bird Baths	Interview

- **Never stop innovating.** Businesses are on one of only two trajectories: they are either innovating and growing or they are dying. Your short-term financial numbers may not reflect it now, but absent innovation in any business, you are killing off your business. Many businesses and business owners may think they are uniquely innovative, but your customers may think otherwise—so use this to your advantage. For example, recent studies have shown that only 14 percent of customers indicate that benefits they receive from business providers were unique or beneficial.[5]

Innovation comes in many forms and is not just limited to one thing. Oftentimes markets can change without the major players keeping tabs on those changes and being able and nimble enough to react to it. For example, for decades many people considered the taxicab business to be a relatively "safe" business until a company named Uber came along and led to the biggest disruption in the history of the taxicab industry—which was enabled by a simple app on a smartphone that most people now have with them everywhere.

Innovation is not just a set of actions but rather a cultural change made throughout an entire business. This cultural change starts with the questioning of the status quo in everything you do by asking simple questions starting with "why." For example: Why do our current customers buy and stay with us? Why are we doing this and why aren't we doing that? Why would our current customers possibly leave us and for what reasons? Why do our customers use a service like ours and what else do they want that we could possibly provide better than their other options? As you can see, the number of questions you can ask are infinite and can come from a myriad of sources including customer interviews, customer-defection analysis, market research, customer and market surveys, etc. Just remember that you can have all of the data in the world, but you have to develop a culture to want to act on that information and not become complacent—and that culture starts with you.

NEVER EAT ANOTHER MEAL ALONE: 1,100 POTENTIAL PROSPECTS ARE JUST WAITING FOR YOU

In most businesses today, referrals are the most effective forms of prospecting. Why? Because referrals provide a higher level of "credibility" and "trust" over all other forms of marketing. Most people commonly refer to these as "warm" leads. Warm leads mean higher rates of sales conversion and better productivity and time management; all of which are key to successful sales growth.

Let's face it; we all get bombarded every day with increasing levels of advertising. **The average person now receives around FOUR THOUSAND marketing messages a day; a nearly 700 percent increase over the past 40 years.**[6] Poor salespeople think like lemmings and follow prospecting trends right off the cliff with other non-successful people. Smart salespeople, on the other hand, always look for ways to differentiate, innovate, and successfully outperform their competition, and there is no better place to start than with your prospecting efforts.

Most of us will eat, and do so three times a day. People love to eat, and the more complicated their lives, the more they love the "release" of eating. Eating and eating out provides release in many different ways. It releases us from our office constraints, the people we work/live with every day, and from the minutia and mundane activities of our jobs and processes that govern our everyday lives. We also love good food, dining environments, and meeting new people.

So here is what I always tell professionals who need more business: **DON'T WASTE YOUR MEALS BY EATING ALONE.** The best way to accomplish this is to focus on the following steps:

First, **set your goals**. Great sales planning is all about developing repeatable and successful sales systems and habits. So if you want to be successful, set a prospecting goal now and measure yourself against it. To keep this simple, set a goal of taking a customer/prospect out to lunch each workday and out for breakfast at least three days a week. Factoring in vacations and time off, this works out to around **368 referral meals a year**. If you were to receive on average at least three referrals from each meal, this would add up to over 1,100 new sales leads. So how would you like to receive 1,100 new "warmer" prospects this year?

Second, remember to **give in order to receive**. In sales, you have to give in order to receive to be successful. Think about it: When you visit a customer and/or prospect in their work/home environments, you are taking their time to sell to them while initially giving nothing in return. You might think your service is the give, but in most cases, this involves a delayed value exchange. And just how much time do people have these days to review all the sales opportunities that come their way? Taking a prospect or customer out to breakfast or lunch (and paying for it) is the most effective way for most people to "give" before you are selling and asking to receive.

Third, **know who to take out**. The biggest mistake sales-people make when taking clients/prospects out to lunch is asking the wrong people to join them. Not every client/prospect is the ideal client—especially when it comes to asking for referrals. The primary people you should be focusing your referral breakfast and lunch meetings with are your PRO-MOTERS. Remember, there are only three types of customers you will ever have: Promoters, Buyers, and Demoters. Of the three, only Promoters will give back to you (in referrals) when you initially give to them. The goal is to identify your Promoters and focus all of your referral meals with them first.

Fourth, **create a personal connection.** Referral breakfasts and lunches should start with building trust and a connection with the customer, and you don't do this by starting right out with asking for referrals. In most cases, you will only have about sixty minutes during meals, so use them wisely. Before your meal, look up information about your customer/prospect;

Google their name and look on LinkedIn—find out what they are passionate about in their lives. If all else fails and you don't know, simply ask them—most people love to talk about themselves. The goal here is to create and foster a personal connection so they will like you and feel obligated to help you. Hold your referral questions until the latter half of the meal. This should give you enough time to build a relationship and not look like you are only there to take from them.

Fifth, **bring referral resources and aids.** How often do you go to meetings totally unprepared? Most people will say never. Well, you need to approach your referral breakfasts and lunches in the same manner. If the goal of these meetings is to ask for referral business, you need to be able to clearly define who your target prospects are and why. Since you are relying on referrals from your contact, you need to clearly spell this out for them and help provide them with whatever will assist them in this effort. This may include a target prospect list or names of people in their own network. If your referral provider is on LinkedIn, connect with them prior to the meeting and show them their connections on the LinkedIn app on your smartphone and see if it helps to jog their memory. Once they start firing off names, write them down.

Sixth, **ask, ask, and ask**. The biggest problem most sales-people have in dealing with referrals is they simply don't ask for them. Studies have shown that 91 percent of customers have indicated that they will provide referrals, yet only 11 percent of people will ask for them.7 Be the 11 percent, and create the habits now to ALWAYS ask for referrals from the right people in the right environments. As previously discussed, the best time to ask for referrals during meals is toward the latter half of the meal; after you have created trust and fostered a relationship and a better obligation to ask and receive. So what do you ask? Simple: **"Can you please tell me somebody (at least three to five people) in your network that could possibly benefit from my services?"** Nail this question down and get it in your head so you don't forget. REMEMBER: **If you never ask for something, the answer is always "NO."**

Seventh, **make sure to follow up**. Most people selling fail due to one simple step: They do not follow up. We know from studies that **48 percent of salespeople never follow up with a prospect** and they will make only two attempts on average to reach them and then stop. Since we know that at least 50–70 percent of sales go to the first person who contacts a prospect, we can clearly see the disconnect here. **The key is to follow up and never give up.** You may need to change how you follow up after repeated attempts, but you never give up. Remember, only 50 percent of qualified leads may be ready to buy when you want to sell to them, so you need a system to stay in front of them until they are ready to buy.

When it comes to following up on your new "warm" leads from your referral breakfasts and lunches, you need to act on and convert them at the highest levels possible. Start by asking if the referrer will help to introduce you to the referrals on your behalf and then let you know when that happens. This is typically the best way to convert your leads and frequently takes place by a phone or by email introduction.

If the referrer is not willing to make that effort, ask them if you can use their name as a source for the reference instead—

most people will agree to this. In these instances, make sure to formulate your messages to your referrals carefully and in a way that will generate the highest levels of credibility and curiosity. Examples could include:

"Hi John, I just had lunch with Jim Smith, who is a customer of mine, and he gave me your name and said we should meet. How does Wednesday afternoon look for you? If I don't hear back I will help by sending you a calendar invite. PS: During our meeting please remind me to discuss how I helped Jim save money this year."

"Hi John, I work with Jim Smith and he said you could benefit from my services. What days and times would work best to meet for fifteen minutes this week? Can I send you a calendar invite for Thursday at 3 p.m.? PS: Remind me to tell you about how Jim is now getting his best customers."

For those referral prospects who fail to respond after five repeated attempts to reach them, put them into a drip-marketing system so you can stay in front of and continue to market to them and get their business when they are finally ready to buy from you.

These of course are just a couple of examples and will vary based on factors such as contact mediums, industries, etc. Either way, make sure your follow-up messages have a **PURPOSE**, are **RELEVANT** and **PERSONALIZED**, include a **CALL TO ACTION**, and generate **CURIOSITY**.

Lastly, make sure to keep your receipts from all of your breakfasts and lunches, for you may be able to write off some or all of these expenses on your taxes at the end of the year.

Make sure to connect with your accountant on these details so you can plan ahead for this. This also brings me to the topic of dinners. Many dinners can include alcohol, and the costs can grow to three times or more the cost of a breakfast or lunch and commonly result in the same outcomes—at a higher cost, of course. You also want to be careful to not compete with your prospect's personal family time as well. My general rule of thumb for professionals is breakfasts and lunches before dinner, and save dinners for your best Promoters ONLY.

KNOW THE BEST TIMES TO PROSPECT

Knowing what prospects to contact and with what messages is not complete until you time it right. People are getting very busy during their days and the attempts to reach them are growing along with it. The number of cold calls attempted to reach the average person has increased from 3.68 attempts in 2007 to 8 in 2013; nearly a 100 percent increase in six years.[7] Business-related emails received are also expected to increase from an average of 108 per person per day in 2011 to 140 per person per day by 2018; a 30 percent increase.[8]

As a result of all these growing levels of contact, you need to get good at picking the best times to get through the constant bombardment your prospects receive. When it comes to **sending emails and newsletters**, the best times for responses are between 8 a.m. to 3 p.m. with **peak times between 8–9 a.m. and around 3 p.m. each day**. When sending emails, some professionals even believe that the best times to send them out are on weekdays between 1 a.m. and 5 a.m. local time since most people start their days by reading emails. For **cold calls**, the best times to call are **between 8–10 a.m. and 4–5 p.m.** and the best days to prospect are **Wednesdays and Thursdays**, with Tuesdays being the worst. As for social media, the best days to distribute content and have it viewed and shared are **Monday and Tuesdays between 8 a.m. and 10 a.m.** As for direct mailing, the best-targeted days for **mail arrival are Tuesday through Thursday, with the most desirable day being Wednesday**.

KNOW YOUR PROSPECTING EQUATIONS FOR SUCCESS

Contrary to what many people may think, effective prospecting is not just about "outworking" everybody else. Effective prospecting is all about creating a plan based on the numbers and executing on that plan consistently, diligently, and relentlessly.

In order to create your prospecting plan, you have four key numbers you need to define. First, **what is your annual sales target or goal?** You should already know this number, and if you don't, you need to revisit your business plans and goals and define one before you go any further. Remember, everything you are using in your business and marketing plan is to support your business goals, and primary among them is your sales goal per year. So don't skip this step.

Second, you need to define your expected **close ratio** for your sales engagements. Don't worry if you are new to this; you can simply use a baseline of 20–25 percent to start with and adjust over time relative to your industry and how you perform. Typically **close ratios in excess of 35 percent are** considered very good in most industries, so if you want a standard benchmark to shoot for as you become more effective, use 35 percent as a future objective while trying to stay conservative in your estimations. Over time, you will be able to modify this number based on your real results.

Third, you need an **average sale size**. Again, this may be newer to you, but you should have a general idea of what your services will cost and how much a typical customer will pay you for it, which will become the basis for this number. If you don't know, look into your market research as to what your target market typically pays for services like yours and/or simply ask similar providers what they receive on an average sale. Over time, you will be able to modify this number based on your real results.

Fourth, you need to calculate your **prospecting activity rate** by the number of calls, emails, meetings, etc., on a daily, weekly, monthly, and annual basis. Let's break these numbers down, starting from the top and working our way back into your prospecting activities. First, let's make a few assumptions. First is that you will work 235 days in a year. This comes from taking your total number of weeks in a year (52) and removing time for vacations, sick days, and unforeseen events. If you end up working more days than that, great—but for your calculations you should always take a conservative approach. Let's also assume an annual sales goal of $500,000, a close ratio of 20 percent, and an average sale size of $4,000. Now that we have our numbers, here are the equations:

- [Annual Sales Goal ÷ (Average Order Size X Close Ratio)] ÷ 235 Days = **Daily Sales Goal**
  [$500,000 ÷ ($4,000 X 20 percent)] ÷ 235 Days = <u>**2.7 Sales / Day**</u>

- [Annual Sales Goal ÷ (Average Order Size X Close Ratio)] ÷ 47 Weeks = **Weekly Sales Goal**
  [$500,000 ÷ ($4,000 X 20 percent)] ÷ 47 Weeks = <u>**13.3 Sales / Week**</u>

- [Annual Sales Goal ÷ (Average Order Size X Close Ratio)] ÷ 12 Months = **Monthly Sales Goal**
  [$500,000 ÷ ($4,000 X 20 percent)] ÷ 12 Months = <u>**52.1 Sales / Month**</u>

Now that we have our necessary sales numbers, we need to calculate the prospecting activity needed to get us to these numbers. No matter what numbers you come up with per marketing source, the goal should always be to try to break down the average to **DAILY GOALS** or as close to daily numbers as possible. Why? Because it is much easier to focus on daily goals and objectives than managing objectives that are variable over longer periods of time such as weeks and months.

Let's start by looking at industry-average response rates (i.e., when your marketing actions produce a lead) for the various marketing tools commonly in use today, and what is needed for each to help you get to your sales goals. For these examples, we are going to use the same numbers (or sales goals) we previously produced of 2.7 sales needed per day and a 20 percent close rate to hit our sales objective. It is also important to note that all of your numbers, including your close rate, may vary per lead type, so over time you should be better able to adjust these numbers to get a more accurate calculation for each.

Direct mail has an average response rate of .05–4 percent.[9] Typically providing the lowest return on investment (7 to 1) of all the major marketing mediums, you can calculate the amount of mail pieces sent to typically produce one lead at: (1 ÷ .05 percent) = 200 mail pieces to (1 ÷ .4 percent) = 25 mail pieces with an average of <u>113 mail pieces a day</u>. If your goal was to produce enough direct mail leads alone to meet a sales objective of 2.7 sales a day, you would need to send out at least **565 direct mailers a day** (113 mail pieces ÷ 20 percent Sales Conversion Rate).

Pay-Per-Click (PPC) advertising has an average click-to-lead conversion rate of 4–5 percent. You can calculate the amount of PPC contacts needed to typically produce one lead at: (1 ÷ 20 percent) = <u>5 contacts a day</u>. If your goal was to produce enough PPC-generated leads alone to meet a sales objective of 2.7 sales a day, you would need to have at least **13.5 contacts a day** (5 contacts x 2.7 sales) by **paying for 300 clicks per day** (13.5 contacts a day ÷ 4.5 percent PPC Conversion Rate).

Phone Calls have an average response rate of 8–12 percent. You can calculate the amount of phone calls needed to typically produce one lead at: (1 ÷ 8 percent) = 12.5 calls to (1 ÷ 12 percent) = 8.3 calls, with an average of <u>10.4 calls</u>

<u>needed a day</u>. If your goal was to produce enough phone-call leads alone to meet a sales objective of 2.7 sales a day, you would need to make at least **52 phone calls a day** (10.4 phone calls ÷ 20 percent Sales Conversion Rate).

Mass (Bulk) Emails have an average response rate of .12 percent (along with a 22 percent open rate and a 2.8 percent click-through rate). Typically providing the highest return on investment (28 to 1) of all the major marketing mediums, you can calculate the amount of mass emails sent to typically produce one lead at: (1 ÷ .12 percent) = <u>833.3 emails a day</u>. If your goal was to produce enough mass-mail leads alone to meet a sales objective of 2.7 sales a day, you would need to send out at least **4,167 mass emails a day** (833.3 emails ÷ 20 percent Sales Conversion Rate).

TV and Radio has an average response rate of around 1 percent. You can calculate the amount of people you need to typically reach to produce one lead at: (1 ÷ 1 percent) = <u>100 people a day</u>. If your goal was to produce enough TV and radios ads alone to meet a sales objective of 2.7 sales a day, you would need to reach at least **500 people a day** (100 people ÷ 20 percent Sales Conversion Rate) with your advertising reach.

Print Advertising has an average response rate of around 1–2 percent. You can calculate the amount of people you need to typically reach to produce one lead at: (1 ÷ 1 percent) = 100 people to (1 ÷ 2 percent) = 50 people with an average of <u>75 people a day</u>. If your goal was to run enough print advertising alone to meet a sales objective of 2.7 sales a day, you would need to reach at least **375 people a day** (75 people ÷ 20 percent Sales Conversion Rate) with your print advertising.

Now that you know the relative volume needed by using one or more marketing mediums to achieve your sales objectives, the next piece of the puzzle it to calculate the **Cost per Lead (CPL)** for each marketing medium. As you can see from the previous calculations, it is possible to meet your lead goals through the use of any one of these marketing options, but that alone is not a clear measure of success. **The goal of any business should be to produce the maximum amount of leads at the lowest amount of cost. This is typically measured on a Cost per Lead (CPL) basis.**

Most of the marketing mediums previously mentioned have various cost factors involved, including things such a creation, production, automation, distribution systems, click costs, labor, etc., that all factor into their overall costs. Once you factor these in, you can then calculate your costs per lead based on the following formula: **(Advertising Spend ÷ # Responses) = Cost per Lead (CPL).**

Last but not least is the calculation of your **Customer Acquisition Cost (CAC).** Your CAC is one of the critical questions investors will likely ask you first about your business since it is a key industry benchmark and **indicator of how well you run your marketing** and your overall profitability, which helps them to determine your equity value. Your CAC is a calculation based on new customers produced from ALL of your combined marketing expenses based on the following equation: **(Total Marketing Costs ÷ Total # of Customers Acquired) = Customer Acquisition Cost.** Naturally, the lower your CAC, the better you are running your business, especially as it applies to your sales and marketing efforts. A lower CAC is also appealing to investors since they will commonly compare your CAC to your industry and use that to measure the sales and marketing effectiveness of both your business and the person running it.

Now that you are able to calculate your Customer Acquisition Costs (CAC), how do you know your **Return on Investment (ROI)** and what your customers are really worth? More important, how do we know that the ROI is actually profitable for your business? After all, why be in business if you can't turn a profit? This is why we need to find the **Return on Marketing Investment (ROMI)** for your marketing spending. Before we get to customer valuation, it is important that we cover ROI and ROMI in more detail.

Return on Investment (ROI) tells you the percentage return you receive from your investment. Applying this to sales and marketing, the ROI for your sales and marketing efforts is calculated as a total percentage of investment return based on sales gained for the investment made by the following equation: ROI = [(Total Sales – Sales & Marketing Costs) ÷ Sales & Marketing Costs] x 100. For example, let's day you generated $500,000 in new sales at a cost of $100,000 in sales and marketing expenses last year. Based on these numbers, you would have generated a 400 percent ROI [($500,000 – $100,000) ÷ $100,000] x 100. The result of this equation is by percentage, but most ROI measurements calculated this way are presented as "# to 1" ratio such as a "3 to 1" or "5 to 1" return on your investment. In this case, you would have a sales and marketing ROI of 4 to 1 (400 percent ROI ÷ 100 percent Invested = 4).

For most businesses and professionals, the next question should be, "What is an acceptable ROI?" This number really depends. On one extreme, an ROI of 1 to 1 (0 percent gain) would indicate that you are producing the same amount in new sales that you invested in, and what's the point of that? You have gained nothing. Conversely, a 5 to 1 ROI (400 percent gain) would certainly be a pretty good ROI. For most professionals a **3 to 1 ROI should be a minimum baseline of success** for any marketing spend. Anything less than that should be removed from your marketing mix and anything more should be viewed as a potential success relative to your other marketing mediums. Of course, this is merely a benchmark and does not tell the whole story. Just because you may be achieving a multiple return on your sales and marketing spend alone does not tell you if you are profitable in that effort.

In order to determine profitability for your marketing efforts beyond your ROI, you can utilize a **Return on Marketing Investment (ROMI).** The benefit of the ROMI is that it provides a better measurement for what level of ROI is truly profitable for your business beyond just guessing and/or using an industry standard. Unlike the ROI, the **ROMI requires that you know the net profit** you can generate from your incremental sales. The calculation for your ROMI is: ROMI = (Net New Gross Profit Generated – Cost of Marketing) ÷ Cost of Marketing. So let's go back to our previous example. In this example, let's assume you have a net profit margin of $150,000 or 30 percent ($500,000 Total Sales – $350,000 Total Costs). Now we can calculate a ROMI of 50 percent [($150,000 - $100,000) ÷ 100,000] x 100.

As a rule of thumb, **any ROMI should be positive to continue with a marketing effort,** and the higher the ROMI the better. If it is not profitable, then kill it. Remember, your business objective is to turn a profit, otherwise you will never grow. As Henry Ford once said, "Business must be run at a profit . . . else it will die." You can calculate a ROMI both at the aggregate level for all of your marketing as well as on a per-marketing-medium basis so you can compare the results of each and determine which ones are in fact profitable (beyond their initial ROI) and which ones are not. ROMIs can be **calculated on both a short-term and long-term basis** as well. Most marketers tend to view marketing ROI and ROMI on a short-term basis since their calculations of customer value tend to be short-term, such as what was sold this week, month, or year as a result. The problem is that not all of marketing is a short-term process.

As we discuss in this book, many customers provide a lifetime of value that cannot be easily captured in one sale alone. Moreover, how will you know exactly what was gained by each marketing source if they were all involved to one degree or another in generating a new sale? For example, what if somebody saw your direct mail and later Googled your name to find a Pay-Per-Click (PPC) that they clicked on, leading them to you? And what if they then left your ad and found your website and then responded to a mass email later that day? Exactly which one of these marketing mediums was attributable to this sale and in what percentage? This is where more long-term ROMI calculations and analysis come into play.

In the instances of more **long-term ROMI calculations,** you need to substitute the Customer Lifetime Value (CLV) for the Gross Profits, resulting in an equation that looks like this: ROMI = [(Customer Lifetime Value – Cost Of Marketing) ÷ Cost of Marketing]. The benefit of this is to better account for any initial loss at a longer-term gain of future business from the same new customer. For example, a dentist may provide a promotion for a teeth cleaning to get a new customer in the door. From a ROMI standpoint, the dentist may have made no profit or even lost money on the ROMI for the initial month and quarter of that new client acquisition, but the one-to-two-year ROMI could end up positive after further repeat services are rendered in the months and years ahead. In any scenario, the higher the lifetime value of continued customer repurchases, the more the Lifetime Value should be considered in this equation.

Now that we have looked at all the major marketing calculations, let's analyze this data in an example of a Marketing Performance Report.

ABC Company Marketing Performance Report (EXAMPLE) can be found in the Resources (page 409). You can download the entire Resources file at: www.TheSuccessfulSalesManager.com (from the "Tools" menu).

In this example for "ABC Company," we can see a company that has a monthly marketing budget of $18,440 and is currently tracking their marketing among fourteen different marketing sources. The report displays a couple of key measurements, including: a Lead Conversion Rate (LCR) of 20.87 percent, a

Cost per Lead (CPL) of $89.51, an average Customer Acquisition Cost (CAC) of $428.84, a Return on Investment (ROI) of 320.3 percent (or a 3.2 to 1 return), and a Return on Marketing Investment (ROMI) of 38.7 percent. All of these numbers together are acceptable at a baseline of a 3 to 1 ROI and a positive ROMI, but certainly not optimal. By looking at each marketing source, we can see the following for ABC Company:

- Public speaking, content marketing, blog and social media, website, email marketing, and lead generation are providing a very strong ROI and ROMI.

- Radio advertising, TV advertising, trade shows, cold-calling, and direct mail are providing the poorest ROI and ROMI and should be either improved or replaced. All of these underperforming mediums add up to $12,400 in total marketing costs (or 67 percent of the monthly marketing budget). In short, 67 percent of the current monthly marketing budget is not properly allocated.

- If ABC Company were to reallocate all of the spending from the five aforementioned poorest-performing market mediums and equally divided that spending to the top three performing mediums (public speaking, content marketing, and blog and social media), all things being equal, they could have seen the following improvements: a Cost per Lead (CPL) of $21.85 (a 410 percent improvement), an average Customer Acquisition Cost (CAC) of $111.75 (a 384 percent improvement), a Return on Investment (ROI) of 1,304 percent (a 983 percent improvement), and a Return on Marketing Investment

(ROMI) of 363.2 percent (a 324.5 percent improvement).

In this example, you can see the potential for dramatic increases in your overall marketing performance, but it all starts with a detailed analysis from the Marketing Performance Report. Absent any of that data, any changes in marketing would be largely based on guessing and not performance. Finally, it is also important to note that increases in better-performing marketing mediums could very well have diminishing returns, so this analysis is not typically static in performance and results for most companies. For example, there may be far fewer speaking venues that provide the type of performance ABC Company had previously received. Additionally, an increase in additional content, blogging, and social media activity may provide fewer incremental results. Ideally, **the best way to reallocate marketing spending is to increase those mediums that will scale the best with further spending—even if they are not the very top performers.**

CHAPTER 3

SALES PROCESS: CREATE AND FOLLOW A STANDARD SALES PROCESS

• • •

Only 65 percent of businesses today indicate that they have a defined sales process. This basically means that roughly one-third of all businesses are winging it when it comes to sales—and these are not the top 20 percent of businesses. Great businesses of any size are run by systems, and those systems are run by people; not the other way around. Sales is not an exception.

The benefits to having a good sales process are many. The most successful businesses are those that are run by systems and processes that make people interchangeable and not the other way around. When it comes to sales, most businesses will always have turnover in staff, will end up hiring good and bad performers, and will see varying results. The goal should be to create and constantly refine your sales process, for a good sales process can:

- Help reduce your costs of sales and increase your sales efficiency

- Help standardize your reporting and performance metrics
- Help simplify sales management and allow you to make better decisions
- Help increase productivity and shared best practices for the entire sales organization
- Help improve the performance and onboarding of new hires
- Help increase sales efficiency through detailed opportunity analysis
- Help increase sales-forecasting efforts for the business

No matter what business you are in, people who buy tend to go through the same psychological buying patterns, which a standard sales process should match. You can modify this process to best fit your business, but as a basis to start from, below are the major elements of a standard sales process. Since a good sales process will follow a set of sales stages (or steps), here are the primary ones to start with.

PROSPECTING

First comes **prospecting**. Prospecting is the most important part of any sales process, for without sales prospects, there is nobody to sell to. We have dedicated a whole section of this book to prospecting and prospecting techniques, but the main points here are still the same: You have to be able to identify your target market, know how you are going to most effectively reach them, and create and follow a defined and disciplined prospecting plan—most of which will be covered in more detail in your marketing plan. The goal of this stage is to try to produce as many high-quality leads as possible with the least amount of time and cost to support your sales objectives.

APPOINTMENT SETTING / CONVERSION

Second is sales **lead conversion/appointment setting.** Now that you are generating sales leads, how are you converting them into a sales opportunity—typically defined by a sales call or appointment? This is a critical part of your sales process that many businesses and professionals fail at doing well. As we will discuss in detail, the timing, processes, resources, and systems in which you can convert leads into sales opportunities can typically have the most dramatic impact on your Cost per Lead (CPL) and your overall Customer Acquisition Costs (CAC).

CUSTOMER QUALIFICATION

Third is the customer-**qualification process.** Qualification of your sales prospects typically takes place during a meeting and/or over the phone, but with the advent of the Internet more people now have access to far more information about the prospect prior to a sales meeting than ever before—so use this to your advantage. During this stage you are trying to uncover key information such as **are they the primary decision maker** and, if not, how are purchasing decisions like this typically made? What are their **goals** that define where they want to be over a defined period of time such as three to five years from now? What are their **gaps** (problems or needs) that you can sell to that are the difference between where they are today and where they want to be (their goals)? **Can they afford your service/s** and do they really need them? **Are they able to switch** to your service if the service is currently being provided by somebody else now, and if not, when will they be able to potentially switch? **Does your service really provide a higher level of value** than what they currently have without it?

The main point to keep in mind here is that poorly run businesses and the people who sell for them typically do not know what a qualified customer is or how to properly qualify a customer, and do not follow a repeatable customer-qualification process. As a result, many people selling think they have a qualified customer when they really do not. The fact that nearly 60 percent of all sales end up in a non-decision should tell you all you need to know about what is really qualified and what is not in today's business world. **We also know from studies that most sales are made or lost within the first three minutes.**[1] which typically involves the time you spend qualifying a customer.

In order to address these key breakdowns, it is always a good idea to create a simple customer-qualification form that you and your people can easily follow to make sure that the questions asked and the order they are asked in are as standardized and repeatable as possible. Once you start adding salespeople, you can start spending more time refining the process instead of just relying on each person to figure it out on their own. This is the quickest way to help build a scalable sales operation. (See the Resources section for an example of a customer-qualification form.)

PRESENTATION/POSITIONING

Fourth comes sales **positioning/presentation**. Once you have determined a potential customer has a need that you can sell to, how do you go about positioning your services to address that need and, more important, how can you articulate that value to that specific customer? This is where things get dicey for many people selling; how do they present their services while also keeping the client engaged in the process? Most salespeople will break into a PowerPoint or some type of canned presentation, which is the surest way to start losing your prospect. Studies have shown that **88 percent of executive buyers want a conversation and not a presentation,** which is where you can now set yourself apart from your competition.[2] By having a conversation instead of a sales presentation, you can then repeat back the key elements you have documented in your client-qualification form and strategically seed that information into your service pitch to make it the most relevant and impactful to your prospect.

Don't be afraid to use visuals in your presentations, but ONLY use them to support your conversation and not the other way around. Remember, **people think in images and not in words because visuals help to create structure and meaning to words.** The problem is that far too many people over the years have become addicted to visual sales tools like PowerPoints in their sales presentations when what most buyers really want is a conversation instead. Use this to your advantage and only try to use visual imagery in a way that supports your conversation with each client, is minimal in use, and is not canned in its presentation.

Finally, remember that **people love to buy but hate to be sold.** So don't sell them anything—help them to buy. The only way you can most effectively do this is by giving them options—whether you end up being one of them or not. The point is that people are always weighing their options and **your biggest competition is always "doing nothing," which is why 60 percent of sales end in no decision.** In order for you to control the sales process, help define the options for your prospects; what they have to gain and what they have to lose by choosing each, and let them decide for themselves. Just make sure not to provide them with too many options; two to three are typically sufficient, because you can start to confuse them with any more than that.

DEALING WITH SALES OBJECTIONS AND DELAYS

Fifth is **overcoming any objections and delays.** Most people have said and heard the following statements: "I have to think about it," "It's too expensive," and "Let me get back to you." Ever heard these objections before? Of course, we all have—people use them every day and they will use them with you, too. When people get to a buying decision, they buy based on two factors: **greed and fear.** Both of these words are based in emotion, and what ultimately compels people to buy is based on an emotional reaction relative to their own "why." It is up to you to discover it and help compel them to want to buy.

The first thing to remember about objections and delays is that you have not lost the deal; the prospect is throwing you a lifeline. The question now is how do you react to it? **Most delays are the result of one or more concerns** that the prospect has that you have not yet addressed. Unless you can address them, in their eyes the value of what you are providing is not worth the value of the money it will cost them to buy it.

The second thing to remember is that prospective customers are **not looking for the cheapest option but rather the highest value.** Ask yourself: Do you buy the cheapest clothes you can find? Do you drive the cheapest car or live in the cheapest house? Of course you don't. Why? Because you find a higher level of value in the clothing, cars, and housing you choose for yourself. How high is too high in cost? Each person has to ask that question of themselves, and a good qualification process will help you uncover it for your sales prospects as well, even if your prospect may not yet know it themselves.

Most price objections end up having nothing to do with pricing and everything to do with something else— most of which you should have been able to help identify through a good customer-qualification process. If you find yourself running into a lot of pricing objections, go back to your qualification questions and see what you are missing before you got to this point and see if this is happening with other prospects as well. The more commonality in objections you are seeing, the more this becomes a process issue you can help address at the sales-process level. In most cases, there is either a lack of need, a lack of trust, lack of value, and/or a lack of urgency on behalf of the customer that you have not uncovered up until this point.

The best thing you can do when you receive delays and objections is what they least expect; **stop selling and start listening.** Most people who sell will react to objections emotionally and start trying to sell them again. Don't do this—reverse psychology is on order here. Here are the steps that will help you better address objections:

1. **Listen intently** to the objection of the prospect, show empathy, nod along with them, and **repeat their objections back to them.** This sense of empathy can send a strong signal to the person you are selling to that you understand and care about their concerns.

2. After you have repeated their objection back to them, **explore deeper into the issue/s to find out what the true reason is for the objection.** Remember, the reason you commonly hear the same types of sales objections over and over again is because they are the easiest for us to remember and use in a non-offensive way. A typical response at this point might be: "I understand. Can I ask you a question? What are your concerns about this decision right now? What is it that you may be uncomfortable with so I can make sure you have everything you need to make an informed decision when you are ready?"

3. Once all objections have been discovered, **address each objection** and then ask them if you have addressed their concerns to their satisfaction.

4. If all concerns have been successfully addressed, briefly recap their goals, gaps, and the benefits provided by your solution and ask them, "Would it now make sense to move forward?" If not, go back again to addressing their needs until THEY indicate they are comfortable moving forward. If they are ready, you can start your closing process. If they still want to delay, simply ask them, "When would you like to start seeing *(repeat back their goals here)*?" If they see no sense of urgency in moving forward now, they clearly don't see the value exchange—which goes back to your sales process.

THE CLOSE

Sixth is the close. Now the fun part; you are ready to close the deal. But are you really? How do you know? The best way to gauge whether a sale is actually ready to close is by asking trial-closing questions. One of the biggest challenges in selling is not in being able to qualify the prospect but rather getting them to close when they are ready. We know that **50 percent of all sales leads are qualified but not yet ready to buy.** Why? Because many times we are trying to close business on our time instead of our customers'. This is where salespeople frequently make mistakes by becoming desperate and discounting and providing other concessions to close what is not yet ready to be closed. This also means that whatever concessions provided to that customer now will be expected by that customer when they are ready to close—at some later time.

Trial-closing questions are a great alternative to simply asking for the close because they are typically non-threatening and highly informative. For example, some of my favorite trial-closing questions include: "Is there anything that might prevent you from moving forward with this decision *(today, this week, etc.)*?" "Have you decided when you would like to start seeing *(repeat goals back to them)*?" "Are you still planning on moving forward with *(repeat back goals)* this *(week, month, etc.)*?" "Are we still in good shape to get started sometime this *(day, week, month, etc.)*?" "If you were in my shoes, is there anything you would be doing differently?" And my all-time favorite is to start a trial-closing question with agreement to action by asking, "Would it make sense to . . . ?"

Once you have successfully used a trial-closing question/s, you should now be ready for the close. So what are you waiting for? Around **78 percent of salespeople will hesitate when it comes time to ask for the sale, and two-thirds will end a sales meeting without even asking at all.**[1] Why would so many salespeople waste so much time and so many resources to prospect, generate leads, and conduct sales meetings and then never ask for the sale?

There is only one final goal in your sales process and that is to close business. How else are you going to attract new clients, pay your bills, and reach your goals if you do not ask for it first? Remember, **if you never ask for what you want in business, the answer will always be "no."** So don't be afraid to ask and build a habit of always asking. Based on the sales process we have discussed, you should already know and have articulated to the prospect the value of their action and inaction and provided them with two to three buying options to consider. Once they have the options in front of them, it is now time for THEM to buy. And here is how you can help.

The first option you have is the **"hard close."** In this case, ALWAYS be confident when asking for a close because your body language and tone of voice will tell them more about your confidence than anything else you can say to them at this point. When you ask for any commitment and/or signature, lean forward, look the sales prospect in the eye, and make sure to repeat back the incremental value they will receive for that price. If they need to sign, hand them your pen while they look down at the sales agreement. Once that is done, **shut up** and continue to confidently look them in the eye and wait for them to talk next. If they talk first, they will typically buy. If you talk first, you could lose the sale. Remember the old saying: **"He who speaks first loses."** So fight the temptation to say anything and confidently shut up and wait for the buying signal, which should always come first from the buyer and NOT YOU.

The second type of closing option is the **"soft close."** A soft close is a more subtle closing tactic that implies to the prospect that the sale is already expected and therefore next steps are now asked of them. In many ways a soft close resembles a trial-close question, only the next step is what typically takes place after the sale is made. For example, if you have to set up a post-sales meeting or appointment with a client, a soft close would be to ask them, "Looking at your calendar, how does next Tuesday look for our first meeting and/or appointment?" Or, "My calendar typically fills up quickly, so when is the first available day and time that we can get started?"

Notice how subtle and non-threatening a soft close can be to a customer. Oftentimes when I have a salesperson I am working with who has a low closing ratio, I will get them in the habit of using soft-closing techniques, which can dramatically increase their close rates as well as their habits and confidence in wanting to ask for a close.

If either closing technique is met with a refusal to move forward, it will usually mean there is an objection that was not adequately addressed in your sales process prior to the close. In those cases, go back in the process and address the objections again as you did before. The trick is to **NOT GIVE UP.** Just because somebody is giving you a "no" now doesn't mean you have lost the sale, yet that it is exactly what most salespeople assume. Consider the following:[4]

- 44 percent of salespeople give up after the first "no"
- 22 percent of salespeople give up after the second "no"
- 14 percent of salespeople give up after the third "no"
- 12 percent of salespeople give up after the fourth "no"

Looking at these numbers, we see that all but 8 percent of salespeople will give up on a sale before they reach the fifth attempt to close it. We also know that, on average, **60 percent of customers will say "no" four times before they say "yes"**

to a sale.[4] So as you can see, discipline in sales is the name of the game, and closing is not only a game of action but persistence and eventually getting to "yes."

ASK FOR REFERRALS

Seventh is asking for **referral business.** Referrals are commonly your best prospective customers because they are typically introduced by a citation that invokes a higher level of trust and credibility before the sales process even begins. Despite this fact, many people struggle with effective prospecting when it comes to asking for referrals. We know that in business today, 91 percent of customers will provide referrals, yet only 11 percent of salespeople will ask for them.[5] This "failure to ask" primarily comes from the following three reasons:

1.) Most salespeople DO NOT *consistently ask for referrals*

2.) Most salespeople DO NOT ask for referrals from the *right customers*

3.) Most salespeople DO NOT ask for referrals in the *right situations and settings*

The most effective ways to deal with these failures in asking for referrals is to change your **habits and discipline** surrounding your potential referrals. Here are a few effective ways to do this:

- There are only three types of customers you sell to: Promoters, Buyers, and Demoters. Of these three types of customers, you need to focus as much time and energy helping your **Promoters,** because if you consistently help them, they are the ONLY customers who will help you in return. Most salespeople stop asking for referrals because they fail to understand that **Promoters are your best potential source for referrals that lead to the fewest rejections.** So start by identifying and nurturing your relationships with your Promoters.

- Many referral attempts fail because of a simple issue of location. If you ask customers for referrals in their home or work settings, you are competing with their time and daily habitual distractions. If you ask over the phone, you are dealing with the same competing interests. But when you **take a customer out to breakfast or lunch,** you have sixty minutes of their time dedicated to you—without distractions. Change the setting and you change the focus, resulting in more and better referrals.

- In sales nearly every agreement involves some form of negotiation. When prospective customers want concessions from you, you should ALWAYS know what concessions you can ask for in return. A great salesperson will always keep a list of concessions (including asking for referrals) in their mind. And never forget that if you never ask for something, the answer is always "no." So **next time a customer asks for a discount, ask for five referrals in return**—quid pro quo.

- If you are in sales, stop acting like you are not. Your customers know you are in sales and therefore they should not be surprised if you ask them for sales-related help. Always end every customer engagement with a simple question: "Mr./Mrs. (customer name), **would you happen to know of any people in your network who could benefit from my products and/or services?"** You may not always get the answer you want the first time you ask it, but if they expect the question again from you during future engagements, watch what happens.

GENERATE REPEAT AND BOOMERANG BUSINESS

Eighth is generating **repeat and boomerang business.** Many of the top 20 percent of business professionals will have a level of repeat customer sales (or client-retention rate) well in excess of 60–70 percent of their business, depending on their industry and tenure. Recurring customer sales are critical to any business due to the high cost of new customer acquisition, which can run seven times the cost of acquiring business from your existing customers. Moreover, the **return on investment (ROI) of client retention activities is typically ten times higher than for new-client marketing.** Therefore, it is important that you not only deliver a higher value of service to your current customers, but that you stay in frequent contact with them as well. A general rule of thumb in your marketing plan is to follow the Rule of 12 and make sure that you reach out and "touch" your existing customers at least once a month by email, newsletter, social media, etc.

You will also have sales that never closed when you wanted them to close. Many of these prospects will typically go quiet or continue to say "no" to your attempts to close them. The longer you are in business, the larger this pool of previous prospects can become. So what happens when most salespeople do not initially close an opportunity? They move on and leave an opportunity that may still be closable in the future. The challenge with most sales opportunity management systems today is that once a lead moves to a sales opportunity and fails to close within a defined time frame (typically defined by the business on a daily, weekly, monthly, or quarterly basis), the opportunity is then "moved out" and often discarded. And when an opportunity is discarded so too is the opportunity to close it again when the customer is ready to buy on their time—not yours.

For most salespeople, the ugly truth is that not all people and opportunities are ready and willing to close **when YOU want them to close.** Because many of our sales processes start by initiating contact with a potential prospect, we know that 50 percent of leads that are qualified are NOT YET ready to close. The surest sign of this happening is when a prospect seems to "go quiet" during the sales process. Just because you or one of your salespeople may need to make a sale and hit your sales objectives this week, month, or quarter DOES NOT mean that the customer is working under the same time frame. If 50 percent of sales leads are qualified but are not yet ready to buy, even the best salespeople cannot get them all to buy on their schedule alone. In the best cases, only half of those 50 percent can be persuaded based on timing alone while the other half cannot. The bottom line here is that **just because the "timing" of the opportunity if off doesn't mean that the opportunity is off.**

When an opportunity is not ready to close, it should be nurtured until it is. **Businesses that nurture leads on a consistent basis typically produce 50 percent more sales-ready leads and at a one-third lower cost.**[12] The problem is that the majority of sales organizations today have no lead-nurturing programs in place. In the case of sales opportunities that fail to close in a forecasted time frame, many of these leads may still in fact be qualified. Therefore, the Rule of 12 should be applied to each. The Rule of 12 comes from marketing research that tells us that you need to be in front of a sales prospect at least 12 times a year for them to "actively" remember you when they are ready to buy. The problem with the Rule of 12 for some salespeople comes from when they initially follow up on sales leads with constant and repeated closing attempts that end up turning many people off. Again, this is the result of trying to close an opportunity before it is ready to close. There is a better way.

When a sale and prospect goes quiet, all of these opportunities should be immediately moved into a boomerang sales process. A boomerang sale is nothing more than an opportunity that is delayed for whatever reason but comes back later to close when the buyer is ready to buy. Since many salespeople cannot predict exactly when this time frame may be, they need to move their sales process from a close to a nurturing stage for each of these opportunities. In short, when the client says "no" and/or goes quiet after multiple closing attempts, they are typically not yet closable and should move into a boomerang communications stage of your sales process. In order to do this, the following are four easy steps any salesperson can follow:

1.) When a forecasted opportunity fails to close after multiple attempts, the opportunity classification should be moved to **a boomerang sales opportunity** in your sales pipeline.

2.) Boomerang sales pipeline opportunities should be ***treated differently*** than other opportunities because you have already engaged the prospect in your sales process and therefore what you are trying to accomplish with them (a delayed close) is inherently different than what you are trying to accomplish with the remainder of your sales pipeline (starting a new sales process). This requires that you classify these boomerang opportunities differently in whatever you are using to manage your opportunities today—CRM, spreadsheets, databases, etc. This new classification will now allow you to quickly filter, manage, and/or export this contact data for use.

3.) Once you segment your boomerang clients out, you need to stay in front of them on a consistent basis that strikes a balance between too much contact and too little. The two most cost-effective ways to do this are through social media and email. Email has a very high level of reach since most people have email and frequently access most/all of their emails daily. Social media is more segmented, so your postings will display chronologically based on user access—therefore, the reach is very low based on the chances of your post being seen at the time of their access. Because of this, a general rule of thumb for boomerang clients is **once a month by email and once a day by social media.** Some social media experts will tell you that three times a day is the maximum reach on social media, but for nurturing leads, this can be both excessive and unrealistic for most small businesses. So should you only use email over social media? No. Email may have three times the number of users as social media, but not all of them can be reached by one medium alone, so it is best to use both if possible for maximum reach.

4.) Finally, your messages to "stay in front" of your boomerang prospects should be **informative and helpful to the prospect—NOT salesy!** The goal of these emails is to keep your name actively in front of these sales prospects and give them additional reasons to WANT to buy from you. In this case, by providing them with useful and helpful information that they can use, you can better establish yourself as a credible and trusted advisor in the eyes of the prospect.

By following these four simple steps, you can convert more of your boomerang opportunities into an active and convertible sales funnel. Based on my own experience, when executed on correctly, I have seen a **20 percent sales bump** on average for those businesses that have adopted this model of better handling boomerang sales.

— CHAPTER 4 —

SELLING EFFECTIVENESS: TURNING YOUR PROSPECTS INTO CUSTOMERS

• • •

THE RULES OF THE VALUE EXCHANGE AND DELAYED EXCHANGES

A sale is nothing more than a simple value exchange; I provide you something of value in return for something of value from you. A simple value exchange is immediate and intuitive; I buy something of value in exchange for an equal value in payment. When the value of what I buy is of less perceived value to me than the cost, I will either ask for a lower price to better reflect the perceived value exchange or simply not buy all together. Conversely, if what I want to buy is of higher perceived value than the price, I will likely buy it now and perhaps in greater quantities to account for any potential correction in future prices. The concepts are simple supply and demand.

Where the value exchange becomes more complicated is when it is applied to the sale of services—especially those services provided by professionals. Why? There are two primary reasons for this. First, most services today are intangible and inconsistent and therefore harder to accurately value until the services have been fully rendered. Second, payments for professional services are commonly paid in part or in full in advance of the services rendered, creating a delayed exchange. **A delayed exchange is the processes of providing a standard of known value (commonly in money) for value (services) to be provided after the initial exchange takes place.**

What makes delayed exchanges different from simple value exchanges is that **delayed exchanges only work based on a level of TRUST.** For example, say you have two different people approach you to do your taxes. The first person is dressed in a nice suit, is professional in his demeanor, and works for H&R Block. The second person is disheveled in his appearance and demeanor and says he is a solo-practice CPA who works out of his home. Which of these two people would you trust to do your taxes and why? Clearly most people would choose the professional from the well-known company because he conveys a higher level of credibility and trust; something you must be able to do as well when it comes to your business.

Most small-business professionals do not work for businesses like H&R Block and therefore start out with a branding deficit; most people cannot distinguish them from other brands. Professionals also tend to offer more fragmented services due to their tendencies to create specialization, resulting in less standardization in the eyes of the average consumer. Finally, professionals typically end up branding themselves, intentionally or not, more as individuals than as entities.

All these tendencies create a **trust gap** that each professional and small-business organization needs to overcome to help increase their sales effectiveness in the delayed value exchange process that is their world. Many of the strategies listed in this book are designed to help you better close this gap and develop a higher level of credibility and trust with your current and prospective customers.

SELL TO YOUR CUSTOMER'S WHY— NOT TO YOUR OWN

Many business organizations today tend to grow and then lose focus of why they had come to exist in the first place. History is riddled with businesses that started out by solving a problem but ended up creating new ones of their own making. As organizations grow in size and resources, they tend to lose their ability to effectively innovate, scale, and grow. As markets mature, so too does the level of competition, often leading to increased levels of commoditization, price sensitivity, and lower differentiation. As a business professional, it is important for you to understand these situations and, more important, how to make your sales and marketing efforts the most productive in any and all of these environments.

A few years back, author Simon Sinek did an analysis of why some organizations succeed and why most fail. In doing so, he developed what he referred to as the Golden Circle.[1] This simple concept was based on the premise that **people don't buy what you do but rather why you do it.** His theory was based on the notion that in most organizations today, the vast majority of people know the "what" of their jobs, fewer know the "how" of their jobs, and very few, if any, truly know the "why" of their organizations. By losing focus of the "why," most organizations will end up valuing process over purpose, and thereby lose their direction and ultimately fail to grow and succeed.

What makes the Golden Circle so powerful is that it equally applies to sales and marketing. As the amount of advertising and constant sales bombardment our sales prospects receive grows each year, people are becoming increasingly jaded to sales activities and less receptive to sales solicitations. As our economy continues to mature, many of the products and services we sell are becoming increasingly commoditized, price sensitive, and more reliant on skilled sales and marketing than ever before. As a result, you need to become more focused on the value your products and services provide to each customer than the old-school notion of letting the products and services "sell themselves." We do this by learning how to better sell to the "why" of each customer.

I teach salespeople to stop talking about product and service features and instead start articulating the value and benefits that those products and services provide to each prospective customer. The most effective way to do this is by training to **sell to each client's goals and gaps.** By understanding a customer's goals, you can determine the "why" of their potential motivations. The gaps are determined by simply understanding what they do now and what else is needed to get them to their goals. Ideally these gaps will then open the door for whatever services you can provide.

Impact Communications recently found that **70 percent of people make purchasing decisions to solve a problem, while only 30 percent do so to gain something.**[2] Knowing

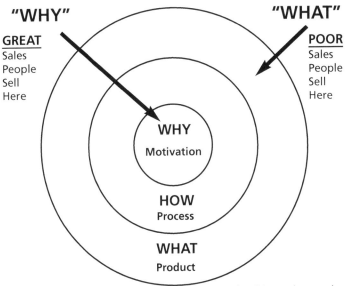

"WHY"   "WHAT"

GREAT   POOR
Sales   Sales
People   People
Sell   Sell
Here   Here

WHY
Motivation

HOW
Process

WHAT
Product

Leads with
Client Value
(Benefits)

Leads with Product and
Process (Features and
Function)

Can Articulate,
Communicate and Add
Value to the Sales Process

Lacks Creativity
and Rigidly Sticks
to a Sales Script

Can Build Credibility and
Trust with the Customer
and
Become Seen as a Trusted
Advisor

Fails to Add Value Beyond
the Product/Service

Fails to Identify and
Uncover Specific Client
Needs

Identifies and
Uncovers Needs

Comes Across as
Just Another Vendor/Sales
Person

Sells to Client
Goals and Gaps

Sells to Solve a Client
Problem/Need

the "why" gets to the heart of each. This is at the core of what makes a great sales process; salespeople can more effectively identify and even create a specific client need, sell to that need, and articulate a level of value that exceeds the cost of doing business for them. This happens best by teaching you and your people to sell to the "why."

When people finally decide to buy, they only buy based on two factors: **greed and fear.** These words may sound pejorative to some, but they are accurate descriptions with the semantic veneer removed. Both of these factors are visceral and ***based in emotion,*** and no matter how many facts you present to somebody about how a product or service works, what ultimately compels them to buy is largely an emotional reaction based on their own "why."

What is also important about the ability to sell to the "why" of each client is that it can be applied to the sale of ANY service. When salespeople get lazy and too process-oriented around the "how" and "what" of their sales, they lose focus of the customer's "why" and, more important, how to better uncover it. One of the best ways to discover this in practice is by walking onto a car dealer's lot and watching the salespeople in action. Automobiles are perhaps one of the most commoditized sales today and the Internet has made it even worse for car salesmen by providing buyers with nearly all the product and pricing details (the "how" and "what") they need BEFORE they walk onto a lot.

For example, when stepping onto a car lot, the first thing that is likely to happen is a car salesman swarming you before you ever get to the showroom. If they are trained, they will ask for your name and repeat it back to you more times than your angry spouse. They will then ask you what you want, show you the car(s) you indicate you are interested in, get a copy of your driver's license (for follow-up), ask you about your job (to gauge if you can afford a car), take you on a test drive, and then try to close you then and there. If they fail to close you before you walk out, the "manager" will typically come in to try to save the day. I have experienced this process many times in my life and I have yet to have one car salesman ask me any of the following questions BEFORE this dog and pony show even begins:

- ***WHY exactly do you need a new car?*** I showed up at the car dealer by driving another car, so I must have a reason for wanting a new one, right? Well, what is it exactly?

- ***WHY did you decide on the car you are interested in?*** If I tell a car salesman that I am interested in a specific make and model of a car—which most of us do—does he/she even want to know why that is? What if I am really looking for something else? What if I really don't know what I should be buying for my needs? If we are a one-car family and I have five small kids, do I really need that new shiny red Porsche Boxster?

- ***WHY did you decide on our car maker over another brand?*** If I have been a Ford guy all my life, why would I be looking at a Chevy dealer? Maybe I am only looking for a better price to take back to the Ford dealer for negotiation. What if I really haven't decided on any brand and I plan to hit every maker before I do?

- **WHY do you prefer a new car over a used one?** A used car costs less than a new one, so why would I really want a new one? In some states, there is no sales tax on a used car purchased from a private party, so do I feel guilty that I am not paying my fair share in taxes? Why not just buy a car from another individual and pay a lot less?

- **WHY is your current car not meeting your needs?** If you were able to drive your current car to the car lot, then your car must be working, right? You got from point A to point B successfully, so what is the problem?

- **WHY did you decide to look for a new car today?** Am I really interested in buying a car today or did my wife just kick me out of the house for a few hours and I needed to kill some time? Did I know there is special financing available this month by watching TV commercials or was I taken in by the ridiculous-looking mini-blimp they have flying over their lot today?

If a car salesman were to ask me these type of "why" questions, I would be not only impressed but far more inclined to want to buy from him/her over the salesperson at the next lot over. Instead of sitting me down after the "what" and "how" process takes place and making me wait forever for their sales manager to haggle a price, why not get to the "WHY" first, where the understanding and sale REALLY begins? If their time is important to them, why begin by wasting it on people who are not really going to buy? Joe Girard was the world's greatest car salesman for a reason—and it wasn't just because he knew how to sell a car.

Sell Me This Pen

For those who saw the movie *The Wolf of Wall Street*, you will likely remember the famous scenes of Jordan Belfort asking people to sell him a pen. He started out by asking this question to friends he was hiring to sell for his new brokerage firm, and the movie ended with him overseas, asking the same question of others he was instructing. When the people at the end of the film started describing the details (the "what") of the pen and "how" it worked, Jordan would pass the pen along to the next person until they got it right. What he was ultimately looking for were people who could sell the "why" of the pen.

Asking people to "sell me this pen" is not a new concept. This question has been asked of people for decades, even during interviews. What makes the concept so simple is that nearly nothing is more commoditized, interchangeable, and replaceable than a pen. Much like selling a car, it is often considered by many to be a "hard sell." But when a salesperson is able to focus in on the "why" of the sale, it can actually get much more interesting, creative, and potentially rewarding. Let me give you an example:

Say I walk into your office one day to sell you a pen. You likely have multiple pens already on your desk, so the net benefit of another pen is initially not compelling to you. In order to generate curiosity, I tell you that I am from one of your favorite lunch locations (Elite Lunch) and wanted to meet with you personally. Now I likely have your attention; how many people from your favorite lunch locations will come to visit with you?

I start by asking you what your favorite lunch spots are. Knowing that I am from Elite Lunch, you will most likely mention my restaurant. At that point, I will ask you why you like our restaurant so much, how often you visit, and what may be keeping you from visiting us more often for lunch. I will also ask you if you typically invite other people to lunch with you and if you like Elite Lunch enough to recommend it to others. I will then ask you what your favorite lunch is and how much on average it costs you. Let's say it is $25 per lunch.

At this point, I will break out my checkbook and write you a check for $25 for a free lunch at Elite Lunch and hand it to you. The only condition I place on you being able to cash this check is that it has to be endorsed by you with my pen. So at this point, how much is my pen now worth to you in cash? Some might initially say $25, right? Think about this for a minute, because how do you really know that this check will actually clear? Knowing that there may be some level of risk involved with this, you may ask me questions to help mitigate your concerns and gauge your level of trust in me. To most, the pen is not worth $25 in cash because of the time it will take you to cash it and any risk premium you may perceive. So let's say the pen may be worth $15–$20 in cash based on your assessment; an initial $5–$10 loss to me.

I then hand you a stack of fifty Elite Lunch business cards with your name written on the back of each one with the pen.

I then inform you that for every new person that eats at Elite Lunch and provides one of these business cards to the hostess with your name written on the back with my pen, you will receive $5 off your next lunch. Now how much is the pen potentially worth to you? $5 x 50 = $250 in free lunches. What if I also tell you that once you run out of the first fifty cards, the hostess will provide you with up to two hundred additional cards that you can only add your name to with my pen? Added together, this works out to $1,250 worth of potential free lunches now. Now how much is that pen worth to you in cash? $100? $200? More? Remember, the average person typically has direct influence over the buying decisions of two hundred and fifty other people, so I know how many cards to give you.

In this example, the pen (the "what") I am selling you is necessary to sign the check (the "how") to get you a free lunch and up to fifty more (the "why"). At this point, how focused are you now on my pen? It is "why" you are buying the pen that is potentially compelling, motivating, and of incremental value to you. What originally cost me around thirty cents to buy and $5–$10 to sell to you could now potentially be worth hundreds of dollars in the eyes of a prospective buyer like you.

Now some may question in this example how initially giving away $5–$10 is good business. How do you guarantee that you will end up receiving anything in return for that investment? The fact is you don't—it's called business and it involves risk. The goal with all business is to try to mitigate your risks and increase your chances for overall success. The $5–$10 I "gave" in order to "receive" in future returns was nothing more than a simple business investment based on a calculated risk. Did I give the money to just anybody? No. I gave it to somebody who fits my ideal target customer profile and knows the value I provide, values the value I provide, and will now have a heightened sense of urgency and incentive to promote that value to others—producing a mutual gain.

In this example, I used the $5–$10 as an investment, or Customer Acquisition Costs (CAC) for future business because it is the simplest way to illustrate the true investment made by all scalable businesses each and every day. Most businesses make investments, directly or indirectly, in order to receive future business. Investors will risk and invest money in future business returns. Owners and salespeople will risk and invest time and/or money into future business returns. Marketing will risk and invest time, money, and resources into future business returns. All of this adds up and reflects the fact that in business, you have to give in order to receive. In business terms, this is commonly referred to as having to spend in order to earn.

As an added "marketing" element to this story, what if I also mentioned that I received your name because you dropped your own business card in our "win a free lunch bowl" and I am stopping in on everybody who did the same thing but I would stop when I ran out of cards (scarcity=urgency)? In the end, you win by earning free lunches from one of your favorite restaurants and helping to ensure that it will remain in business for you to continue to enjoy. Elite Lunch wins by generating more business at a five-to-one return on our marketing investment. In essence, you are now buying the ability to earn up to

$1,250 worth of free lunches while Elite Lunch can make an incremental $5,000-plus from up to 250 additional clients after your expenses. And that is how business is done, folks; through something as simple as selling a pen.

BECOME AN "EXPERT" AT WHAT YOU DO

Ask yourself a simple question: If you found out your daughter had a brain aneurysm, would you rush her to a primary care physician? Hell no, you wouldn't! You would try to find the best brain surgeon you could find and quickly. Why? Because a primary care physician does not specialize in treating brain aneurysms and this is your daughter's life on the line, so you would want the best brain surgeon you can find. Now ask yourself: If your daughter was severely injured during surgery due to malpractice at the hospital, would you be better off contacting your local hometown attorney or somebody who specialized in medical malpractice injuries?

These questions illustrate a very simple point: Our economy, society, and professions are becoming increasingly specialized. Many of the top professionals today provide literally hundreds of thousands of product and service options to consumers. Absent any level of specialization and authority citations, how will people really know who to choose? One of the first questions I ask attorneys when I start working with them is, "How are you different than the other 1.2 million attorneys in the US, and why should I choose you?"

One of the most effective ways to set yourself apart from others is by setting a goal of becoming an "expert" in your respective profession. By becoming an expert, you are sending a signal to your target market that you are uniquely knowledgeable, credible, and considered to be an authority in what you do. Since nobody can truly proclaim themselves to be an expert, traditionally the best way to become a credible expert is through credentialed sources. In higher education, experts are commonly credentialed through the level of degrees they are awarded, the papers they publish, tenure they have received, and the speeches they deliver. In the military, experts commonly are credentialed through levels of training, experience, rank, and honors bestowed on them. But for many professionals today, credentials alone are not enough to make you an "expert" in your chosen field. Here are a few ways you can change that:

First, **specialize as much as possible within your given profession.** If you find that there is a growing level of competition in your chosen field, try to focus further into a segment of your profession. Focus can allow you to master this segment through education and experience and become known as the go-to person for that particular need. The other benefit of segmented specialization is that it allows you to potentially become an early adopter, thereby eliminating some or all of your competition and allowing others to proclaim you as the expert in that area of your profession.

Second, set a goal to **study, read, learn, teach, and gain more experience** about the area of your profession you want to be known as an expert for than any potential competitor.

Third, **speak and present** about your expertise to others. This is one of the most effective ways to build your credentials as an expert. For example, many professions such as legal, real estate, accounting, etc., have continuing-education credits that have to be earned to maintain a license to practice. These credits are typically earned through coordinated speaking/training engagements by other professionals who, in many cases, have to participate to receive their credits. Becoming a regular speaker in your area of expertise for continuing-education classes may be pro bono work for you but can go a long way in establishing your credentials as a known expert. Speaking at smaller continuing-education classes can help you become a better speaker and lead to larger speaking opportunities as well.

Fourth, **write and publish your work.** Today, anybody can become a writer and publish information quickly and effectively thanks in large part to modern technology and innovation. Mark Twain was famous for getting his first writing job for a newspaper over a century ago by initially offering his services for free so he could prove his value. With the Internet and expanded publishing services, you can now accomplish the same objective without having to work for a newspaper. Today, most professionals will start their writing experiences on their own websites, blogs, and social media, and further expand their publishing reach to trade publications and news organizations. In addition to writing and publishing articles, nothing can be potentially more impactful in becoming an expert than **publishing a book.** As a published author, many find it much easier to get speaking opportunities and access to key people than ever before. What makes book publishing so unique and special is that many people would love to write a book, but very few actually end up doing it. As we discuss later, there has never been an easier time to publish a book, and the old excuse of not having a publisher for it is now ancient history.

Fifth, start a **media and PR campaign** for you and your area of expertise. Practicing, speaking, and publishing are all great, but they lack the full leverage and reach that can be gained by rapidly extending yourself to the masses. Nothing propels professionals into the limelight and instant recognition faster than exposure through mass media. The ability to speak on radio and TV talk shows, get on the news, and be mentioned in major newspapers can be the difference between becoming an overnight celebrity expert and somebody who has no more visibility than a billboard in a cornfield. There are a number of PR companies that can help you as a professional jump-start this process, as well as a number of great books that can help teach you the tricks of the trade. The major benefits PR companies can provide over books are customized strategies, up-to-date information, and access to the key media contacts for your area of expertise. PR companies don't typically work for cheap, so it is not unusual for professionals to initially engage them to get started and then cut back on their services as needed once they get a good system in place that is working for them.

Sixth, **establish your brand expertise** in everything you do and with everybody you know and work with. Don't be afraid to project your expertise in your branding as long as it also comes across as professional and in good taste. Make sure that what you want to be known as an expert for is conveyed in everything you do, from your business cards, website, emails, publications, speaking, etc. It should also be included in the way people present you to others. If you have an assistant and/or people who refer calls and business to you, **make sure they announce you and your level of expertise to others before you have to do so yourself.** Remember, people largely trust the opinions they will receive about you from others, even if they work for or are closely associated with you. You can convert significantly more business as a result of this simple yet effective process.

GIVE IN ORDER TO RECEIVE

One of the most important aspects of sales I teach to any person in any industry is the simple rule of reciprocity; the ability to give in order to receive. If you Google the term "give in order to receive" you will likely end up with a lot of biblical references and related websites. Giving is a charitable act and leads people to feel obligated to return the good will. What works so well in these religious teachings works equally as well in selling, regardless of your religious beliefs.

Giving should not be confused with selling, which is where many people who are selling can get into trouble. Giving materially in direct return for an action is considered unethical in many industries and, depending on the extent of the give, considered a bribe. In sales, giving should ideally be part of the relationship-building process and not directly tied to a specific business transaction.

There are three key aspects to making giving an effective part of your customer relationships. First, **giving should be unique and unexpected.** One of my favorite memories growing up as a young child was watching my father send out Thanksgiving Day letters each year to all of his contacts, both personal and professional. Every year he would write a highly personalized letter about the past year and what he was thankful for. We would then help him fold, address, stamp, and lick the envelopes for the thousands of letters that went out each year. One year when my father's health was failing he did not send out the letters, and what followed was truly amazing. All of the people who had previously received his letters were reaching out to find out what was wrong and to let me know that his letters were one of the things they looked forward to most during the holiday season.

What this experience taught me about giving was that the best way to give is to not follow the sheep but to be creative and stand out from the crowd. Think about it: What do most people do around the Christmas holiday? They give Christmas gifts and cards. Remember the famous scene from the movie *Christmas Vacation* when Clark Griswold brings in a gift for his boss and the reaction he received? Not only was his gift nearly identical to the other gifts on the table, but his boss's reaction was to tell him to "put it over there with the others." Now what if Clark Griswold were to have provided a different gift to his boss at a time of year when nobody else provided one? What do you suppose his boss's reaction would have been then and, more important, what sense of obligation would that have created?

There are many ways to give, but like most people, we tend to give like lemmings; the top 20 percent act differently, though. Giving can be beneficial at any time if done tastefully and unexpectedly, so **always shoot for the unexpected and give when others typically don't.** When starting a relationship, don't be afraid to give free initial advice if they are not expecting it. When thanking a customer, give in a way and at a time they do not expect from other businesses and professionals. When speaking and publishing information, don't be afraid to give useful information in a way your audience would not initially expect, such as a discount on services for mentioning the speech, etc.

Second, **the best giving is personalized giving.** Say you receive two letters of congratulations from two highly esteemed people in your profession; one is handwritten and the other it typed. Which one means more to you? Which one will you remember the most? If the answer is so obvious to most people then why is it that most of us will not send handwritten letters?

One of my favorite stories about personalized giving comes from one of my favorite salespeople of all time: Joe Girard—the World's Greatest Car Salesman. Over the course of twelve years, Joe sold thirteen thousand cars. That works out to six cars sold a day when the average car salesman sold five a month. Joe gave out sixteen thousand "uniquely designed" business cards per month when the average salesperson gave out five hundred standard ones. Joe gave out fifty-dollar referral fees (two-hundred dollars in 2014 dollars) for new-customer referrals when most other salespeople paid nothing. Joe constantly asked for referrals when only 11 percent of salespeople ever do. And most important, Joe learned about and appreciated his clients and wrote each one of them a handwritten, personalized note each month when the average car salesman did not. And what were the results of all these efforts? Nearly 70 percent of Joe's customers came from repeat customers or people they knew.[3]

Giving in order to receive can also take time, so **be patient;** your returns may not be immediate but will pay off over time. When I was in Boy Scouts, we had a simple motto to "do a good deed every day." In sales, you should have a similar motto: **"Give a good deed every day."** Watch what happens to your results. Remember, people will only respond to your prospecting efforts through a sense of curiosity, obligation, and urgency. It feels good to most people to give to others and it can feel even better when your prospective customers give back in return.

Giving applies to marketing as well. Many businesses today will use giving as a way to help grow awareness and usage of their services. For example, Uber currently offers a "Get Free Rides" promotion to in effect turn their current customers into marketing agents for the company. In this case, the Uber app allows current customers to invite non-users to try Uber and become new Uber customers. When the recipient receives the invite, their first ride with Uber is free (up to $20). Once they take the offer, the current customer who invited them also receives the same $20 deal. Uber knows that the average lifetime value of a new customer should far exceed these initial costs and uses this promotion as a very effective loss leader in doing so. Moreover, by giving to both their current and future customers to help grow their customer base, everybody wins.

ONLY SELL TO THE "RIGHT" CUSTOMERS

As previously discussed, you only have three types of customers: Promoters, Buyers, and Demoters. The reason for the
segmentation is that **one of the cornerstones to growing a
successful business is selling to the right customers.** You
need to focus your sales and marketing efforts on selling to
the RIGHT customers for you.

Now that we have defined the three segments for your
potential and current customer base, you need to segment
your customer list for you and/or your people to operate
from. Start by listing each of your customers on a spreadsheet
and add a column for Client Segment (see Resources for an
example). In this new column, assign a P (Promoter), B
(Buyer), or D (Demoter) next to each client name. Once completed, instruct yourself and your people to handle the customers listed in the following ways:

- **Increase time with your Promoters.** If your business
  has a standard way of handling customers, instruct
  yourself and your people to treat your Promoters
  BETTER. Always find ways to add increased value to
  a Promoter so you can make them feel important and
  always try to exceed their expectations. The more you
  invest in these people, the more they will help you sell
  to and succeed with others. Furthermore, by creating
  strong personal relationships with Promoters, they
  will not want to lose their relationship with you and/or
  your business. The result is typically a much higher

willingness on their part to provide referrals to other Promoters and Buyers who you can sell to. Remember, **91 percent of customers indicate that they will provide a referral, yet only 11 percent of salespeople will ever ask for one.**[2] Having you and your people ask for referrals from your Promoters first will help you gain the confidence and experience to then ask from others as well.

- Decrease your time with your Demoters. If your business has Demoters, make sure that you and your people DECREASE your time with them as much as possible. This may sound logical in theory, but in practice, most people do the exact opposite. Whenever Demoters start complaining, the first thing most people do is drop everything else and try to make them happy. The more Demoters you have, the worse this problem becomes. If you have too many Demoters, it will affect the confidence and productivity of you and your people and hurt your sales numbers. You need to be able to explain to your salespeople that they CANNOT make these people happy and WHY they should instead be spending more time with people they can.

NOTHING SELLS BETTER THAN SCARCITY

Have you ever wondered why nearly every commercial or infomercial that is trying to sell something to you always has a deadline to order or, in the case of QVC, a limited-inventory countdown clock? Or how about auctions on eBay that will list both the remaining quantities and time left in an auction to bid on a product? How about the limited time for ordering your favorite seasonal coffee at Starbucks, like the Pumpkin Spice Latte around Halloween? Or how about retailers who publish coupons and coupon codes that expire within thirty days? These are all examples of how businesses utilize scarcity to increase sales.

When it comes to selling, nothing sells better than scarcity because **people will demand more of what they can have less of.** What makes scarcity so powerful in sales is that it helps create a sense of urgency that leads to action—oftentimes when a business needs sales the most. This typically includes times when seasonality can lower sales volume, when resources and inventory are too high, or when you simply need more sales to hit your sales goals. No matter that your needs, scarcity can do what in many ways even price discounting cannot; namely to get people to buy fast and now!

As we previously discussed, the two things customers must know to create urgency and action in sales is the benefit of the action and the opportunity cost to them of inaction. Unlike most other sales tactics that are designed around the benefits to a customer, scarcity is the opposite due to its **focus on the cost of inaction.** For example, in 2003 British Airways announced the end of their Concorde flights between London and New York due to costs. The result: Sales following the announcement increased dramatically for the remaining flights. Why? Did the service somehow improve over the last few flights? No. What changed was scarcity and people knowing that this may be the last opportunity to experience a Concorde flight. The inherent value of the flight didn't increase after the announcement but rather the value to the customer based on scarcity of the unique flights remaining.

Scarcity can be used in the sale of any product or service **as long as there is uniqueness to the offer.** If you plan to make something scarce in selling, it has little or no effect if your customers have alternative places to buy it from. This is especially true in today's business environment where nearly anything can be found and ordered over the Internet. But don't worry if you sell similar services to others, for scarcity in uniqueness can be applied to anything, such as a unique service, unique delivery and fulfillment options, unique timing, and unique incentives and pricing.

In the professional services industry one of the **most valuable resources is time.** And since it is limited, it can be used very effectively to your advantage. For example, if you are a service provider, when was the last time you contacted a prospective customer to let them know that you have a rare opening in your schedule to potentially work them in next week and you were contacting them first? If they don't take it, somebody else will. What did you just do? You used scarcity of access by letting one or more prospects know that they can uniquely take advantage of this scarcity in the opening of your schedule for a limited time.

Another example would be a scarcity in pricing. When was the last time you were offered a discount on services from another professional, such as a discount on dental work, insurance, websites, tax preparation, etc.? Most people receive these, but they are still not compelling enough because they are not unique in service and/or typically don't **include a short deadline for action.** In fact, many discounted offers include no deadline at all, and if they do, the time frame is often too long—sometimes a month or more. Why does this not work? Because without a shortened deadline, people will typically procrastinate and make the easiest decision of all by doing nothing. How do you combat this? By providing greater incentives with shorter deadlines.

Think about it: What do you do when you open and sort through your mail? You are quickly making a decision of action or inaction. If I have one piece of mail offering a 10 percent discount on services that I can use any time versus another that offers a 25 percent discount for the same services but expires in 5 days, which one is more unique, compelling, and likely to get my attention and action? This brings us to the final part of using scarcity, which is the **expectation of uniqueness.** In this example, how many times will I see the 25 percent discount offered, and how many times is too many times to where I then feel compelled to wait for the next expected offer to arrive in order to act—if I act at all? Moreover, if I receive these with such high frequency will I never again utilize services from this service provider at full price instead of waiting to act on these discounts alone? Just look at all the pizza coupons still sitting in your drawers to help illustrate this point.

The idea here is to make sure that whatever scarcity you create to sell is not an expected scarcity that repeats with commonality. If people regularly expect an offer from you to compel them to buy, then you are now competing based largely on price—which, unless you plan to scale your business large, you cannot win at in the long term. So be careful and calculated with your scarcity offers so your customers are not expecting the scarcity you wish to create based on pricing. Here are a few ways to do this:

First, make sure any unique pricing offer you provide is **not repeated for at least 6–12 months.** In order to maintain a level of expected uniqueness in your pricing offers, you should not have too high a frequency, which can lead your customers to consistently expect them in order to buy from you. If you do have a need to increase your frequency of unique offers, then change the parameters of the offer such as the pricing discount relative to the deadline, with the higher discounts offered in the shortest time frame and vice versa. Remember, if your customers see the same offers too often and learn to expect them in order to act, you are becoming a business who now competes where nobody wants to: based on price. In short, don't become another pizza company in your marketing.

Second, make sure any pricing offer has a **VERY short deadline,** such as a week from the expected time of delivery. **Giving people too much time to decide is helping them make the easiest decision of all, which is to do nothing.** Since most purchasing decisions end in no decision, you are in effect helping your biggest competitor sell against you by giving deadlines that are too long or, worse yet, giving no deadlines at all. Good scarcity marketing requires action, and without a compelling deadline, most customers will choose inaction instead.

Third, **DO NOT accept expired pricing promotions** when used. Be firm on your published deadlines, for they will set a precedent for the uniqueness of your offers and how people will react to future pricing promotions from you once received. Any exception to this rule sends a clear signal to your customers and prospects that your pricing offers are far less unique than you want them to be. Moreover, by not accepting them you are enforcing an opportunity cost of inaction, which is the basis for effective scarcity marketing.

Fourth, when possible, **offer higher pricing promotions for shorter deadlines** and vice versa. If you want people to act now, give them a good reason to do it. If your service costs $500, how compelling would a 1 percent discount be as opposed to a 30 percent discount? In each professional business, you need to determine what that percentage or dollar value is that will tip the scales for you and compel customers to want to buy. If you don't know what this is, start asking your current customers, provide a survey, and even try a couple of smaller targeted marketing campaigns at different price points and see which ones receive the highest response rate. If you have created a detailed Company Marketing Performance Report (see Resources), you can also calculate the total amount of profitable discounts allowed by marketing source based on the Return on Marketing Investment (ROMI) calculations. Naturally the best pricing discount will be a balance between the total number of leads and new sales produced relative to the total cost of sale for the business.

THE ATTITUDE OF THE SELLER IS MORE IMPORTANT THAN THE ATTITUDE OF THE BUYER

Have you ever watched one of those English-accented, high-energy salespeople pumping the latest crap on infomercials and sales channels like QVC with more energy and excitement than a kid in a candy shop? How amazing is it that no matter what product they are selling, they consistently act like the poster child for caffeine addiction? After watching the same guys doing this over and over again, many people ask how they could possibly believe this much in every single product they are paid to sell. The answer is simple: Selling is more about the attitude of the seller than the buyer.

For those who may be old enough to remember, selling commercials really hit center stage starting back in the 1970s when Ron Popeil's company Ronco hit the airwaves with the highly energetic Ron pushing products like the Pocket Fisherman, Mr. Microphone, the Electric Food Dehydrator, and other unnecessary products that had a useful shelf life rivaling that of a bowl of ice cream. Here again we have the great attitude of Ron Popeil stirring his audience into a frenzy over the new hope of dehydrated fruits and meats; and it worked!

What all of these great salespeople showed us is that the attitudes of the buyers are not transmitted to the seller but the other way around. If you are expecting to sell your services to others, don't expect to walk into a happy and receptive audience of people who are excited to hear another sales pitch. Remember, you are not selling the next smokeless ashtray that they can see and touch but rather a service that is largely invisible to them. **When you sell services you are selling a relationship and a promise of results** based on their goals and objectives, and that relationship starts and ends with the attitude you have when you first walk in the door. Your attitude can be conveyed in many ways including your body language, your movements and gestures, your voice, and even your facial expressions.

In a recent research study, university students were shown pictures of actors' faces but some were able to view them for only a fraction of a second. They were then asked to rate each picture by attractiveness, likability, competence, trustworthiness, and aggressiveness. Two very interesting findings came from the study: First, the strongest correlation of results was around **"trustworthiness,"** and second, the students who were given unlimited time to view and rate the pictures produced largely the same results, although they become slightly more negative over time.[4]

Judging people by their facial features and expressions is nothing new. Studies on facial features and trust have shown that people **view "happy" people with higher levels of honesty, reliability, and trust.**[5] Taking this a step further, the facial structures we tend to subconsciously assign greater levels of trust to just so happen to mirror a "happy-looking" face.[6]

To illustrate this point in a less scientific manner, when you first meet a dog up close, notice how they react to a happy face versus an angry face. I have done this with dogs countless times to see just how quickly they will subconsciously react to my facial expressions, and it works almost every time.

So how can you as a salesperson apply this information to help you improve your own sales? Here are a few tips:

- **Don't meet with new clients and prospects while you are in a bad mood.** Bad moods internally will often be reflected in how you act externally, and it will show—especially on your face. If you are having a really bad day and you have important sales meetings, simply reschedule them for a time when your bad mood goes away.

- **Train yourself to smile more around other people.** If actors can train themselves to do this on stage, you can train yourself to do this in real life. Always start your greeting with anybody new with a smile, eye contact, and a firm handshake. Make everybody you meet with feel like they are the most important person to you at that time.

One of the most amazing parts about a smile is how it can affect your attitude, confidence, and sales results. When a salesperson starts out with a good sales month, they will commonly end with a great month all because of their attitude and confidence that they then carry into each subsequent sales meeting. So make your attitude shine and watch your sales grow; it all starts with a smile.

STORYTELLING
CONCEPTUALIZES THE MESSAGE

There is an old saying in sales: **"Facts tell, but stories sell."**
Most salespeople tell facts to their prospects in the wrong way
and at the wrong times. As a result, what the facts make you
feel is typically the opposite of how customers really think of
you when you are providing them. While using facts may
make you feel smart, important, and informed, your prospective
customers may really be viewing you as condescending,
confusing, and unlikable; all the qualities that will help you kill
any sales opportunity. When was the last time you heard a
salesperson spewing out all of his lovely facts to you and
ended up turning you off as a result? It happens to everybody.
Don't be that guy, and learn from their mistakes.

Facts are great in a sales process but only if they can help
conceptualize a message. The most effective way to conceptualize a great sales message is through a story. Without a
basis to support the fact in the mind of the customer, it
only leads to annoyance and confusion, and a confused
mind always says "no."

Storytelling is powerful because it also provides meaning
and relevance to information, and **people cannot remember
anything without giving it meaning.** Think about it: If I were
to say four numbers to you, would you remember them? Most
people would quickly forget because they know the numbers
but cannot associate a meaning with them. If, however, I told
you I had the four numbers that make up the password to your
bank debit card, I would have your attention since the numbers

now have meaning. This is also why **stories are memorable and statics are not.** Studies have shown that after a sales presentation, 63 percent of the attendees remember the stories told while only 5 percent remember the statistics.[2]

There are a number of reasons why stories are so impactful in the sales process. Here are a few tips to help you understand why:

First, stories **best tell the "why" of your services.** When it comes to selling services, people don't buy what you do but why you do it. You might be the greatest dental periodontist in the world, but if you tell me that you treat periodontal disease it is of no value to me unless I can associate my problem of oral inflammation to it and know there is a way to treat it. If, on the other hand, you were to tell me the story of a patient who had a problem with oral inflammation, the challenges he had with it, and how you were able to help him fix the problem, then you would have my attention. Another example is with attorneys who practice highly specialized areas of law yet can't convey their value to consumers. For example, does the average person know what services an elder-law attorney provides? Most of us have aging members of our family or soon will; by 2025 nearly one-fifth of all Americans will be sixty-five or older. Yet do they know who can help them with Medicare and Medicaid planning or managing financial matters for family members struck with Alzheimer's, or dementia? This is the difference between telling me "what" you do versus explaining "why" you do it within a story I can relate to and understand; especially if my needs and/or situation are similar.

Second, stories help **avoid confusion by conceptualizing your message** in simple terms that people understand and can relate to. Most people are initially skeptical during a first sales meeting, and stories help to quickly mitigate this skepticism by providing something that is more believable, interesting, and even entertaining to the prospective customer. People like to buy from people they like and it is hard not to like a good story. Moreover, the more complex the services you offer the better the chance a story will be able to explain what you provide in the easiest way possible to the average person.

Third, stories allow you to **differentiate yourself from others.** Since most people selling today are poor storytellers, becoming a good one gives you a distinct sales advantage. Facts and data still rule the day for most salespeople, which can end up leading most sales conversations quickly to price. Those who sell by telling stories and framing data within their stories are much better able to articulate and sell based on customer value and results and not on price.

Fourth, nothing is more powerful than a **customer success story,** especially when it is first told by your customer. It is always powerful to memorize and be able to regurgitate these stories, but getting your customers' stories on video is even better; especially when they are posted on your website and YouTube for all to see. No matter which way you choose to promote a story, start by writing it down so you can better memorize it and train your memory to better process it for when you need it most: during a sales meeting.

When formulating your sales stories, the **goal of each story should be a call to action.** If your goal is to sell your services to other potential customers, tell stories that lead you to that sell. A story should also have a defined structure to be most effective. Ironically the structure of a good story will mirror a generic sales process, starting with identifying a **problem,** describing what **challenges** resulted from those problems, and then providing a **resolution** that compels the listener to want to act—preferably in your favor. The best stories told will be those stories that are most relevant and evoke an emotional reaction in the listener. We know that the decision to buy is largely an emotional one, and stories are the best way to evoke that reaction in your listeners.

CONSISTENCY AND CONSENSUS BREED CREDIBILITY

How often are you and your service/s seen in your target market? Many people buy based on the exposure and the buying actions of others; if they see others buying your services, they become more curious about why and see you with a higher level of credibility and trust. **But just because they may see or know you doesn't necessarily mean they know what they see in you.**

People like to stay in their comfort zones and tend to buy in a similar manner. This is the reason people who frequent the same stores and restaurants will buy the same clothes and order the same food; they know what to expect each time they buy. **That expectation is the promise the seller creates for the buyer that it will happen all the time, every time.** For example, when was the last time you went to your favorite restaurant and ordered your favorite meal only to have it come out different than previous experiences and not to your liking? Or how about the last time you went for a haircut with your favorite barber or hair stylist only to have them not perform to their usual level of service? How did that make you feel, and why did you feel that way? Unlike a new experience, your expectations were higher since your experience and expectations told you to expect a similar and desirable outcome each and every time. When that failed to happen, the business failed to provide you with your expected exchange of value.

As a business professional, your customers will have the same expectations of you and your services. If they refer you to one of their family, friends, or acquaintances, they are putting their own credibility on the line with the expectation that you will deliver the same level of service to the referral that you provided them. If they engage you for additional services, they are expecting the same level of value and service as previously provided. The bottom line is that no matter what you provide as a professional, it should at least be as consistent and of the same level of value as possible with every customer you work with no matter what. Remember, most people would not rank McDonald's hamburgers as their favorite, but when you walk into any McDonald's anywhere across the United States, you know and expect the same results each and every time. This is how they were able to sell billions of hamburgers and how you too can better grow your business and your promise to your customers.

When it comes to consensus in sales, it is pretty straightforward when selling services to consumers (B2C) since most decisions fall on a single decision maker and sometimes include their spouse. For professionals selling to businesses (B2B), this can become much more complicated since we have always been taught in the past to identify the key decision maker and do whatever you can to get in front of them and sell them—for they are the ones who make the final decision. If you are selling services to businesses, this is nothing new. After all, who wants to spend all their time selling and reselling to multiple people before you finally get a decision? The problem today is that the typical B2B buying decision **has to be signed off on by an average of 5.4 people to make a sale.** So who should you sell to and why?

Studies have shown that **decision makers within businesses consider widespread support for the supplier to be the number one impact on their buying decision.**[7] Think about it: Most decision makers in businesses today make a lot of decisions in a short amount of time and, depending on the size of the organization, they commonly have to defer to others to help. By potentially bypassing users and influencers within a business, you may be passing the very people who have the greatest influence on your sale.

The most effective way to deal with the question of who is involved with any decision-making process is to ask any and all people who work with the targeted customer, **"How are purchasing decisions like this typically made in your family/businesses/organization?"** The answers should help guide you in the right direction and to the people who can buy and help influence the buyers' decision.

Consensus can benefit your marketing efforts as well. Have you ever projected a desired outcome and expectation on a customer or prospect? For example, if I published a reference to the fact that "91 percent of our customers would recommend our services to others" or "95 percent of our customers are repeat customers" as part of all my customer communications, how would you respond to that and why? Not only would you deduce that we likely have happy customers, but when the business asks for referrals and renewals, how much more willing will you be to help provide both? This is the same reason hotels place those little "protect the environment" cards in your bathrooms to help get you to reuse your towels. When you see them what are you more compelled to do? Clearly the hotels will save a great deal of money on reduced laundry costs so you know that altruism alone is not the only motivation here. The messages are clearly designed to influence a desired decision-making process by the customer and is something you can successfully do as well.

LEARN HOW TO SELL YOURSELF FIRST

One of the key observations I made early on in my sales career is how the best salespeople will typically be the best salespeople no matter where they work or what they sell. I would constantly see great salespeople move from companies with superior products and services to companies with vastly inferior offerings and vice versa, and the results were almost always the same: These people could successfully sell nearly anything. So how did they do it? And what about all those excuses you may hear from people about how if only our products or services were better they could be the top salesperson as well? All of this starts with your people and a clear understanding that **HOW YOU SELL is more important than what you sell.**

People buy from people, especially people they like. Likability comes from a number of factors including similarity, compliments made, and your willingness to be helpful and cooperative. For most professionals today, you and your employees who represent your brand are in many cases literally becoming their own brand while selling yours. As our economy continues to mature, we are faced with increasing levels of competition and commoditization of services. When commoditization takes place, the greatest differentiator often comes down to price—unless you and your people can add more personal brand value to the process than your competitors, that is. As a result, the person or people representing your service/s is likely to have a greater influence on your customer's perception of your value than the services you provide. We also see this from customers who now indicate that fully 35 percent of the value they receive comes from the person selling the products or services.[8] This applies to brand loyalty as well. You can build the most powerful brand in your service industry that everybody may know, but the brand alone does not know your customers—you and your people do. Because of this, **your customers will typically be much more loyal to you and your people than the brand you represent.**

For example, I worked with two very prestigious law firms over the years and both were highly credentialed and exceptional at their work. Each, however, provided very different experiences to their customers, and the results showed it. In the first firm, the minute a prospect or client walked in the door they were treated like a king. They were greeted by name with a happy "we were expecting you" by the receptionist. They were then offered premium drinks and snacks while they waited until they were finally whisked into a conference room with their name prominently listed on the door. Each person in the firm knew each client by name and always greeted them with a smile and a handshake. Once someone became a client of the firm, they would receive thoughtful gifts and handwritten cards from the attorney/s containing personal information that was important to them such as birthdays, anniversaries, deaths in the family, and milestones in their children's lives. The other firm was a whole other story.

When you walked in to the second firm's office, the experience was a total opposite of the first. Prospects and clients had to sign in at the front desk and wait, often for long times, sending a clear signal to the customer that the attorney's time was more important than theirs. While waiting, they also had to listen to their crabby receptionist answer phones calls in a very impersonal and rude manner, sending another clear signal as to how they could expect to be treated as well. When the attorney finally arrived, they were spoken to no differently than a doctor reading off of a chart to their patients. The attorneys and the staff were **very cold, impersonal, and businesslike with their customers.**

Both of these firms offered the same legal services, but the experience in working with the people in the firms was vastly different. One firm made their customers feel very important while the other did not. One firm made sure that everybody in the firm acted in a way that made customers feel important while the other firm did not. The primary difference was the culture that was created and fostered in each firm around the desired experience of the customer. It all starts and ends with you and your people.

In order for you and your people to better sell your services, you need to be able to sell yourselves first. You can do this by first understanding that you and your employees are both critical and unique brands in and of yourselves, and you must develop ways to better build credibility and trust in the eyes of your customers. You also need to take steps to better develop the perceived value that ALL OF YOU provide in your relationships with your clients. This is commonly done when you and your people are able to do the following better than your competition:

- Provide reasons to buy from you beyond just the services that you offer. This often means providing additional value-added experiences and services to help support the sale. It is important to remember that in sales, **you have to give in order to receive**.

- **Ask intelligent questions** of your customers in a way that allows you to understand your customers' issues and needs better than your competitors.

- ALWAYS make your customers **feel like they are the most important people** to you and your business when you are taking their time to deal with you. Every customer interaction should be designed to exceed your customers' expectations and make them feel as important as possible.

- **Connect personally before you sell professionally.** Salespeople often talk about being "in control" of the sales process, but they often fail at knowing when the appropriate time to take control is. There is an old saying—"People don't care what you know until they know that you care." People have an inherent need to feel important, and the best way to make them feel important is to start out by personally connecting with them. Look for areas of similarity and common interests, and offer compliments. When you begin any sales meeting with a prospect, make sure to make a personal connection before you jump into business. If they have a problem and/or need, acknowledge it, understand it, empathize with it, and connect with it. If I find a customer is upset, I always let them talk it out and reply with a simple response: "I don't blame you one bit for feeling the way that you do. If I were in your shoes, I would likely feel the same way." I ONLY start to control a sales process after a connection is first made. This requires getting any negative emotions and/or fears out of the way, and I will often let people talk themselves out before I ultimately steer them to where I want to go.

In summary, most professionals cannot count on their services alone to be their differentiator in the market in today's business climate. Moreover, when you develop a sales process for your business you will find that the execution of that process is what truly sets you apart from others, and the people who make that execution happen are the key.

DITCH THE PRESENTATIONS AND START A CONVERSATION—DIAGNOSE BEFORE YOU PRESCRIBE

The sales profession largely has a bad stigma about what people perceive the typical salesperson to be. Through decades of movies involving slick salespeople and cutthroat sales tactics, many people are naturally skeptical when dealing with new salespeople. Why? Because there is little or no initial credibility and trust for most new salespeople today. And how do most people selling start out a sales meeting with these skeptical people? They break open a PowerPoint or some other canned presentation and start talking and pitching. **Most sales are made or lost within the first three minutes,** and when you make a presentation, you are talking to your prospect instead of *with* them: the surest way to kill any sale before they even pay attention to your products or services.

Another challenge with salespeople today is that they think they know more about their products and services than their prospective customers—which in many cases they will—and seem to want to impress their sales prospects with their vast knowledge. The primary problem here is twofold. First, people don't care what you know until they know that you care about them. Second, people selling need to understand that **knowledge in and of itself isn't power. Rather, the communication of that knowledge is where the true power**

lies. This why proper communication is so critical when selling to others.

Recent studies have indicated that fully 88 percent of executive buyers want a conversation and not a presentation. Because of this simple fact, you need to design your initial sales interactions as a conversation. One of the best ways to do this is to create and follow a simple sales client meeting guide (see example in the Resources section) that provides a standard conversation format for your initial sales meetings with your prospective customers. By using guides such as these, you are better able to have a conversation with your sales prospects while CONSISTENTLY capturing key sales information you will need to help identify any goals and gaps they may have that you can then sell to. In short, you need to diagnose before you prescribe.

For example, think about what would happen if you were to walk into a doctor's office with severe migraines. You may tell the doctor what the problem is and he/she will run a series of tests and ask you a number of questions (diagnose) before they suggest any treatments for your problem (prescribe). Now, what do you suppose would happen if the same doctor, upon hearing your head hurt, immediately broke out a prescription for a pain medication and told you about all the advantages of this new drug and why it is so great? In this second example, how much less confident would you be that the doctor truly under-stood your needs and is prescribing what will cure the source of your problem? So why it is that so many salespeople do exactly the same thing with their sales prospects? Remember, **in health as in sales—diagnose before your prescribe.**

There will be times, however, when a prospect may request a PowerPoint or presentation. In these instances, you need to understand that visuals can be very powerful but not when they include a dense amount of text to accompany them. Most people today will literally read from PowerPoint slides and in effect turn a good opportunity for a sales conversation into a bedtime story. Don't do it. Keep your slides brief, remove as much text as possible, and use visuals to reinforce your conversation, not take the place of it. Moreover, when using visuals, make the images compelling—not the text.

When used properly, good visuals are powerful because most people think visually and not in text. Therefore, **visuals can be processed 60,000 times faster than text**[9] and help give your sales prospects a point of visual focus for their thoughts as you are selling to them. Because of this, it is helpful to use highly relevant and compelling visuals for your prospects to look at when they are processing your sales information. In many cases, the best visuals are those that match the prospect's gaps and goals, which you can uncover during an initial sales conversation. For example, what if a dentist has a patient who complains that she cannot get dates because of her bad teeth? How compelling would two visuals be that help this customer see the before and after pictures of cosmetic dentistry work along with pictures of famous couples who also have near-perfect teeth? Or how about a criminal defense lawyer who is meeting with a prospective client who could be convicted of a serious crime that could involve prison time, a failed marriage, and possibly losing custody of the most precious part of his life—his children? How compelling would the visualization of a new life in federal prison be versus pictures of his potential post-acquittal where he could be playing in the park with his children? The examples here are potentially endless but all are based on a visual perception of the goals and gaps for each unique customer and how your products and services can potentially help them solve their problems in the most powerful way: visually.

USING LEVERAGE IS THE KEY TO SALES GROWTH

Business growth is all about leverage, and so is sales growth. By definition, leverage is the ability to multiply the outcomes of one's efforts through the highest and best use of resources. Earlier in this book, we discussed the importance of knowing what your time is worth relative to other alternative people, processes, and resources that could be utilized to your benefit. Most leverage in small businesses today is achieved through the delegation of resources. For example, most business professionals' time is worth more than a receptionist's so they delegate those tasks to lower-cost resources, thereby freeing up more of their time for higher-earning functions. This happens throughout all business functions, ranging from customer support, marketing, sales, finance, etc.

Most successful businesspeople will create business plans that include detailed resource costs, utilization, and returns. From this information, they will design what their organizations will look like in detail based on their end goal and then build up into that model from today forward. Sales and marketing should be an integral part of this plan and provide a clear picture of what will be needed and the details for each position.

For example, most successful attorneys today will bill around $500,000 in annual billings, with very few ever eclipsing the $1,000,000 per year mark. Why? Because most attorneys, like other professionals, have a hard time delegating to create leverage in their businesses. They do this for a number of reasons. First, **most professionals know what they do but many don't have a clearly defined picture of who they ultimately want to be.** Second, most professionals fail to understand what it is that they are really good at and do not find ways to delegate everything else out to other people and resources. Third, most professionals simply don't know how to properly delegate because they fail to learn and fully understand what each task or position entails and how to create a repeatable system that others can follow to support it.

One of the biggest mistakes you can make as a professional is **thinking you can do it all yourself.** The challenge today for most small businesses in the US is that they operate as sole proprietors; meaning they choose to go it alone. Of the 28 million small businesses currently in the US, fully 22 million (or 79 percent) currently employ no other resources beyond themselves. Once the initial excitement of a new small business wears off, reality will set in and you will quickly realize that you cannot successfully do it alone and if you continue to try, **you will likely burn yourself out and your business will fail.** Sound familiar? The goal should be to hire people who are good in their respective areas of work—especially those areas you are not the best at—and grow your business with the help of others.

In the end, leverage is what allows you to scale not only your sales and marketing but your business as well. Without it, you will simply be creating more responsibilities and work for yourself at a lower return for your time. This is one of the main differences between growing a successful business as part of the top 20 percent and the remaining 80 percent who will fail. Moreover, this is where a business's greatest potential value, its **equity value,** is created.

ALWAYS MAKE SURE THAT YOU ARE IN CONTROL OF THE SALES PROCESS

In the previous chapter we discussed the importance of following and executing on a defined step-by-step sales process. But simply learning these steps alone is not enough for most salespeople. They also need to learn how to control the sales process that manages them and how to do it in a way that creates control without coming across as being too pushy to their customers. Most people don't react well to "pushy" salespeople, yet most people will never successfully sell unless they assert some type of control over their sales process with a prospective customer. Ultimately you need to strike a fine balance between the two if you want to be successful. Ideally, the fault for having to be pushy in sales is on the salesperson and the business, not the prospect. If the sales process is followed, the customer is qualified, and the value exchange is clear and compelling to the customer, there should be little or no need to push a prospect to buy beyond what should already compel them to want to buy. However, in reality, most businesses today do not operate in this perfect world.

A simple rule in sales is to make sure that **the person selling is in control of each step of a sales process and not the customer.** This means that objections and delays at each step need to be overcome in order to move as many sales as possible successfully through your sales process. One of the easiest ways to address objections is to clearly identify them as quickly as possible and address them with the customer in a way that moves you successfully to the next step. One of the most effective ways to do this is through the use of trial-closing questions after addressing each objection.

For example, most sales break down between the customer presentation and the closing stages of a sales process. As a result, a customer can "go quiet," simply state that "the price is too high," etc., and the result for most salespeople is to simply give up without fully addressing the objections and move to another closing attempt. Many people are naturally fearful of objections and therefore it is a course of least resistance to follow this path; even though the top 20 percent do not. Ironically the same people who tend to give up on these objections also tend to give up on controlling the other process-step breakdowns that can happen in all stages of sales, ranging from lead follow-up, prospecting rejections, sales-meeting rescheduling, setting follow-up sales meetings, asking for the close, asking for referrals, and consistently staying in front of current clients and stalled sales prospects.

— CHAPTER 5 —

CLOSING THE SALE: WHERE IT ALL PAYS YOU

• • •

Who can forget the famous scene from the movie *Glengarry Glen Ross* when Alec Baldwin tries to motivate a group of salespeople by telling them to **"A"** Always, **"B"** Be, **"C"** Closing? The point was to make sure that no matter what happens in a sales process, they are always pushing to the same defined objective: the close. As entertaining and disturbing as this scene may be to some, it does help illustrate a part of the sales process where ironically most people do in fact fail to execute effectively.

Of all the steps mentioned in a sales process beyond prospecting, none is more important than the close, for absent the close, there is no sale and no new customers and revenue to support and grow a business. As previously discussed, around **78 percent of salespeople will hesitate when it comes time to ask for the sale and 66 percent will end a sales meeting without asking at all.**[1] Worse yet, 44 percent of salespeople will give up on a sale after only one "no." So why do many businesses and professionals waste so much time and so many resources to prospect, generate leads, and conduct sales meetings and then never ask for the sale?

Many salespeople will often confuse the goal of creating a new client relationship with the sales goal of closing a sale. We all want to make friends, be liked, and be accepted, but far too many people will place this priority over their fear of a possible rejection and therefore will not ask for a sale. When you ask most salespeople why they are in sales, many will tell you that they like to work with and meet new people. So there is an inherent potential conflict of interest here when on one hand you need to close sales to support your business and on the other you want to work with people and don't want to potentially jeopardize those relationships in doing so. Moreover, if you have worked hard through the sales process to create credibility and trust with a prospect, you now have to potentially put that status at risk by asking to close a sale.

These problems can be overcome with proper training, management, recruiting, and even sales resources alignment. For example, many larger sales organizations are increasingly bifurcating their salespeople based on function and aligning them to the various steps of the sales process. Car dealers have done this for years when, during some negotiations, in addition to the floor salesperson, they bring in a "closer" who is emotionally unattached to the customer relationship and has an easier time pushing for the close. Good sales managers and business owners can also act in a similar manner because in addition to having a non-emotional attachment, they can bring a higher sense of authority to the close as well, thereby further strengthening their position with the customer.

WHY CLOSING DECISIONS ARE MADE

Recent studies have shown **that 70 percent of people make purchasing decisions to solve a problem while only 30 percent do so to gain something.**[1] But when people finally decide to buy, they only buy based on two factors: **greed and fear.** Both of these factors are *based in emotion* and no matter how compelling your business's case to buy is, **the final decision compelling them to buy will be largely emotional.** Because of this, you need to understand the psychological state of your buyer's mind at this critical time of the sales process and make sure that you are addressing and closing to their emotional needs and concerns instead of just the rational.

For example, many of us know what it is like to purchase a new home. For most people, it is the largest purchasing decision we will make in our lives. When looking for homes, most buyers have a logical criteria (greed) in mind for their new home, and when they find it, their emotional reaction will commonly be to buy it quickly due to their now-emotional connection to the property and the thought of potentially losing it (fear). In these situations, the emotional connection and the potential fear of losing a property is the compelling event to buy now; the higher the emotional connection and levels of competition and/or the risk of loss, the greater the fear.

Another example would be the future transition of the family farm upon the death of a parent. Most people don't want to think about the death of any family member, but it is the one common ending we all share—it is just a matter of how and when. Because of potentially high estate-inheritance taxes, many farmers could end up losing their family farm that they would rather have been inherited by their children. An estate-planning attorney might explain how to set up trusts to help protect these family objectives, but how much more motivated would they likely be to act on it if they knew that a parent's death could come any day now? Moreover, how could that heightened emotion be used to help trigger an action to set up a trust today as opposed to continuing to wait?

These examples exist in any business and further illustrate the power that emotion truly has in closing business. Many salespeople fail to recognize this fact and when a customer emotionally objects to a sell the salesperson will try to continue to close them based on facts. That is the surest way to sell to the wrong source of the objection and need.

CONFIDENTLY DISCUSS PRICES

When it comes to business, **you can only end up competing based on service or price, but not both.** If your goal is to compete on service, then price will still matter but only in relation to the value of the service you can provide. If you want to compete on price, then your profits and survival will be based largely on how you can scale your business to control costs relative to your competition. In either situation, price will be a part of your sales process and therefore you have to understand when it is best to discuss it, how to discuss it, and why. For many salespeople today, price is not something that they like to discuss, which is why you will commonly see salespeople get uncomfortable and act defensively when a prospective customer asks, "So how much does this cost?" The top 20 percent do not have this problem.

Salespeople will frequently struggle when talking about pricing for the following reasons:

- They feel the price is too high themselves (questioning the value of what they sell)
- They are **afraid of rejection** or putting the relationship they are forming with the sales prospect at risk
- They are afraid of potentially starting a pricing negotiation process
- They are unsure exactly when pricing should be discussed in the sales process
- They **don't understand the true value exchange** they are providing to each individual client

The economics for pricing is simple: The more perceived value you can provide a prospective customer with your products and services, the greater the price (or cost to the prospective customer) you can command. If your business is running successfully, you should always strive to find the right supply (value) and demand (buying customers) balance to produce your sales objectives. If you price your services too high relative to the value you provide, demand (buying customers) will decline. Conversely, if you price your services too low relative to the value you provide, demand (buying customers) will exceed your ability to supply them. In both cases, if you lack a clear understanding of the value you can provide to each customer, it is hard to determine the "right" pricing.

When a prospective customer asks you for a price, what he/she is really trying to do is determine in their own mind the potential value you are providing to them. If the value of your products and services is not immediately apparent to them, then providing price before value is one of the quickest ways to kill a sales opportunity. Think about it: If pricing precedes value, then the buyer will process the "known" value of their own money versus the value they already perceive you are providing them before they ever really know or you have had a chance to fully articulate to them. This is where many sales fail before the sales processes ever begin. **Starting off initial sales meetings by pitching and presenting instead of learning about your customers' needs and the value you can provide them is the fastest way to get to a discussion about pricing.**

Because of this problem, most sales situations should lead with value and end with pricing when possible. If the price of your products and services are at the high end of your market, leading with value first is especially important—because how else are you able to discover and present a fair value exchange with a prospective customer absent the value they already know their money to be worth to them?

Depending on how long your sales process is, there may be instances where discussing price may need to happen early in the cycle; the longer the sales cycle, the more important this may become. Why? Because your time is worth money and you don't want to waste their time and yours trying to sell to somebody who in the end cannot afford your products or services. In these situations, you may be better served by providing a full price range or simply discussing what other "known" customers are also paying for similar services. It can also be helpful to ask prospective customers probing questions about pricing such as: "Is there a budget in place for this purchase?" "How much have you typically had to pay for services like this in the past?" "Do you have an idea yet as to where your comfort zone is for a service like this?" Etc.

Now that we have addressed *when* to discuss pricing, the next part it to discuss how to discuss pricing. First, whenever your pricing is provided make sure that both your verbal and non-verbal communication conveys nothing but confidence. **Present your price, stand firm, don't fidget, don't make excuses for the price, look them in the eye, and then SHUT UP.** The next person who speaks should be them and not you. The more you talk to try to justify the price after presenting it, the more concerns they may have in making a decision and accepting your price as presented. No matter what questions they may ask you after your pricing is presented, be prepared for all of them, learn from past situations, and always remain calm and confident in addressing all questions and concerns. In some instances if I notice that the room is too tense preceding a "What is the price?" question, I will use reverse psychology on the buyer by stating, "Two million dollars." At that point I will smile, hopefully get them to smile, and lower the level of anxiety before I present the real pricing.

Finally, remember that people love to buy and hate to be sold. For this reason, it is helpful to give your prospective customers more than one potential option (with different price points), and explain to them the value differences between each. Ideally, **most people will react better to two to three buying options and no more.** If you provide a greater number of options beyond that, some people will get confused and not be able to decide. Once the value for each option is articulated, the buyer should then be able to make their own price-versus-value comparison and choose the right one for them. If you have developed a high level of credibility and trust with the buyer up to this point, don't be surprised if they ask you which of the options is the best deal; in which case you are exactly where you want to be.

For example, in one of my previous software companies, we fully modularized components of our systems so they could be bought as both a bundle of services or as add-on modules to our core system. In those instances when price objections came into play, our first responses where simple: "No problem, we can certainly bring the price down to where you are comfortable. What price do you want to be at so we can then remove the modules that will help get us down to that point? We can always add those modules back later once we have proven our value to you."

As you can imagine in these instances, most buyers were not prepared for this nor were they prepared to remove services to bring the price down; now they wanted them all because up to that point we had clearly showed them the value of each. In this case, we sent a clear signal that we were confident in the value of our services provided but were nimble enough to quickly adjust our delivery models based on price. Moreover, at that point in the decision-making process we quickly empowered the buyer to make the value-exchange decision—not us. In the end, we NEVER once had to discount our services as a company; all because of how we presented pricing and designed our products and services to help support it. Now, how many businesses can say that?

NO, YOU DIDN'T LOSE THE BUSINESS BECAUSE OF PRICE

When people buy anything ranging from cars, clothing, food, etc., they are paying a price based on their perceived value. Additionally, most people don't buy the "cheapest" products and services they can find because the value is not there for them. Therefore, most people will wear higher-priced clothing, drive nicer cars, and eat at better restaurants not because of price but because of value. If you ask these people why they buy at these higher levels, most people will not mention price but rather other reasons having to do with the perceived value to them such as looking more presentable in public, enjoying their commutes, and enjoying their dining experiences with others. That's of course when you dig deeper into their "why" instead of receiving the more common "it was too expensive" rejections.

Most people will tell you that a sale was lost because of price for two reasons. First, it is commonly the first and easiest thing a prospective customer can use to say "no" without really saying "no." Second, it can allow salespeople to better excuse the loss by using the business as an excuse for what was really a poor sales process. In short, the salesperson was likely "told" that he lost because of price and then "told" the business the same thing. **In reality, most sales are not lost** because of price but rather other reasons. In addressing the "pricing" objection with prospective customers, it is a good idea to fight any fears of objection and giving up. For as the old saying goes, "There is no last word in diplomacy."

Any time you receive a pricing rejection make sure that you don't argue with the prospective customer. Instead respond with a simple, "Okay" (a little reverse psychology never hurts here). Next, **ask the prospect if the price is their only concern or if there is anything else that may be involved with the decision (there usually is).** If they continue to come back to pricing, ask them how they know it is too expensive. Compared to what other options? Again, using reverse psychology, you can now apologize for failing to articulate the value of what you were selling and for wasting the prospect's time. If you then discover the "real" causes for the objection, indicate that you would have handled things differently.

If during this objection questioning you uncover the real reasons for the objection (beyond price), then address those issues with the customer and make sure they are all addressed before you attempt to move the customer back through your sales process and try to close on them again.

NO, THEY DON'T NEED MORE TIME TO THINK ABOUT IT

Most buying decisions are made or lost before a customer ever needs to "think about it" or "get back to you." We know from studies that **most sales are made or lost within the first three minutes** of the presentation/meeting, so there really is not much left to "think about." The final decision to buy will be based more on emotion and not based on further thinking. What they are really telling you through this rejection is that they either don't see the compelling value to act now and/or they are not emotionally comfortable making this decision now; and that is on you to address as part of your sales process.

In dealing with this rejection, it is good to address it head-on now so it is not lingering out there any longer. For example, you could respond with: "Okay, I understand. Can I ask you a question? What are your concerns right now about this decision? **What is it that you may be uncomfortable with so I can make sure you have everything you need to make an informed decision when you are ready to buy?"** Notice how you can handle this in a non-threatening way and work to uncover the true issues he/she may be dealing with there.

In some instances, you may need to let the prospective customer have the time they requested for various reasons, which is okay. If you know the true source of their concerns, then you can better address them during this time by providing them with further support during their "thinking" period. It is also a good idea to make sure you set a date and time to follow up with them as part of a give-and-take for this delay. In asking for a good time to follow up, you are also trial closing them to gauge their true level of interest. Their response—or lack thereof—to your request could be all you really need to know about where you truly stand with the prospect.

KNOW WHEN YOUR PROSPECTS ARE READY TO BUY

One of the mistakes people commonly make when selling is not knowing if a prospective customer is ready to buy or not. At a certain point in any sales process, if your buyer is ready to buy they may tell you in ways that are not so obvious to you or them but through questions and reactions that can help tell you they are ready without them overtly coming out and saying, "Where do I sign?" In sales we refer to these questions and reactions as "buying signals."

The most obvious buying signal is, "Okay, where do I sign?" If you miss this buying signal you might as well stop here and hire somebody else to sell for you. For everybody else, there are a few things to know about buying signals, when to look for them, and most important, how to react to them when they happen. In all cases, you have to learn how to observe and listen to your sales prospects in order to pick up on these signals. If you end up talking and not listening, you will be limited to only one of the two types of buying signals you are looking for.

The first type buying signals are **non-verbal buying signals,** which are the physical reactions your prospect will show you while you are selling to them. Typical buying signals such as these will include:

- Leaning forward during your discussions
- Looking you in the eye

- Nodding, smiling, and agreeing with you
- Handling or experiencing your product or service

The second type buying signals are **verbal buying signals,** which require you to ask enough questions and at times to shut up long enough for them to ask you questions in return. It is these questions, or lack thereof, that they ask of you that are the quickest indication of their real interest in your product or service. So make sure that when they start asking these types of buying-signal questions, you clearly understand where they are psychologically in the buying process at that time. Typical verbal-buying-signal questions to look for include:

- How soon can you/I . . . ?
- How quickly can you deliver . . . ?
- What are my payment options?
- Do you offer any discounts or promotions?
- Who else uses this product or service?
- Can you tell me more about this?
- Do you offer any guarantees or warrantees on your service?

In addition to these questions, you many also hear objection questions that, in reality, may be buying signals as well. Remember, when people make final buying decisions, it is largely based on emotion, so they may also expose any of these emotionally based fears they may have. You can address these at this point as well. In reality, most people have been sold something in the past that they regret and may still have a bad taste in their month from that experience and don't want to repeat the same mistakes. Examples of these types of buying-signal questions can include:

- I had a bad experience in the past buying a service like this. Here is what happened and how do I know it won't happen again with you?
- Is this really the best price you can offer me today?
- If I buy from you, are you sure this really will help me with . . . ?
- Who are your major competitors and how are you better?
- What happens if I buy this service and it ends up not working?

In all of these buying-signal situations, you need to recognize what these questions really are and when they happen, because when these questions come up, you need to stop selling and start closing because they may now be ready to buy. If unsure, ask trial-closing questions to see if they are ready to move into the close. Trial-closing questions are a great alternative to simply asking for the close because they are typically non-threatening and the prospective customer simply might not be ready to buy yet, so you don't want to make them feel uncomfortable. For example, some good trial-closing questions to use when you see buying signals can include: "Would it now make sense to . . . ?" "Are you comfortable at this point with moving forward?" "Is there anything else we need to discuss before you would want to move forward?" If they are ready, start your close or you may oversell the prospective customer and blow the whole deal.

A CONFUSED MIND ALWAYS SAYS "NO"— PROVIDE SIMPLE, FEWER OPTIONS

Many of the products and services sold today can be confusing to the average user, especially those that are technology driven. As professionals, you have become experts in your chosen fields, meaning that the training and knowledge you have received will commonly far outweigh that of your customers'. Because of this, salespeople tend to want to create a level of credibility and trust by puking their special knowledge all over a prospect when in reality all they may end up doing is making their prospect feel stupid and inferior during the sales process.

Most sales will end up in inaction, and many times this has to do with the confused mind of the buyer. If your sales prospects are not clear on the value proposition you are providing to them, they will likely not give you a second chance to explain it; most people are busy enough. Instead, they will commonly "go quiet" or simply tell you that the price was too high so they can get you to stop the sales process with them.

The job of a salesperson is not to be smarter than your prospective customers. In reality, the job of a salesperson it to take your vast store of knowledge and be able to translate it in a way that the prospective customer can clearly understand.

This means not using special acronyms, jargon, and other forms of communication that the client does not understand. You have to be able to speak at their level first so they can understand your value exchange and, in doing so, also build up credibility and trust so they can better rely on your expertise to handle the more confusing aspects of your products and services. Remember, **people don't want another salesperson—they want a trusted advisor.**

THE KEY TO THE CONVERSION IS IN THE FOLLOW-UP

Have you ever wondered why marketing and salespeople frequently don't get along in many larger organizations? Consider this: In most businesses today ***48 percent of salespeople never follow up with a prospect*** and ***30 percent of leads are not followed up on*** at all.[2] Think about that; roughly a third of all leads lead to nothing, and nearly half of all prospects are never followed up with by a salesperson. Talk about a glaring problem!

Another critical aspect to lead follow-up is timing; you need to act fast on leads in order to maximize your lead conversions. How fast? We know that **the rate in which leads are considered qualified drops by 600 percent in the first hour that they are not acted on.** Breaking this time frame down further, you can also increase your likelihood of lead conversion by nearly 400 percent by responding in the first minute, 160 percent in the second minute, 98 percent in three minutes, and 62 percent within thirty minutes.[3] Think this happens in most sales organizations today? Nope; the average company takes over forty-six hours to pick up a phone and respond to a lead![2] But guess where you will not see this commonly happening: with the top 20 percent.

Another critical aspect of follow-up is **frequency,** or how many total times you tried to reach your lead. The average person selling will only make 1.3 attempts to reach a prospect and then give up.[2] These people are not part of the top 20 percent. What makes this even more troubling is that we know that conversion rates of leads to opportunities are directly correlated to the amount of attempts made to reach a lead.

The need for additional follow-up attempts to reach a prospect has grown from 3.7 attempts needed in 2007 to 8 attempts today. Additionally, we also know that 80 percent of sales require at least 5 follow-up calls after a meeting to close them.[1] The good news is that persistence can pay off here when fully **93 percent of leads that can be converted are done so within 6 call attempts,** compared to a 48 percent conversion rate for those leads that are called only once.[3] This basically works out to around a **100 percent increase in lead conversion just by increasing the timing and frequency** of your follow-up attempts alone.

So what are best practices for following up on leads and how should you do it? For phone follow-ups, you should try three attempts on the first day (one minute, thirty minutes, and two hours after receiving) and one additional attempt on days five, fourteen, and fifteen after receiving the lead. For cold-call follow-ups, the best times to call are between 8–10 a.m. and 4–5 p.m. and the best days to call are Wednesdays and Thursdays, with Tuesdays being the worst. For emails, you should send an email each day starting with day one (within thirty minutes) and then emails on days four, eight, fifteen, and twenty-two. When sending email follow-ups, the best times for responses are between 8 a.m. and 3 p.m. with peak times between 8–9 a.m. and 3 p.m. each day. The benefit of following this **"coordinated" follow-up schedule can result in a 16 percent increase** in the chance of reaching the lead by phone, in addition to the overall conversion-rate increases gained by the timing and frequency of the attempts. If you have a prospect's mobile phone number, you can also drive up your conversion rates further on this schedule by texting at the same intervals as your emails (download example below). This new lead-conversion schedule is recommended as a starting point for your business and should be modified through additional use and testing to best fit your business and industry.

The New Lead Conversion Schedule can be found in the Resources (page 411). You can download the entire Resources file at: www.TheSuccessfulSalesManager.com (from the "Tools" menu).

A perfect example of how good lead-conversion systems work is by looking at the bigger mass-tort law firms in the US today. These law firms will commonly buy and/or market for their leads from many different sources and intake them in bulk; something smaller law firms cannot typically handle. As a result, they will set up rigid and scalable lead-conversion systems and workflows to get the highest levels of conversions out of the leads they pay for. The reason these larger firms succeed in lead conversion when many smaller law firms fail is that they know the process, grind, and what it takes to squeeze lemons into lemonade. Since smaller-sized law firms don't typically have the time, resources, systems, and processes in place to produce the same results, they typically get much worse results and return on investment (ROI) out of their leads.

The main thing to keep in mind with conversion is that a system and process must be defined and consistently followed in order for it to be successful. The good news is that there are a growing number of good conversion management automation systems on the market today as well as outsourced lead conversion/call center companies that can greatly assist you in these efforts. For most professionals, the benefits are huge. A potential increase of converting nearly 100 percent more of your current leads that you are already paying for and/or working hard to generate on your own into prospects should be compelling enough. Few, if any, aspects of marketing today can provide these types of returns.

CREDIBILITY COMES FROM STRONG AND RELEVANT CITATIONS

Most salespeople will tell you that the best tool you can arm them with is happy customers. Why? Because happy customers create the strongest credibility possible; namely proof of the value you are trying to sell to others. And that is the name of the game in sales: rapidly developing credibility and trust with your buyers during the buying process. For example, if I wanted to buy a new service but did not know for sure if it would work or not for me, how much more likely would I be to buy if the salesperson told me that he had two hundred other people just like me who he could call right now to tell me how much they love their service versus having only one or two clients he could reference by name only? Remember, the final decision to buy is largely a decision based on emotion, and **the strongest emotion is fear.** Any chance you have to address a potential buyer's fears in their mind means more decisions to buy. That is what customer references and citations can provide for you.

Developing strong customer references requires a defined process to execute on; it is not just something you "want to do" in business but something you "have to do" over time. The first step is to make sure that you stay in contact with your customers. If you have a smaller customer base in a smaller geographic radius, this may be accomplished with simple recurring customer calls and meetings. For businesses with a larger customer base and/or customers spread out over a wide geography, one of the most effective ways to do this is by providing them with a Net Promoter Score (NPS) survey by email, phone, and/or mail. An NPS survey is one simple question you can ask all of your customers: "On a scale from 1 to 10 (1 being the lowest, 10 being the highest), how likely are you to recommend our products or services to a friend or colleague?" By asking this simple question, you can learn which customers are most likely to become references for others, how their opinion trends over time, and how much value your customers truly perceive from your products and services.

Once you have identified who your stronger potential reference customers (or Promoters) are, you should then ask each of them if they would be willing to do any of the following:

- Would they be willing to **provide a testimonial** (written or video) about your products and/or services that you could then use in your marketing to others?
- Would they be willing to have you **publish their success story** in using your products and services for publication in white papers, on your website, in a video, in press releases, etc., to help promote your services to others?
- Would they be willing to **receive calls or emails from other prospective buyers** about their experiences in working with you and your business?
- Would they be willing to help **refer other new customers** to your business?

Once you have identified these potential promoters and their level of involvement, you should then act on these initiatives with the goal of developing and maintaining enough of each to support your sales efforts moving forward. In asking for these Promoters to "give" you these valuable citations, you should also be willing to "give back to them" in return for their efforts; not only to thank them but to help encourage more of it in the future.

Finally, once you have developed your customer testimonials, references, and citations, start using them in every sales process—especially with your new customer sales. Good salespeople will frequently "name drop" and cite examples of happy, similar customers to help assure prospective buyers that what they are selling does in fact work for others, how it has been working, and why. This process of invoking other customers into a current sales process also helps to rapidly build credibility for the seller and business as well as ease the emotional state of fear many buyers will have when they are ready to close. Using good customer references in a sales process in effect says to a prospective customer, "You can be confident in your decision to buy this product or service because you know it has delivered on the value promise to others who I know or can relate to."

NEGOTIATION—A GAME OF GIVE AND TAKE

The business definition of a negotiation is the bargaining (give and take) process between two or more parties. But this simple definition far too often fails to happen when it comes to most sales negotiations today. Sales negotiations are a natural process with many of the services we sell today, but too many people walk into a negotiation process unprepared and unskilled as negotiators, which leads to the resentment of this process instead of using it to their advantage.

When it comes to sales and business, you will find yourself in many negotiations, whether you like to negotiate or not. Some people tend to come to negotiating more naturally while others do not. When people negotiate, they typically do so to get a better deal, but what they really want to gain is the feeling that they "won" when they purchased. **So don't be** offended if some people feel the need to negotiate with you. In many instances, it only helps to support their desires to want to "win" when they buy and feel a sense of accomplishment in doing so. When it comes to sales negotiations, there are a number of key points you should remember and use to your advantage.

First, **don't start negotiating until both parties agree on exactly what you are negotiating over.** By starting out each negotiation with a clear understanding of exactly what is on the table, you can help eliminate any surprises that could creep up during the negotiation process that you were not expecting or prepared for. To use a gamblers' analogy, you should always be playing (negotiating) for only the "table stakes," which is everything you have on the table and nothing more. For example, say you are selling a home and your buyer wants you to discount your sales commission by 1 percent to help them close the deal. After you agree to the concession, the buyer may then want the seller's agent to do the same and have the seller pay 100 percent of the closing costs. If you started your negotiation with a clear understanding that your 1 percent concession alone would allow them to close, then you could have helped to avoid any further issues with the buyer wanting even more concessions after you thought your negotiation was completed. By simply stating beforehand to the buyer, "Just to be clear; if I offer you a 1 percent discount that is all you will need to close on this house today. Is that correct?" you could have helped to avoid this problem before it ever started.

Second, remember that **the prepared negotiator is the one who usually wins.** Before you start any negotiation, always try to learn as much as possible about the buyer—their current situation, any needs, pains, etc. The more information you can arm yourself with about the prospective customer's situation, the better the position you will be in to negotiate with your prospective customer before any negotiation begins.

Third, when a prospective customer starts by asking for a concession, **always begin by asking why they want the concession in the first place.** Your job in selling is to qualify a prospect, align your products and services to their needs, and get the prospect to clearly understand the compelling value of what you provide to them. Because of this, any further concession requests should be understood from the customer's perspective, which will better allow you to fully understand "why" they are really making the request. Furthermore, repeated similar concession requests from others could indicate a pattern that you can learn from and help further refine in your sales processes with others. So when people ask for a concession, simply ask them why, listen, and don't get defensive. The feedback they provide you could be priceless in more ways than one.

Fourth, understand that **most people will ask for more than they really expect and will settle for,** so don't immediately settle for what they initially request. If you ever watch other people negotiate, you will likely see a trend where many people instinctively try to "meet in the middle." There is that give and take in a negotiation process. Absent any knowledge of how the person across from you will negotiate, it is a good idea to start with the notion that they, like many others, will likely settle at a "meet in the middle" point when negotiating. Because of this, always try to make sure that your middle is where you too are comfortable at settling. For this reason, consider their low to your high and measure the middle. If their low was too low to meet in the middle for you, counter their low to a higher point and continue to a counter until they and you are comfortable meeting in the new middle to close the sale.

Fifth, **don't negotiate against yourself by providing unilateral concessions; always give only when you get something in return.** This is perhaps where most people who sell will fail in negotiating. Why? Because when selling a product or service, most salespeople are fixated on using only one bargaining tool (the sale of their own product or service) in return for one concession from the buyer (commonly in price). Because of this, salespeople will commonly "sell against themselves" by giving more and more concessions (typically in price) without asking for anything in return for those concessions other than the final transaction itself. For example, when a customer starts by asking for a 10 percent discount, many salespeople will concede and only counter with the close. This may go back and forth until the buyer finally buys—commonly at a lower price point. What should happen is when the customer starts off by asking for a 10 percent discount, the salesperson should ask for something of equal value in return. These asks can include such things as 5–10 new customer referrals, a press release, a written customer testimonial, etc.—all things that are of value to the salesperson and/or business. By knowing what you can ask for in advance and knowing that each give requires a take, you will be much better prepared to negotiate and will end up giving as much as you receive.

Sixth, know that the objective in any negotiation is for you to **offer smaller concessions first and save the most costly concessions for last**—and don't start by negotiating the price. These can include non-monetary concessions such as better delivery times, added services, PR, shorter contracts, better payment terms and options, etc. Remember, **most people are buying your services for a reason and it is not because of the price.** If you are able to offer a high-value service and experience to your customers, then that could be far more valuable than a price discount alone. As a business owner, the added benefit of such negotiation tactics can include a higher average order price and customer value—leading to a higher potential business valuation as well.

Seventh, always know that **time is your greatest ally in any negotiation,** so use it to your advantage. The worst thing you can do in any negotiation is lose the time advantage. Any lack of time or working on a short deadline can cause you to give more and gain less. Short timelines can also cause salespeople to try to prematurely close on a sale that is not yet closable commonly by offering incentives when the prospective customer is not yet ready to buy. And guess what happens to your prospective customer when this happens? You can then lose any and all of the credibility and trust you had previously developed with that person as well as setting a new lower price point in their mind for when they are ready to buy from you; all of which is bad. The goal here is to take time pressure off of you as the seller by having more alternative opportunities to close while putting more time pressure on your buyers by giving them deadlines and reasons to want to buy from you now by using incentives such as time-driven promotions, limited inventory, and expiring offers.

Eighth, **always be prepared to say "no" and walk away from any sale.** Nothing is more powerful and potentially convincing to a buyer than a seller's willingness to walk away from a deal. Remember, not every customer is the "right" customer for your business and the first indication that a prospect could end up being a bad customer is when they are difficult and unreasonable to sell to. The worst thing any business and salesperson can do is to limit the number of prospective buyers they have. The more prospecting and buying opportunities you have to choose from, the more you can run the risk of potentially walking away. That is why businesses and salespeople that have strong marketing and prospecting activity are able to better attract and sell to the "right" customers; because they have enough "right" buyers to be able to say "no" to the wrong ones.

Ninth, always remember to **keep your cool, be confident, and don't show emotion until after a sale is closed.** Negotiation is largely a psychological battle and you must be able to control your own mind, emotions, and reactions first if you plan to do better than your buyer. Your buyers are not only buying your product or service but also reading and buying the seller during a sales process. You can use that to your advantage against the buyer by using reverse psychology on them. For example, what if your buyer asks for a concession from you, and you wince or firmly say that there is no way the business could support that? Then you shut up and wait for a response; something they won't be expecting. In this example, the message you are sending to the buyer is that what they are asking for is overreaching. Most buyers will then react by either making more of their own concessions in response or becoming uncomfortable and trying to rationalize it; all of which is to your benefit.

Tenth, always remember that **there is no last word in diplomacy,** and negotiation is all about diplomacy. When selling, you will successfully negotiate sales and will lose on others. But just because you may lose a negotiation now doesn't mean you ultimately lost the customer. Many times, a customer will walk away only to come back later—it happens all the time in business. In sales, we tend to get very short-sighted on narrow sales objectives when, in reality, if the value of your services is truly there for your prospective customers, they will eventually buy from you in the weeks, months, and years ahead. Some of the most successful salespeople I have worked with over the years never gave up on a client even after multiple "nos." It was often their tenacity and commitment to pursue these buyers that ended up convincing the buyers that they were eventually worth buying from. So don't give up on any negotiation, and remember that a "no" can become a "yes" later if you don't give up.

PEOPLE LOVE TO BUY BUT HATE TO BE SOLD— GIVE THEM CHOICES BUT NOT TOO MANY

Most people love to shop and buy. Shopping malls, retail stores, and online e-tailors are full of people who are buying goods and services each day—and most enjoy the hell out of doing it. Many people simply find pleasure in buying, and studies of the human brain show that shopping, along with dancing, eating, sex, gambling, and other activities, will actually stimulate portions of the human brain where pleasure is felt. So then why can selling be so hard for some people when so many of us love to buy?

When it comes to buying, **people love to be in control and make choices; especially the right choices for themselves.** In many sales situations today, salespeople want to take this control away from buyers and limit their choices—largely to their own. Because of this, many people can feel uninformed and uncomfortable with a purchasing decision, leading to lower sales close rates.

To counter this problem, the goal of any sales process is to control the sale but still let the buyer feel that they are making the best "choice" for themselves when buying. Absent any choices, a buyer can feel like they are being sold. **With choices, people can feel more empowered and comfortable in their buying decisions.** But make sure that you are not giving them too many choices, for that can lead to indecision and confusion, and a confused mind always says "no."

For example, most fast food restaurants have around one hundred (give or take) menu items and thousands of potential ordering configurations to choose from. In order to ease the buying process, these restaurants have created combination meals (or bundles) of their products so people can easily and quickly choose the right meal combinations for them. Absent any of the combination meals, many people would struggle in making quick purchasing decisions. Similarly, many businesses today offer their own combination of services (or bundles) for the same reason, resulting in higher average order values in many industries.

For the typical consumer, it is best to provide them with a limited number of services and service bundles when possible, with around two to three options (give or take) being ideal. Even if the options presented are your own, this still empowers the prospect to "buy" instead of being sold only one option and takes away the anxiety that can go along with it. If you know that the prospect will be evaluating other competitors, this is also your chance to help define those competitors relative to you in advance of their own evaluations. Some companies will even provide a buyer with a competitive matrix and questions to ask competitors, knowing that they will likely result in a favorable outcome to their business. Again, you are helping people buy while still retaining enough control of the sales process to close.

YOUR BIGGEST COMPETITOR IS DOING NOTHING

Every time I ask a professional or business owner who their biggest competitor is, they almost always get it wrong. The irony is that for nearly all businesses it is the same competitor: doing nothing. Most sales end in no action at all and these no-actions can far outweigh any losses to another business. Why? Because **"doing nothing" is the easiest thing for people to do,** and that is what you are up against. In order to create urgency and close business, your customers must be able to clearly answer two simple questions.

First, **what is in it for them?** Your prospective customers must clearly understand what problems you are solving for them and/or what are they trying to gain that they need your products and services to achieve. Most salespeople come at this side of the sales equation more naturally because most businesses train salespeople extensively on their own products and services.

Second, **what is the opportunity cost to them of inaction?** This is where most sales deals will stall and where your largest competitor (doing nothing) commonly comes in. When a prospect understands the problems or gains you are addressing for them, their gaps and goals must be compelling enough to make them want to take action over inaction. In some cases the expected results are simply not strong enough. In others, there can also be a cost of inaction that is not well understood by the buyer during the sales process.

For example, people have choices when visiting a dentist. They can brush and floss and get their teeth cleaned regularly in hopes of preventing cavities. If a cavity is discovered by a dentist, the patient can get it fixed now or wait until the cavity becomes so bad it requires major dental work to repair and/or replace. In each instance, the patient is making a choice based on the value of action now versus the value of inaction in the future. For most people, the cost of action now (cleaning and filling) will outweigh the inaction cost of major dental work and the cost that comes with it.

One of the best ways to help uncover the cost of inaction is for your salespeople to have a good understanding of each prospect's business and needs as part of the sales process. This starts with moving away from initial product pitches and presentations and moving toward the "diagnose before you prescribe" sales process we had previously discussed.

When it comes to your business, **you need to clearly articulate and address both the cost of action as well as the cost of inaction if you want to be truly effective.** If you find a large number of your sales opportunities end in inaction or are trending in that direction, make sure you go back to the opportunity costs in your sales process to help address this issue.

— CHAPTER 6 —

MARKETING SUCCESS: HOW TO MAKE IT RAIN

• • •

Ask ten different people what the definition of "marketing" is and you are likely to get ten different answers. Don't know ten people to ask? Then simply type "marketing definition" in Google and look through the 311 million different answers instead. The bottom line is that the execution and planning of successful marketing is just as fragmented as the definition of marketing itself, which is why so many professionals and small businesses will typically set themselves up for failure before they ever begin.

Businesspeople commonly think that marketing only deals with sales and advertising, but marketing is about everything dealing with the acquiring and retaining of customers. The four "P's" of marketing are Product (or Service), Place, Price, and Promotion. For service professionals, this simply works out to **putting the right service in the right place at the right price at the right time.** This marketing "mix" is critical because a failure in any one of these key elements will cause your marketing to fail to reach its full potential.

In the United States today, many medium-to-large-sized companies have marketing departments and dedicated marketing employees. Contrast this with companies in Japan, which typically do not. Why? Because most Japanese businesses realized a long time ago that **marketing is not a department of a business but rather is the business itself.** Because of this "departmentalization" of marketing functions in the United States, there is often a misconception as to what marketing truly is and how it should permeate all aspects and resources in a business.

Because of the departmentalization of marketing, many companies have a difficult time in successfully coordinating their sales and marketing resources together. To help combat this, senior-level managers such as Vice Presidents (VPs) will be assigned over both sales and marketing. While this can be effective for some companies, many will continue to struggle in this capacity and often see the role of marketing as being largely incongruent to their own functional success. As a professional and small-business owner, you have a unique opportunity to now recognize this inherent problem and overcome this hurdle in your own business; and it all starts with a plan.

The cause for why most small businesses fail can be traced right back to marketing or a lack thereof. Most lacked a clear and concise marketing strategy and plan, which is a cornerstone of nearly all successful businesses. You might be the greatest attorney, dentist, doctor, CPA, etc., in the world but if nobody knows that, how do you expect to succeed without customers?

The challenge for professionals and small-business owners today is that most do not have the marketing experience, departments, and dedicated employees to help guide them in their marketing efforts. This means that marketing is yet another skill many small-business owners have to master on their own. The problem is that while a small percentage of professionals and small businesses will excel at marketing, most do not and are left wondering why others have reached higher levels of achievement while they continue to struggle daily to attract and grow their business.

In order to become successful in your marketing efforts, you need four key elements. First, a **MARKETING PLAN** to provide you with a roadmap for success. Second, **DISCIPLINE** to keep you consistently executing on your plan. Third, **MEASURMENT** to allow you to know what is working and what is not relative to your goals. And fourth, **REFINEMENT** to provide you with the flexibility to modify your marketing plan relative to performance and your overall business objectives.

YOU MUST HAVE A WRITTEN MARKETING PLAN

If you want to be part of the top 20 percent, you have to have a plan to help guide you there. Some professionals may start out with a business plan but most will lack a marketing plan, which in many respects is far more important. Why? Because **a marketing plan spells out how you plan to attract and keep profitable customers.** Where a business plan may be more based around the WHY of the business, the marketing plan defines HOW it will happen.

When creating a written marketing plan, the following are essential elements and the questions you need to be able to address before your plan is ready. This process and exercise is not meant to be easy nor is it fast, so take your time and you will find you can learn more by asking yourself these questions then you can by winging it. In my experience most professionals who have failed could easily go back to these fundamental questions and find out exactly where they failed to properly plan. So it is up to you; learn now to become part of the top 20 percent or wing it and learn the hard way.

THE NINE KEY ELEMENTS OF YOUR MARKETING BUSINESS PLAN

Marketing Goals and Key Performance Indicators (KPIs) for Your Company—Questions to ask yourself: What do you wish to achieve (be specific) in your business and how will you know when you get there? What kind of sales/revenues do you want to achieve and by when? What is the desired level of brand awareness you wish to create in the market and when? How many clients and what level of revenue and profits do you want to achieve and by when?

Target Market and Geography—Questions to ask yourself: Who are your ideal customers and where are they located? How do they buy similar services like yours and what are their major problems and needs in their work/life? What is most important to these people and how it is related to your services? How much do they typically spend on services similar to yours and how are those decisions typically made? Is your target market small enough to narrow in on specific needs yet large enough to meet your growth objectives? Do you have both a primary and secondary market you want to target? What is the total market size of your target market in dollars?

Service/s Provided—Questions to ask yourself: What service/s do you plan to provide that are desirable, useful, and perceived as being valuable to your targeted customers? How will your services help solve the problems and needs of your target market and why? Have similar services been offered to this target market before—if so, how will yours be more successful, and if not, why are you the first to offer it?

Service/s Pricing—Price is a very important element of your marketing plan that many professionals fail to research and get right; especially when they are first to market. Questions to ask yourself: Does the perceived value of your service to your target customers exceed the cost of their purchase price? If the price is too high and you need to lower it, can you still be competitive, profitable, and meet your goals? If the price is too low, what additional value can you profitably provide to increase the value exchange with your customers and get them to want to buy more of your services at a higher price? What target-market research have you completed to support your proposed pricing model?

Key Messages—The key messages about your services must be unique, inviting, intuitive, easy to understand, compelling, and impactful. Most important, your messages should be focused and speak to the value your services will provide to your targeted customers. Questions to ask yourself: What are the key problems and needs of your customers and how does your service/s address those issues? How will you brand your firm to support your key messages and keep that branding consistent in all of your marketing efforts?

SWOT Analysis—A SWOT analysis is a simple breakdown of the Strengths, Weaknesses, Opportunities, and Threats to your business. Questions to ask yourself: What will you uniquely provide (Strengths) to your target market that they do not receive today? What are the areas in which you are at a disadvantage (Weaknesses) relative to your competition? What are the additional needs in your market (Opportunities) that you could potentially provide? What elements (Threats) are out there now or in the future that could cause trouble for your business?

Marketing Budget and Breakdowns—In order to execute on your marketing plan, you must first allocate the necessary funding to pay for it. Many professionals fail to do this and as a result end up severely underfunding their business. Questions to ask yourself: How much money will I need to spend on a daily, weekly, monthly, and annual basis to support my marketing plan? What percentage of my revenues/billings will constitute my marketing budget moving forward as I grow? What do other similar professionals in the top 20 percent spend on their marketing as a percentage of revenues?

Marketing Tools and Resources to Use—In this section you want to spell out the specific marketing mediums you intend to use to support your goals. Questions to ask yourself: What marketing tools and services are needed to help support each of my business goals and Key Performance Indicators (KPIs)? What are the most cost-effective tools to use based on the various budgets I have as a percentage of revenues? How do I optimally allocate my marketing-budget dollars to the most effective marketing tools and services? What vendors and/or in-house resources do I need to obtain to help meet my marketing objectives? What marketing tools do I have the most experience with and which ones do I need the most help with? Once you have these questions answered, you can then create a Marketing Performance Report to list each marketing medium and how they are tracking to your performance expectations.

ABC Company Marketing Mix (Example) can be found in the Resources (page 407). You can download the entire Resources file at: www.TheSuccessfulSalesManager.com
(from the "Tools" menu).

Marketing Timeline—A marketing timeline is a twelve-month display of the expected marketing activities and plans by week and/or month for your business. The value of this process is to give a high-level view of your overall marketing mix and how best your tools and resources are allocated and coordinated throughout the year. Questions to ask yourself: Are all of my marketing mediums displayed on the timeline and is the frequency and consistency enough to support my goals? Are there any gaps in time, mediums, and/or resources in my marketing efforts that need to be addressed before they happen? Is the coordination of all of my marketing activities properly aligned to work together? Is my marketing plan optimally aligned to support my desired sales goals on a daily, weekly, monthly, and annual basis?

Once you have created your marketing plan and have addressed each of these key areas, you should have much more clarity about your real market opportunity, positioning, and direction; far more than you likely had if and when you created your business plan and everything was viewed through rose-colored glasses. Your marketing plan can take time and can be difficult to complete, but it is necessary if you want to be part of the top 20 percent!

The Monthly Marketing Calendar (EXAMPLE) can be found in the Resources (page 410). You can download the entire Resources file at: www.TheSuccessfulSalesManager.com (from the "Tools" menu).

MARKETING VERSUS INSURANCE COMPANIES AND THIRD-PARTY PAYMENT PROVIDERS

Good marketing can be critical to the success of those professionals and small businesses who accept insurance, legal aid, and other forms of third-party payments of their services—often at a significant discount to their current market rates. For example, it is not unusual to see small businesses today that will take insurance payments at a 10–50 percent discount on their regular service rates. This happens because insurance companies will commonly consolidate your potential market of customers, bundle and/or re-price your services, and then sell them back to you; often at a discount to what you could charge on your own. The insurance companies in effect do a large part of your marketing for you but at a much steeper cost than what you would pay to market directly to your own potential customers. For example, instead of you paying 10 percent of your annual revenues to directly market to your customers, you are in effect paying insurance companies to do it for you at rates that can be one to five times the cost of marketing on your own.

Insurance payments can also create a deadly cycle for many small businesses who end up finding themselves on a hamster wheel of work with very little control, reward, and profit. Excuses you will commonly hear business owners use to help justify this are, "I have to keep my employees busy" or "I don't have a choice." **The reality is YOU DO have a choice, and it all starts with your own marketing.** You may not be able to escape all insurance payments but you can control which ones you will accept and at what percentage of your business. The answer is to measure all of your marketing sources based on a return on investment (ROI) with the goal of generating enough of your own business through your own marketing efforts and at a higher ROI. Then you can be selective as to what insurance carriers and payments provide you with the highest ROI and eliminate those that don't.

Active marketing is also important because it can help keep you from falling into the insurance markets due to customer attrition. **The average business today will lose around 10–20 percent of their customers each year for various reasons.**[4] You have to prepare for this level of attrition by having a marketing strategy in place to not only retain as many of your current customers as possible but to be able to replace those customers who leave through your own marketing efforts as opposed to those of the insurance companies. **Absent any marketing, a professional could expect to replace 100 percent of their customer base every 5–10 years.** If the insurance companies are your only source to replace them with, you might as well admit who you are really working for when this happens.[1]

Another important aspect of direct marketing has to do with the equity value of your business. **The more customers you can directly generate and grow, the more valuable your business will be to potential buyers of your business.** For example, let say your business currently generates over 50 percent of your business from insurance carriers. If I am putting a value on your company, not only will I look at your valuation based on a multiple of earnings, of which 50 percent will be lower due to insurance adjustments, but I will also look at the risk to the business if those insurance carriers decided to lower rates and/or drop coverage all together. On the opposite extreme, if you were able to produce enough business through your own direct marketing, thereby negating the need for insurance business, your business will create a lot more potential equity value for most buyers.

Other forms of third-party payment can come from government agencies and authorities. Much like insurance companies, they will "price" the market for your services; often at a steep discount to your regular rates. In most cases, they will not fairly compensate you for your services relative to other alternatives, thereby **treating you and your services as a commodity. And the only way you can be successful selling commodities is through cost control and scale.** So ask yourself: Is that why you decided to become a professional? Most would say "no," but by falling prey to third-party payment cycles, a commodity is exactly what you can become. The answer is direct marketing. By having an effective marketing plan, you can help avoid this trap and become a true marketing leader in your business.

WHAT YOU SHOULD SPEND ON MARKETING

One of the first steps in developing a successful marketing plan is to have a defined marketing budget for your business. The most common way to develop a marketing budget is based on a total percentage of "desired" annual revenue (or billings). In the **United States today, the average business will spend around 10.2 percent of their annual revenues (billings) on marketing.**[2] These percentages vary greatly based on factors dealing with industry, target customer profiles, growth, geography, competition, etc. For example, the typical attorney will only spend around 3.7 percent of their annual billings on marketing. A good attorney will bill around $400–$500K per year, meaning they should expect to spend at least $14.5–$18.5K per year on marketing. However, attorneys competing in more competitive locations and in more highly competitive practice areas can spend at many multiples of their industry average. Dentists, real estate agents, CPAs, and many other professionals will spend based on the same factors, commonly ranging from 3–10 percent of their annual revenues (or billings).

The goal in defining any budget is to first define your desired annual revenue targets and base your marketing budget as a percentage of that target—not what you are making now. Remember, marketing is about growth, so your marketing budget should be used to help lead you to your ultimate revenue number and not the other way around. **As the old saying goes, you have to spend money to make money.**

Next, you need to make sure that you maximize the return on investment (ROI) on whatever marketing budget you create. Your ROI will help tell you what is working in your plan, what is not, and what needs to be replaced. Your overall ROI will also tell you if you are reaching the point of diminishing returns in your marketing spend. In short, if each additional dollar spent on marketing provides a lower ROI, you have reached a point of diminishing returns and need to consider reallocating your marketing spend to other higher-yielding marketing vehicles and/or cut back on any further increases in your marketing budget. So how do you determine what is acceptable?

Marketing is all about ROI. Therefore you need to make a return on what you spend, otherwise why market to begin with? Many people will provide different answers as to what a good ROI for marketing is, but as a general rule, **a 3-to-1 ROI (or return) should be a minimum basis for an acceptable ROI.** Anything at or above a 3-to-1 return should be considered "acceptable" with the highest returns being "preferable." The goal here is to continue to refine and drive up your ROI numbers as high as possible and replace your lowest "acceptable" return vehicles with your highest "preferable" return vehicles over time.

In driving up your marketing ROI, you should also accept the fact that adjustments and changes are the name of the game in marketing today. With the recent adoption of radical and disruptive technology changes such as the Internet, mobile devices, and the like, you should expect your marketing plan to continue to evolve over time despite how well it may be performing today. To illustrate this point, just ask all the people who bought Yellow Pages advertising a decade ago how much business they still receive from it.

UNDERSTANDING FREQUENCY AND REACH

There is a simple marketing formula when it comes to successful advertising: **Reach x Frequency = Results.** Reach is the total audience that you can touch while frequency is the amount of times you will touch them. Most professionals inherently understand the concept of reach when they see an advertisement for a service on a TV commercial, billboard, etc. What they all too often fail to understand is the importance of frequency. For example, it is not unusual to see professionals who will run one or two TV or radio advertisements, mailers, blog posts, newsletters, speaking engagements, emails, etc., and then QUIT. The key to successful marketing is to **develop a marketing plan that balances both reach and frequency** in a way that maximizes your marketing results and return on investment (ROI).

For example, I once worked with a professional who had been running a large-scale marketing campaign using multiple marketing mediums with a very large reach (city-wide in a major metro). He would run these marketing efforts in force for 10–20 days per year with a tremendous level of reach, only to give up after spending his entire marketing budget in this short period of time—with very poor results, I may add. This professional was all about maximum reach with no frequency. Sounds familiar? Well, after creating a more balanced approach, the professional was able to use the same budget by narrowing down his reach and increasing his frequency to a monthly rate. The results of this increased focus on frequency allowed him to get better results, build up his brand value, and achieve a much higher ROI.

When creating your own marketing plan, **always make sure you have a clear understanding of both the reach and frequency being provided to you by each marketing medium**. If you want to find out if any of your marketing campaigns that typically reach larger numbers of people are not in balance with a proper level of frequency, then find ways to segment your reach down and increase your frequency so you can track the results for each adjustment. Just keep in mind that increased frequency can also lead to increased brand equity, which may not be as traceable short-term as more immediate sales but still adds value over time in many other ways, including higher future sales conversions.

It is also a good idea to make sure that you question the balance achieved in reach and frequency when working with vendors as well. Remember, many advertising vendors will be more than happy to sell you on the total potential customers they can help you reach by using their products and services for a short-term gain to both you and the vendor. But frequency can be a less glamorous sell and requires discipline and planning, which is why any services you receive should be retained to support your own marketing plan and not one created for you in part or in whole by people who may have other interests that are not similarly aligned. Moreover, frequency and reach are best when coordinated among all marketing vehicles in use, which most vendors alone cannot support. In short, **there is only one person who truly owns your successful marketing plan and that is you.**

THE RULE OF 12 IN MARKETING

We all love to close business, but as with many businesses today, don't be surprised when upwards of **50 percent of the leads you produce may be qualified but not ready to close.** Additionally, we also know that close rates on leads can increase based on the frequency of the touches you have with your prospects over time. Finally, your customers are increasingly bombarded each day with more and more competing marketing messages. Because of these issues, the original Rule of 7 in marketing, which was developed decades ago, has become the Rule of 12 today.

When a sales opportunity is not ready to close, it should be nurtured until it is. Just because it is not ready to close now does not mean that it will never be closable at some future time. Because of this, **companies that nurture leads on a consistent basis typically produce 50 percent more sales-ready leads and at a one-third lower cost.**[3] The problem is that the majority of professionals and small businesses today have no lead-nurturing programs in place. In the case of sales opportunities that fail to close in a forecasted time frame, many of these leads may still in fact be qualified, and therefore the Rule of 12 should be applied to each.

The Rule of 12 was derived from marketing research that tells us you need to be in front of a sales prospect at least seven times a year for them to "actively" remember you when THEY are ready to buy. The concept of seven touches was developed many decades ago, before the proliferation of the Internet and more advanced forms of advertising, which has exponentially increased the amount of the information that bombards us each day. So what may have required a mere seven touches decades ago now requires at least twelve today (or once a month).

The Rule of 12 is important based on how we react to and filter information that we receive in our everyday lives. The human brain gets bombarded with far more information than it can fully process at any one time, so it chooses to subconsciously filter important from non-important information through its own reticular activating system. But when the brain recognizes a familiar stimulus that it sees and/or hears more often, it will react differently to it—which can be developed through the use of the Rule of 12.

For example, think about the last time you walked into a busy restaurant. How many conversations were you able to consciously or subconsciously listen to at any one time? Now what would happen if you walked through a busy restaurant and somebody mentioned your name; what would you do? Most people will subconsciously react by immediately looking for the person saying their name, which comes from the reticular activating system of their brain telling them that something important and familiar has been said that is worth recognizing. This is exactly the type of reaction you want to receive for you and your business, and the Rule of 12 helps to promote this type of reaction in the minds of your customers.

For many professionals, the problem with the Rule of 12 starts when they follow up on sales leads by trying to close them on their time. When most people receive constant and repeated closing attempts when they are not yet ready to buy it can end up turning them off and having them go quiet or, worse, providing an angry refusal. Again, this is the result of trying to close an opportunity before it is ready to close. There is a better way.

When a sales prospect goes quiet after a sales process is complete, all of these opportunities should be immediately moved into a nurturing or "boomerang" sales process. A boomerang sale is nothing more than an opportunity that is delayed for whatever reason but comes back later to close when the buyer is ready to buy. Since many salespeople cannot predict exactly when this time frame may be, they need to move their sales process from a close to a nurturing mode for each of these opportunities. In short, when the client says "no" and/or goes quiet after multiple closing attempts, they are typically not yet closable and should move into a boomerang communications process. Once in this process, the goal should be to reach them with a frequency of at least once a month or twelve times a year (Rule of 12).

FOCUS ON BOTH BUSINESS GENERATION AND CONVERSION RATES

Far too many professionals and small businesses today pay way too much for new business and leads while doing a poor job of handling the ones they have already received. How many times have you yourself responded to an advertisement by email or phone while receiving no immediate response? Or how many times have you called another professional and service provider only to get a voice mail to leave a message so they can call you back on their time? Better yet, isn't it fun when you call a business only to get to a phone triage system that seems to take forever to get to a live body? Or how about everybody's favorite: when the phone and cable companies expect you to be at home from 8 to 12 or 1 to 5 so they can show up at their convenience and not yours? How does all of this make you feel? And more important, **how less likely are you to want to do business with these people and companies once this becomes your first experience with them?**

One of the least understood and fastest growing areas of sales and marketing has to do with lead conversion. For most small businesses and professionals, it is far easier to advertise and pay for leads than to successfully manage the process of receiving and converting them into clients, which commonly involves numerous steps and processes to successfully execute. Unlike advertising, conversion management also tends to be less standardized based on the unique aspects of each professional's resources, markets, goals, and limitations. In short, a good deal of conversion today can be automated, but the processes to support the automation typically requires some level of unique customization and/or education that most small businesses lack.

The economics of conversion can be very compelling if fully understood. **Even a mere 5–10 percent increase in conversion rates can equate to thousands and even millions of dollars of incremental revenue to many professionals**

and small-business owners. So let's use an example. Say Jim the attorney currently bills around $500,000 per year in his practice. In order to produce these results, Jim has a coordinated marketing campaign that ends up costing him around $200 per lead and each new client is generating an average of $9,000 in billings per client. Since Jim typically converts around 20 percent of his leads into new clients/cases (pretty typical for attorneys), he would have to generate around 23 leads per month (or 278 per year) to hit his revenue projections. The calculations look like this:

$500,000 Annual Billings ÷ $9,000 Average Billings per Client = **55.55 Billable Clients Needed per Year**

55.55 Billable Clients per Year ÷ .20 Percent Conversion Rate = **277.75 Leads Needed per Year** (or 23.2 leads/month)

As previously discussed, not every lead that is qualified is ready to buy when you want them to buy, and studies have shown that this may be the case in up to 50 percent of qualified leads. But what about the other 50 percent who are? If attorney Jim is only converting 20 percent of his leads (or 40 percent of his closable leads), what would the financial impacts be to him based on a higher conversion rate?

Using the previous example, let's say attorney Jim implements a conversion management process and is able to raise his conversion rates from 20 percent to 30 percent. In this example, a 30 percent conversion rate means that he can now pay for 93 fewer leads per year (277.75 leads – 185.2 leads) to maintain the same level of billable income at a savings of $18,600 (93 leads x $200 per lead) in leads purchased.

$500,000 Annual Billings ÷ $9,000 Average Billings per Client = 55.55 Billable Clients per Year

55.55 Billable Clients per Year ÷ .30 Percent Conversion Rate = **185.2 Leads Needed per Year** (or 15.4 leads/month)

If, however, Jim decides to receive the same amount of leads (277.75 leads) at the higher conversion rate of 30 percent, then the overall increase in lead conversions alone can result in total billings of $749,970 (a whopping $249,970 INCREASE in billings in one year)! Put another way, the opportunity cost of Jim not increasing his lead conversion rate to 30 percent is around a quarter of a million dollars per year!

$749,970 Annual Billings ÷ $9,000 Average Billings per Client = 83.33 Billable Clients per Year

83.33 Billable Clients per Year ÷ .30 Percent Conversion Rate = 277.75 Leads per Year (23.2 leads/month)

And what if Jim wanted to double his annual billings to a million dollars based on the same number of leads he was paying for at his current $500,000 in annual billings? Simple; he would only need to increase his lead conversion rate to 40 percent. At a baseline return on investment (ROI) of 5 to 1, this would mean that Jim could afford to invest the following amounts into his lead-conversion efforts based on a his desired increase level of lead conversion over 20 percent based on the following equation:

Desired Conversion Rate = Total Annual Conversion Investment [(Incremental Billings – Conversion Investment) ÷ Conversion Investment)] x 100

25 Percent Conversion Rate = $20,827 Annual Conversion Investment [($124,960 – $20,827) ÷ $20,827)] x 100

30 Percent Conversion Rate = $41,661 Annual Conversion Investment [($249,970 – $41,661) ÷ $41,661)] x 100

35 Percent Conversion Rate = $62,482 Annual Conversion Investment [($374,890 – $62,482) ÷ $62,482)] x 100

40 Percent Conversion Rate = $83,333 Annual Conversion Investment [($500,000 – $83,333) ÷ $83,333)] x 100

So as you can see, most small businesses have ways in which to increase their revenues without having to simply buy more business and leads. In my experience, **most professionals today, on average, will convert less than half of their leads received due to poor lead-conversion processes.** As we have demonstrated in the previous example, by doubling Jim's conversion rate from 20 percent to 40 percent, he was able to double his total billings (revenue) based on the same number of leads previously provided.

As we have previously discussed on the importance of following a sales process, there are a number of ways you can increase your conversion rates as well. These include:

- **Respond to leads received immediately and without delay.** Thanks to the Internet and mobile devices, most buyers today start out in control of their buying process, which means you should expect competition for all leads received the first second they contact you. More people are now researching you online before they ever contact you and **when they do contact you, they expect to be responded to without delay.** So how fast is fast? Consider this: The rate in which leads are considered qualified drops by 600 percent in the first hour that they are not acted on. Breaking this time frame down further, you can also increase your likelihood of lead conversion by nearly 400 percent by responding in the first minute, 160 percent in the second minute, 98 percent in 3 minutes, and 62 percent in 30 minutes. Think this happens in most sales organizations today? Nope! The average company takes over 46 hours to pick up a phone and respond to a lead! Use this to your advantage.

- **Don't give up on leads.** Many leads fail to convert because most professionals and small businesses give up on trying to reach and convert them far too quickly. The average person selling will only make 1.3 attempts to reach a prospect and then give up. We also know that *48 percent of salespeople never follow up with a* *prospect* and *30 percent of leads are not followed up on at all.* **The need for additional follow-up attempts to reach a prospect has grown from 3.7 attempts need in 2007 to 8 attempts today.** Additionally, we also know that **80 percent of sales require at least 5 follow-up calls after a meeting to close them.** The good news is that persistence can pay off here; fully **93 percent of leads that can be converted are done so within 6 call attempts,** compared to a 48 percent conversion rate for those leads that are called only once. This basically works out to **around a 100 percent increase in lead conversion just by increasing the timing and frequency of your follow-up attempts alone.**

- **ALWAYS have a live body answering your phone calls.** Like it or not, we live in an increasingly impetuous society where people expect more immediate results; especially when they try to contact you! We know in many industries today that fully 80 percent of new callers will hang up when they receive a business's voice mail. Additionally, far too many professionals still use a voice mail for their overflow calls and calls received during off-hours. This is often one of the first places most professionals should start with when it comes to conversion. The goal should always be 24/7 coverage of calls received by a live body, period. Too busy to answer these calls yourself? Hire a phone answering service to do it for you.

- **Provide a superior overall customer experience than your competitors provide.** The minute a potential customer contacts you by phone, meets with you, or arrives at your location, they are making decisions about you based on EVERYTHING and EVERYBODY they experience about your business. Is your phone receptionist helpful and friendly or rude and disrespectful? Do they **answer phone calls within the first three rings** or immediately place you on perpetual hold? Is your office in a good location and are customers treated as being important the minute they walk in or are they simply asked to wait with the others? And how does the entire experience of working with you and your business compare to major competitors in the area based on the objective accounts and experiences of your customers?

- **Automate your lead management.** Thanks to the advent of the Internet and advanced automation, lead-management systems are more plentiful and affordable than ever before. There are no more excuses for professionals today to be managing leads manually nor can it support an effective coordinated and integrated lead management and marketing approach. As for the customization of lead-management processes, many lead-management systems are now becoming more industry specific with workflow and automation design based on the unique needs of many industry verticals.

- **Measure what you manage.** Once you set out to improve your lead-conversion process, keep tabs on your status and continuously audit your results for improvements. When possible, record calls received by your business and review them regularly for quality and consistency. Test out your business's own customer experiences by having others make periodic "secret shopper" calls and visits and report their results. Survey your customer base using a trending Net Promoter Scoring (NPS) measurement model.

Hire a professional. Despite the increasing levels of automation options, many professionals simply don't have the time to fully design an optimal lead management system for their business. Moreover, some of the problems may actually start with you, so it is a good idea to hire an independent consultant to help take a truly objective look at your entire business and help design processes, automation, and education around what will work best for your business. Good consultants will oftentimes bring a level of experience with other businesses, industry contacts, and knowledge that can prove to be invaluable when compared to the results of your time and resources in dealing with conversion management.

— CHAPTER 7 —

MARKETING RESOURCES: SO MANY CHOICES!

• • •

Marketing for small-business professionals has changed dramatically over the past few decades due in large part to the ever-growing number of technology-driven marketing options at your disposal. The Internet and mobile technology has caused the most dramatic disruption in the history of marketing and it has all happened in a very short and rapid period of time. Because of this disruption, many professionals have become confused as to what options they should utilize today, how they compare, and which ones can provide them with the best results. Gone are the days of relying on simple print publications like Yellow Pages and newspapers. Welcome to the new world of converged marketing.

Prior to the Internet, most marketing was based on a premise of interrupting consumers. Advertising through such traditional conduits as TV, radio, print, mailings, billboards, etc., were designed to try to capture the attention of prospective customers in their everyday lives. These forms of advertising were typically very broad in focus and relatively expensive, especially for smaller to mid-sized businesses selling their services in larger markets. And then came the technology revolution.

When it comes to marketing and advertising, the first way technology changed things was by allowing people to limit the levels of interruptions in their lives. TV commercials can now be skipped through the use of DVR devices. Telemarketing has now been limited through Do Not Call registries and caller IDs. Broadcast radio advertising is being circumvented through satellite radio and mobile iPods. Email solicitations are increasingly targeted and filtered with email SPAM-catching automation and federal legislation. And finally, newspapers and phone books are being replaced by websites and the Internet.

The second thing technology has done is dramatically change the way we buy as consumers. Thanks to the Internet and the increasing levels of information, products, and services offered online, **consumers are increasingly in control of where and when they now buy. Need a good book? Go on Amazon.com and read the book reviews of others before you decide to buy.** Need a car? Go on Edmunds.com or KBB.com to see what other consumers think about a specific car and get detailed pricing before you ever go onto a car lot to buy it. Need to hire an attorney, CPA, doctor, dentist, insurance agent, real estate agent, etc.? You can now go online to both find and research professionals in your area before you ever have to contact them. What if you get a referral? Great! Go online again to see if others rate the referral you received as high as the person who provided it to you.

The bottom line is that **consumers are now initially in control of the buying process** and what were once marketing mediums for mass interruptions are now becoming mediums for increased brand management and part of a larger overall converged marketing strategy where all of these resources can now work better together as a whole rather than separate and on their own.

The overall benefit of these dramatic changes in marketing is that the results and economics of marketing and advertising have now reached the masses. **Anybody with even a very limited budget can now do effective marketing, which was only a dream for most small business owners only over a decade ago.** Moreover, the leads produced from these new types of inbound marketing now typically cost 61 percent less than the more traditional forms of interruption marketing.[1]

Below is a list of many of the most common marketing resources in use today by professionals and small businesses. Each description is designed to provide professionals and small-business owners with a general overview of the merits and challenges in dealing with each as well as best practices to consider.

WEBSITES AND BLOGS

Most businesses today now realize that they need a website. Websites have become the virtual storefront for most businesses, with an increasing number of small businesses even doing away with their brick-and-mortar presence all together in lieu of their new online existence. Since most business professionals provide a service, the service delivery will typically take place either at their own establishment or those of their customers. Whether you have a physical establishment or not, **over 89 percent of consumers now indicate that they expect all businesses to have a website, regardless of size.**[2] But just having a website alone is no longer enough.

Now that a growing number of businesses have websites, a greater focus is being placed on the quality of your website both by consumers who review you and the search engines that index you. Recent studies have shown that 39 percent of consumers have indicated that they will leave a small-business website if it provides a poor customer experience.[3] The search engines like Google have also made changes in their search-ranking algorithms to take into account things such as website structure, mobile-friendly compliance, and content quality. In short, your website is quickly becoming the first and even last chance you may have to generate business and convert customers. As the old saying goes, **"You never get a second chance to make a good first impression."**

Case in point: A few years back I was working with a well-known professional who had very strong brand recognition and was frequently cited in the news as being an expert in his field. I had encouraged him to build a website and he continued to refuse by indicating that "if anybody wants to learn anything about me, they can look me up online." And they could—except for the fact that everybody was controlling his branded footprint online but him. One day a very prominent potential client received his name as a referral, along with the names of two other well-known professionals. They had a nice meeting and then he heard nothing from him afterward. I received a phone call a month later from this professional, indicating that he was now ready for a website. When I asked him what had changed his mind he said that he recently ran into that same potential client he had lost and when he asked him why he didn't hire him, his response what that after his meetings he looked up all three of the referrals online. Since he was the only professional who didn't have his own website, he thought he might not be as up on his profession as the others and hired one of the other professionals who did have a website instead.

On a growing number of professional websites today you will also see a blog. Most blogs today are deployed as part of the main website and typically utilize the same design characteristics in their layout. Blogs have become useful for businesses and professionals because they allow for the ease of user content publication along with easy syndication and indexing on the search engines. Unlike a website, a blog utilizes a special "ping" mechanism that sends a signal to the search engines each time new content is added to a website. Once received, the search engines will commonly read and index the new content within a matter of seconds, resulting in much faster content distribution. Without a blog, content placed into a website requires indexing to take place at the mercy of a visiting search-engine spider, which will commonly index a typical professional's website on its own every month or two.

Another benefit of a blog is the ease with which an average Internet user can quickly publish new content to their website with little/no technical expertise. Unlike the days before blogging when content needed to be updated to a website by a website programmer, **blogging now allows for the quick access and publishing of timely information by virtually anyone.** Finally, most common blogs in use today allow for the automatic Real Simple Syndication (RSS) of blog content to external resources and social media sites such as Facebook pages, Twitter feeds, LinkedIn pages, news aggregators, etc. This ability to automatically distribute active blog content through this added reach provided by RSS makes blogs even more beneficial, especially if you have a social media presence.

Finally, you will commonly hear the term Search Engine Optimization (SEO) associated with websites. SEO is the process of getting websites and online properties highly visible on the search engines so consumers can more easily find you in a search. In many professions today, consumers will begin their search for professional services online. These "non-branded" searches can lead to a significant level of new business generation for professionals online and, as a result, businesses now will commonly spend large sums of money on SEO professionals and services to help them increase their visibility for these searches.

It should also be noted that SEO should not be confused for pay advertising online such as Google's Pay-Per-Click (PPC) advertising. Instead, SEO has to do with the onsite and offsite performance of a business's website in the search engines. Onsite SEO deals with things such as webpage structures, website conversion, content management and syndication, etc. Offsite SEO deals with the authority assigned to that website based on the linking and citations provided by third-party sources. When done properly and within the rules provided by the search engines (white hat SEO), **SEO can be a highly effective marketing strategy yielding some of the best return on investment (ROI) in all of marketing today.** The problem with the SEO industry is that it is still highly fragmented, un-standardized, and subject to constant change and penalties by the search engines like Google. Since Google makes the vast majority of their revenues today from online advertising that accompanies (and competes with) natural search results, it is in Google's best interest to keep their ranking algorithm both secret and ever-changing. For you as a business owner, this also means that SEO is a never-ending battle that is judged only as a journey and not a destination.

Pros:
- Very high potential return on investment (ROI).
- There is more long-term equity value in a good authority-building growth.
- Good brand-management capabilities.
- Good online conversion capabilities for all marketing mediums in use (TV, radio, email, print, etc.).
- SEO leads typically have a 14.6 percent close rate, while outbound leads (such as direct mail or print advertising) only have a 1.7 percent close rate.4
- Effective local search exposure through local citations.
- Google provides for rapid content indexing from blogs.

Cons:

- o Complicated and inconsistent search-engine-ranking algorithm changes.

- o Potential Google "black hat" penalties.

- o Inconsistent results provided by a largely fragmented and non-standardized industry of SEO providers.

- o Relatively high initial production costs requiring multiple skills and competencies.

- o Authority online tends to favor consistency and longevity, which is typically harder for new businesses to overcome.

- o High levels of competition in competitive markets (legal, dental, etc.).

Best Practices:

1. **Build a website based on how you WANT to be perceived.** For many business professionals, your website is now a reflection of your brand, and the good news is that you can help control that reflection with a professional website. For many customers **your website is your first and last impression, so make it as professional as possible.** I have worked with professionals for years who, despite their budget restraints, built world-class websites that accurately reflected what these professionals wanted to be. Conversely, I have also seen countless professionals considered by many of their peers to be some of the best in the field who had websites that were in no way

a true and accurate reflection of their work. Remember, **a website should be a reflection of who YOU WANT TO BE,** so you must project that in the best way possible and build your presence and brand online based on that future destination now, not later.

2.   **Make sure your onsite SEO is good.** Search engines will send out their website-crawling spiders to index websites and therefore SEO people will commonly build websites to best "court the crawl" of these spiders. The best way to help describe this process is by relating it to books. Search engines will read and index a website similar to how we read and buy books. We give prominence to the spine and cover of a book similar to how the search engines give prominence to title tags and meta descriptions on each web page. When buying a book, most people will look at the front and back covers and glance at the chapters to look for importance and relevance. Search-engine spiders follow a similar process by looking at prominent tags, site maps, word density, page structure, etc. Over time, onsite SEO has evolved, which means **you should expect to have your onsite SEO reviewed annually for updates.**

3.   **Start building authority for your URL and website now.** Many business professionals wonder why some websites rank high in search results while others do not. Since more and more professionals are doing a better job these days with their onsite SEO, the great

differentiator for rankings has traditionally come down to good offsite SEO (or authority building). As of the publishing of this book, Google has around 65 percent of the total search market, and the name "Google" has literally become a verb for finding information on the web. When Google was first introduced, it was unique in how it ranked websites in their search results pages. Unlike other search engines that ranked website pages largely based on content, Google added a unique "page rank" search-ranking algorithm that took into account the authority websites received from other websites and online resources.

What started with measuring authority based on simple inbound links into a website has now become far more dynamic based on the quality and relevance of links and has grown to include additional citations from other sources beyond just links alone. Over time, this authority-building process through inbound link building led to a lot of people gaming the system by building and buying inbound links against Google's own policy of growing them naturally. As a result, Google has recently released a number of bad-linking penalties under the guise of their "Penguin" algorithm updates. Because of these recent changes, authority building has become much more dynamic and potentially damaging as a result. When building authority and links into your website, most professionals find success in doing it gradually and over time.

Links should ideally come from relevant websites (i.e., lawyer-related website links to a lawyer's website, dentist-related website links to a dentist's website, etc.), come from web pages with a higher Google page ranking (on a scale of 1 to 10 with 10 being the highest), come from as many different websites as possible (multiple sequential links from the same URL address will be of lesser value), and send the same signals to the search engines about you (same business name, address, phone, etc., from multiple locations). If you need to build authority into your website, the good news for you is that inbound links are also hard to hide, especially on competing websites. For example, if you have a competitor who has good authority and search-engine results, you can see their links in detail on free link-analysis websites like opensiteexplorer.org. You can also utilize offsite SEO experts that can help you through this process. But be careful and make sure that their work will yield the results you need without potential search engine penalties. Whichever path you choose, remember that you cannot afford to ignore offsite SEO results if you wish to achieve visibility on the search engines. Moreover, a large proportion of online searches to a professional's website will be parochial in nature, meaning locally-focused offsite sources like Google Local, Yelp, and others are now integral with your website and your overall visibility online.

4. **Stick with .com URL (website) names and buy to scale.** Since first rolling out .com website (URL) names, we have seen an explosion of different types of URL addresses ranging from .net to industry-specific names ending with .lawyer, .accountants, .photography, .contractor, etc. When it comes down to it, **always try for a URL name ending in .com first; even if the best names are already taken.** Why? Because building up a brand name using anything other than a .com only ends up helping the business who owns the .com, which is how most people will think your website is addressed. Another thing to consider is the URL (website) name you use. If you plan to grow the business over time, the last thing you want to do is to have to change a URL (website) name when a business partner leaves or your service focus changes. **Any change in your URL (website) address means you have to rebuild your authority and citations to that new URL all over again, which can take a lot of time and money.** It is best to pick a URL name that can survive any future changes in your business and ownership, thereby better protecting your online investment and building a potentially transferable asset.

5. **Focus on website conversion.** Most website designers and SEO experts know that search engines like Google historically index content on a website. Because search engines will read and rank based on content, the web has exploded over the past decade with content and websites full of deep content. The problem

for most professionals, however, is that most consumers don't like to read as much as the search engines do. In fact, they prefer to watch. Based on my own work, a typical user's time on a professional's website (measured in average time onsite) is only around two minutes. This means that the average visitor to your website will only spend enough time to maybe read a paragraph's worth of content before they move on. So what we have today is a disproportionately large amount of website content to improve visibility for a bunch of website visitors who largely don't want to read much content. Because of this, the average website conversion rate measured in total visits to contacts and/or purchases is only around 1.9 percent, when it could be much higher.

To overcome this problem, you need to think about ways to increase the conversion for the website visitor traffic you already receive by providing them with information in a way that they want to receive it. For example, **Americans love to watch videos** yet most professionals' websites don't utilize them. Experts have indicated that around 1.8 million words can be conveyed in a one-minute video.[5] How many words do you think a visitor can read on your website in the same amount of time? **Videos also have a 41 percent higher click-through rate than text content and can have a measurable brand impact of 32–65 percent in as little as 3–10 seconds.**[6] Another benefit of videos is how they allow you to potentially connect in a more visceral manner with your potential customers; something that most content cannot do. When creating videos for your website, make sure to keep them **topically specific and no longer than 60–90 seconds in length.** Anything beyond 90 seconds and you will lose the majority of your audience.

Another aspect of conversion is how you proactively help support visitors while they are on your website. A growing number of websites now utilize online chat capabilities to answer customer questions while on your website and help convert them into clients. Online chat is inherently no different than when a customer walks into a store and somebody is there to greet and assist them; only with chat, this takes place online. Chat also allows you to potentially provide assistance during off-hours visits since, unlike a physical office, websites don't close their doors at night and on weekends. Another aspect of website conversion has to do with the **design, structure, and flow of your website.** For example, how easy is it for a customer on your website to quickly contact you, find your location/s, buy your products or services, schedule a visit, receive help, and learn more about you? Many websites built for small-business professionals are created by website developers who do not understand your business and your unique buying processes. Remember, you hired a website developer to build a website and that is all they typically do well. Because of this, it is not unusual to find different professional websites that may appear to the average owner as being seemingly similar yet producing radically different results.

To help address this problem, you need to analyze and fully understand the customer experience on your website, what your goals are for your customers on your website, and how you can improve it. Changes could be as simple as how professional your website appears compared to your competitors' or may include more complex changes such as how phone numbers, social media links, page structures of your website, etc., are positioned and displayed on your website and pages. As an example of more complex conversion options, we know from studies that website-contact-form conversions can increase by 50 percent simply by reducing the fields on the "Contact Us" form from four to three.[7] This is just one of many ways you can make improvements to your website performance.

6. **Build for mobile and the future.** In April of 2015, Google created their first mobile search penalty for websites that are not considered by Google to be "mobile friendly." This means that websites that do not have a mobile-friendly version of their website can expect to receive decreased visibility in searches taking place on mobile devices. This becomes increasingly important since many web experts expect visits to websites from mobile devices to exceed PC visits to websites sometime in 2015. Google has already indicated this has happened in searches. The problem

for many professionals who already have websites today is that many of them were built for PC access and not mobile access, meaning their website is not designed for the increasing levels of mobile interaction and search. We also know that **people who visit websites through mobile devices also tend to behave differently on mobile devices than through PCs.**

For example, most traditional websites include a "Contact Us" form, while most people on mobile devices prefer a "Click to Call" option. We also know that the screen size limitations of mobile devices tend to render many traditional websites too small and dense for the average user to read. Because of this and other factors, studies have shown that fully **80 percent of users will abandon a website if they have a bad mobile experience.**[8] We also know that 88 percent of mobile users will take action within one day and 77 percent will contact a business in the same time frame. Finally and most important, we know that mobile is pervasive and here to stay. **80 percent of smartphone users will not leave their home without their smartphone** and people will check their smartphones an average of 110 times a day, with some people checking as many as 900 times a day.[9] When factoring all of this in, it is important that any existing or new website you utilize be fully mobile-friendly and compliant.

If you are unsure of your website's current mobile compliance, you can check it through Google's "mobile-friendly" webpage. It is also important to note that at the time of this book Google has endorsed **"Responsive Design"** as the only mobile platform it recommends for optimal mobile rendering. The benefit of responsive design technology is that it will change the rendering of your web pages to fit literally any resolution and size of mobile device that can access your website. With the growing number of different mobile devices in use today, this becomes increasingly important and is why your website should utilize responsive design today for mobile device access.

7. **Create and execute on a strong content creation and syndication strategy.** Prior to 2012, many SEO strategists indicated that more traditional SEO tactics were the number one driver of traffic to websites. But with the advent of Google Panda (bad content) and Penguin (bad linking) penalties starting around this time frame, **content creation quickly became revered as the top driver of website traffic** moving forward. Prior to Google's content penalties, referred in the industry as the "Panda" updates, the web was awash with duplicate and poor content; most of which was created, manipulated, and misused in order to game the search engine for traffic and authority. Because of this, Google took a stand starting in 2011 by indicating that penalties would be applied to websites who utilized poor quality and duplicate content.

With this new content penalty the message was clear: **Only author and publish your own content, and make it useful.** The good news is that this penalty happened to take place around the same time that many professionals were beginning to add blogs to their websites for easier content creation and syndication, along with the rapid growth of social media and content-hosting websites. So the natural questions at this point include: What content should be created? Who should create it? How should it be published? And how should it be measured? This is where an effective **active-content strategy** becomes into play. **An active-content strategy is a portion of your marketing plan that spells out the how, when, and what of your content strategy moving forward.** The goal is to create as much useful content to your targeted customer base as possible with the ideal balance of frequency and reach.

On a website, you have two types of content: static and active. Static content is simply content that is posted to your website as a website page. Active content is content published on your blog that includes the added benefit of rapid indexing and syndication. When considering how much content to create, keep in mind that more is usually better. The analogy I commonly use in describing this is to think of your content as a fishing net; the more content you have, the larger your net. Recent studies have shown that businesses with **websites of 401–1,000 pages get 6 times more** leads than those with 51–100 pages.[10] The depth of content as it applies to search-engines rankings is also a factor. Other studies have shown that the average content length for a web page that ranks in the top ten results for a keyword on Google has at least two thousand words.[10]

Content also becomes important for non-keyword specific searches since over 60 percent of search online is considered to be "long-tail" search—meaning it is more descriptive in nature and typically includes more than three words. The reason **long-tail search** is becoming more important is because as the Internet grows to include billions and billions of new web pages, people have to become more specific when searching to quickly get to exactly what they are looking for when they search. Long-tail search also means that as people get more descriptive, fewer repeatable phrases and terms are used to find the content and information they need. Because of this, **the more content you have to potentially match all of these different permutations of search, the better chance you have of picking up these long-tail searches.**

Another benefit of long-tail search is that because it's more specific in intent, it also tends to **convert at a higher rate than simple vanity-type searches**. So when you create your online strategy, it is a good idea to create a good mix of static and active content as well as a good number of syndicates for your content beyond just your blog. Social media also helps to syndicate your content through **Real Simple Syndication (RSS) feeds from your blogs, so the content you publish can automatically reach your followers and potential customers through your social media properties.** Where most professionals fail in managing an active-content strategy is in the consistent execution of the strategy; they simply don't see it as an ongoing priority. This problem goes back to expectations we typically have today and our increasing need as a society for instant gratification. **Active-content strategies are typically slow and take time to grow.** Think of an active-content strategy as watering a plant; if you water it and provide sunlight, you know it will grow, but it won't happen instantly and neither will your content results. Because of this, **you have to schedule your time and resources around content creation and make it inflexible.** If you do not have the time to keep up with this commitment, hire somebody who can write on your behalf. One of the dirty little secrets about blog content today on professionals' websites is that a large percentage of it is written by other professionals and shadow writers. As a general rule of thumb, I typically suggest that **active content be written and published no less than once a week** in order to create a baseline and acceptable minimum level of frequency. The bigger and better your syndicates, contacts, and followers, the greater the reach your content will receive.

8. **Use a professional.** The aspects of website design, strategy, and marketing have grown increasingly complex and confusing for most business small-business professionals over the past few years. Even various aspects of the website design and marketing processes have become specialized to deal with the various aspects of each discipline. Additionally, search engines like Google make hundreds of algorithmic changes each year. That—along with the recently rapidly developing markets of social media and mobile devices—alone is simply hard to keep up with for the average small-business professional. Because of this growing level of complexity, an increasing number of small businesses today rely on other experts in the other professions of website design, SEO, and marketing to help them get this all right. These **website professionals are also getting increasingly niched in the various service industries** so they can better incorporate the unique aspects of these businesses into their own website and SEO strategies for success.

SOCIAL MEDIA

Social media is perhaps one of the most intriguing yet highly misunderstood forms of advertising and marketing today by small business professionals. For years I have been giving speeches to professionals on the use of social media in their businesses and without fail most people I run in to continue to be confused about the true value provided by social media in their business. The typical questions I receive include: "Isn't social media something my kid does?" "How do I keep my personal life separate from my professional life online?" "Everybody tells me we need to use social media, but I still don't know how and why."

Therein lies the problem.

When it comes to social media and business, it is important to understand that **the primary interest in social media has to do with its reach, or the staggering number of people and the amount of time they spend on social media today.** Advertising is all about visibility and eye-time and the use of social media for businesses is inherently no different than TV commercials or traditional billboards on a major freeway. The only difference is where people's eyes are now (on the web and social media) versus where they were limited to in the past (print, TV, and commuting).

There are literally thousands of social media tools in use today, but most people access and use social media sites like Facebook, Twitter, YouTube, Dropbox, Pinterest, etc., for personal reasons, while they use other sites like LinkedIn and Google Plus for professional purposes. That contrast, however, is graying over time. The challenge is "how" they all work together and in conjunction with a website and a blog. When creating an **active-content strategy,** a blog is considered the primary content generator with the website as the primary conversion tool. In between is the distribution (or reach) for your content through the use of social media. In other words, social media gives your content that is created on your blogs reach by putting it in front of readers so they can see it and eventually be converted to customers and/or repeat business. Without social media, your blog may be nothing more than a billboard in a cornfield. In order to accomplish this strategy, you can connect and automatically distribute your content from your blogs to your social media through the use of automated Real Simple Syndication (RSS).

Building an Active Content Strategy

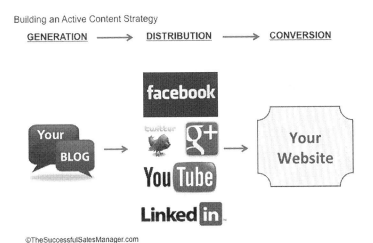

©TheSuccessfulSalesManager.com

Beyond social media, there is now a growing list of additional places you can publish your content to, as we will discuss below—but this general illustration provides a good understanding for most small-business professionals to visualize how all these pieces work best together based on their resource limitations.

Unlike other forms of marketing, **social media has a relatively low conversion rate of around .71 percent,** which means the frequency of your advertising efforts on social media needs to be higher to account for the lower levels of conversion. This has to do with the relatively high levels of overall content and information shared on these social media sites today that compete with your content. Moreover, many social media sites display content and updates chronologically—so your ability to reach users is dependent on when each user will access their social media tools; the more often you post, the greater the potential reach.

On a final note, it is important to point out that social media is not something you can just ignore as a professional anymore. Fully **93 percent of Americans now indicate that they expect a business of any size to have a social media presence** and social media users of Facebook alone have indicated that they are more likely to buy from brands that they like and follow on Facebook.11 Therefore, social media is both an opportunity and an opportunity cost for you as a small-business professional, so it is up to you to determine which one you want it to be for your business.

Pros:
- Effective way to build large networks of people, customers, prospects, and referrals.
- Rapid active-content distribution and reach from your blog.
- Relatively low setup and maintenance costs.
- Demographic-based advertising options versus Pay-Per-Click (PPC), which is largely keyword based.

- Good brand-building capabilities.

Cons:

o Relatively low conversion rate of direct traffic at .71 percent.

o Can be hard to track a direct return on investment (ROI) and lead source from.

o Most businesses still do not set up effective social media strategies.

o Relatively low click-through rates (CTR) on paid advertising.

o Infrequent and lower levels of reach requiring higher levels of content frequency.

Best Practices:

1. **Create a Facebook Business Page.** When most people think of social media, **Facebook** is the first vehicle they will mention, and for good reason; over half of all Americans have a Facebook account and half of those people (one-quarter of all Americans) will access Facebook each day. The average Facebook user not only frequently accesses the site but will spend an average of 8.3 hours a month on Facebook; a number that quickly gets the attention of anybody in marketing.[12]

What makes Facebook interesting for businesses is that each Facebook user will typically access the site and start out on their own "news feed" page, which will include a chronological update for all of the people and pages (including business pages) that they follow. Because of this, every business should have their own Facebook business page so users can easily find and "follow" your page. This will then include your business in their news feed. The more people who follow your page, the more news feeds you can potentially reach. This also leads to the potential viral-sharing benefits of social media. When users see a post from your business page that they may find useful, they can "like" or "share" that information with other people they are connected to on Facebook, further extending your reach and visibility to additional people who could end up following your page and/or buying your products and services as a result.

Facebook also captures demographic data on their users such as their location, interests, careers, personal status, marital status, etc. Unlike more traditional forms of online advertising that are limited to keywords, social media advertising allows for targeting based on user demographics and interests. In short, **if you are able to identify the demographic details of your Target Client Profiles, social media tools like Facebook can allow you to potentially target them based on it.** For example, it is well known that policemen typically have higher rates of divorce than the average person. Because of this, I have had divorce attorneys who have advertised to people who had "liked" police department pages on Facebook, knowing that this demographic could be a good fit for their services.

2. **Create a Twitter account.** Twitter is commonly referred to as a micro-blog and allows users to post information up to 140 characters in length; which is not much. This character-length limitation has helped lead to the abbreviation of many words like "You" to "U," "In my honest opinion" to "IMHO," etc., so it can fit into this shorter space. Twitter also incorporates the use of hashtags (#) in front of words to help index content based on that word. For example, if you use a word like "Lasik" in a tweet and place a hashtag in front of it ("#Lasik"), this allows other Twitter users to find your tweets when they look for the mention of "Lasik" in other people's tweets. Where Twitter can become useful is in the ability it provides for anybody to easily find and follow your tweets from your Twitter account. When users "follow" your Twitter account, they are then receiving your tweets in their Twitter feed.

For example, I once worked with an attorney who was considered an excellent courtroom litigator. He was so good in fact that other law firms would send their associates down to court to watch and learn from him in action. What Twitter allowed him to do was provide real-time tweets of his upcoming courtroom appearances that other attorneys who were following him on Twitter could see so they could quickly learn of and view his appearances. Another benefit of Twitter is the news-information feed it provides to people in the media. Many reporters want breaking and timely news information, and by following the Twitter feeds of newsworthy people, they are quickly able to see and report on real-time events, press conferences, etc., of key people. Clearly people of vanity and fame are the primary benefactors of Twitter-account activity while many of the more "normal" people will set up a Twitter account and not stay active with it. Unlike other social media sites like Facebook, the adoption rate of Twitter users is not widespread. However, you will find many people devoted to Twitter, so it should not be ignored. Because of this, I typically suggest that, **at a minimum, professionals should create a Twitter account and publish their active content (from their blog) to it.** To help keep the account active with tweets, you can simply feed it automatically with your blog posts through the use of Real Simple Syndication (RSS) feeds from your blog. At a minimum, this will help keep your Twitter account active for those people who are devoted Twitter users.

3. **Create a LinkedIn profile and page.** LinkedIn is a business-networking website that has in effect become **the world's largest resume and CV for professionals online today.** LinkedIn has also grown in authority whereby simple Internet searches for professionals by name will often result in their LinkedIn profile pages appearing toward the top of many search engine results. At the time of this book, there are roughly one billion people-searches conducted on Google each

day. Job recruiters in the professional placement space also rely heavily on LinkedIn to find good candidates and recruit them away from others. What LinkedIn effectively does is allow you as a professional to **present yourself professionally to the world and, in turn, connect with other professionals to help build your business network and branding.**

Since it is commonly believed that there are six degrees of separation from any one person to another, sites like LinkedIn allow you to strategically build your network online and shrink your degree of separation to your target customers and influencers.

As a professional, LinkedIn allows you to both create profiles for you and/or your employees and create business pages for your business—similar to a Facebook page. When creating your personal profiles, make sure they are 100 percent complete, accurate, and professional. Use a high-quality picture on your profile and make sure your career history and achievements are well documented. LinkedIn also allows you to **create one free LinkedIn business page per business** and allows other people to follow it. You can also create additional "follow" buttons for placement on websites and other online sites. LinkedIn company pages allow you to post active content and have your followers see that content in their own chronological news feeds in LinkedIn; similar to Facebook. Because of this, you can republish your blog content automatically to your LinkedIn company page through the use of a Real

Simple Syndication (RSS) feed from your blog to your LinkedIn company page.

Additionally, LinkedIn recently added the ability to personally publish unique-content articles directly to LinkedIn. This content must be considered unique content to publish here and in doing so can provide added reach to your network of business professionals who may now be able to see your articles on LinkedIn through your own personal business connections to them, as opposed to having them follow your blog or social media pages to see it.

Once your LinkedIn profile and company page are created, your next step is to build your connections and audience. The "advanced search" feature allows you to quickly and dynamically look up people in your network and those you want to be connected with. You can also write and receive recommendations and provide testimonials as well as join common-interest and industry-specific groups. When building your connections, LinkedIn allows you to send direct connection requests to "second degree" connections, which are people who are connected to your direct (or first degree) connections. Because of this, **it is a good idea to first get connected with well-connected and well-known users in your industry who will in turn allow you to more easily build your network through their connections, and so forth.**

LinkedIn has also become a very effective sales prospecting tool for many professionals. Prior to

LinkedIn, the ability to reach out to and find a prospect's contact information could be very difficult. Today, with the help of LinkedIn, you can easily look up and send connection requests to virtually any sales prospect that has a profile on LinkedIn. Depending on your account level (free or paid), this can go beyond simple connection requests to also include personal messages through LinkedIn to a non-connected prospect.

Many talent scouts and professional recruiters have increasingly become dependent on LinkedIn to search for good job candidates. Unlike the old days when recruiters would typically advertise a position and rely on responses and job boards, LinkedIn now allows recruiters to proactively search, discover, contact, and recruit people who may not even be aware of a new opportunity and/or may not be actively looking for a new opportunity. This has in effect **allowed the job market for professionals to become an "open market"** whereby employers cannot hide their good employees from other people and companies anymore.

4. **Create a YouTube page.** YouTube is currently the world's largest video hosting and sharing website. Founded in 2005, YouTube was acquired by Google one year later for $1.65 billion dollars. If YouTube were its own search engine today, it would be the second largest in the world only to Google, its current owner. Today over 1 billion people use YouTube and watch

over 4 billion videos per day there. **Only 9 percent of small businesses in the US currently utilize YouTube,** and that is ultimately your greatest opportunity. Here's why:[13]

The greatest value YouTube can bring to your business is the ability to scale your sales and support while increasing your online conversions. YouTube allows for the **free creation of a YouTube channel (or page), which you can customize for your business** and manage all of your videos from. YouTube channels are relatively easy to create and, once created, you can upload, modify, and report on your videos from your page. You can also get the code to **embed your videos from your YouTube page on to your website** and other web properties where you want to publish your videos. Finally, you can also optimize your videos to help generate high visibility in organic and video searches.

YouTube also allows you to potentially monetize the popularity of certain highly watched videos by paying you to support Google-paid advertising around your videos. Finally, YouTube will also allow users to add comments and start discussions about each of your videos. From your channel, you can then monitor and remove comments made by others about your video as well as review detailed statistics for each video on YouTube.

5. **Create a Google Plus account.** Google Plus is a social media engine that many people refer to as Google's

answer to Facebook. The primary difference between the two is that Facebook allows people to have friends and pages to have followers without any further segmentation. Google Plus took this a step further by creating "circles" of friends, thereby allowing people to more effectively segment where information can be shared. Despite this difference, Google Plus had largely failed to attract the same level of social media usage that Facebook has achieved and as a result started to require people have a Google Plus account to do other things on Google such as claiming local business listings, write customers reviews, etc. At that point, the number of Google Plus accounts grew exponentially, but many professionals are still confused as to its overall value beyond that.

At the time of this book, Google Plus is going through some changes, so instead of getting too granular, it's best to keep it simple here. In short, it is free and relatively easy to set up a Google Plus account for your business, and all of your information should be complete and optimized. Once created, you should then **claim and optimize your Google Local listing/s from your Google Plus account.** From your account, you can manage reviews, add videos, add pictures, and add posts. Unlike many other social media sites, your Google Plus page does not currently allow you to republish your blog content on your Google Plus page via a Real Simple Syndication (RSS) feed. This means that, currently, the content you post there has to be original to this location.

6. **Link your blog to your social media accounts through an RSS feed.** One of the benefits of creating an active-content strategy is the ability to automatically distribute content written on your blog to many of your most popular social media sites such as Facebook, Twitter, LinkedIn, etc., via Real Simple Syndication (RSS). Most popular blogs in use today currently support RSS feeds—some of the most popular RSS-feed "connector" sites include Twitterfeed.com and HootSuite.com, among many others.

7. **Actively promote your social media sites.** Social media is all about gaining greater reach and visibility. Therefore, setting up your social media sites and creating an active-content strategy alone is not enough. Far **too many businesses and professionals today spend precious time and money on their social media without any focus on building up their audience for it.** As a result, the work and resources they put in are largely unnoticed, especially by their customers and prospects who don't know they are there.

Once your social media is in place, it is time to publish your links to your social media in EVERYTHING you do. The general rule of thumb I use for professionals is if it's important enough to publish a phone number on, it's important enough to include all other forms of communication, including your social media links. This means **publishing links in your email signa-**

tures; on your business cards and stationery; on your receipts; in emails and advertisements; on your websites, blog, and other social media sites; etc. In other more traditional forms of advertising, this should also include mentioning them in any TV, radio, billboard, print, and other forms of advertising you do. If you are a frequent speaker, make sure to mention and include links to your social media sites at the end of each speech. Social media sites like LinkedIn, Facebook, and Twitter also allow you to create customized "Like" and "Follow" buttons that you should prominently add to your online properties like your website, blog, and other online publications.

Another way to help build up your followers for your social media sites is to create promotions and incentives for your customers and prospects to "like" or "follow" your social media pages. Examples can include a 10 percent discount off your next service if they "like" your Facebook page. Other examples include a contest or giveaway to users who become a fan of your page. You and others can also "suggest to friends" your business page or any other page on Facebook that you like. Finally, sites like Facebook also allow you to advertise for page "likes" by paying for the total number of "likes" received. Just be careful in paying for these "likes," since the costs can add up quickly and you need to be able to target your ideal clients, which you may or may not be able to do through these kinds of advertisements. Either way, always check the social media site's guidelines for advertising and getting followers, as the rules and capabilities frequently change over time.

TV AND RADIO

Radio and TV advertising first become popular starting with the rapid adoption of each new form of communication and entertainment in the 1930s and 1950s, respectively. Both forms of advertising were based largely on the interruption of users through commercial advertisements that were interceded throughout regular programing. Because of the relative and historic scarcity of available time slots and the relatively high cost to produce these forms of advertisement, most small business professionals simply could not afford to compete with larger and better-funded businesses for these precious timeslots. For example, before the advent of cable and satellite TV, the "big three" TV channels were the only TV option for decades. Additionally, TV and radio are commonly referred to as "mass marketing" because the audience for each is typically very large in number within most media markets. This also poses a problem for many small business professionals who ideally want to better segment their target-client base based on factors such as more refined geography and detailed demographics. The resulting "spillage" of advertising to these untargeted prospects is simply a factored-in cost of this type of advertising, leading to its higher price. With a **historic response rate of around 1 percent, most businesses would have to reach 10,000 people by TV or radio to receive 100**

responses (or leads). Finally, TV and radio advertising typically requires a higher level of frequency to help build brand recognition and familiarity with your audience. This means that one or two advertisements alone are typically not enough to be effective and a more long-term and costly program will be necessary.

With the adoption of cable and satellite TV over the past few decades, the scarcity of the "big three" TV channels has now evolved into hundreds of new channels that are largely more demographic-specific. Because of this dramatic increase in supply of new special-interest channels, you can now better target your local TV advertising around home-improvement shows, cooking shows, real estate shows, etc., at a much lower cost than historically possible. There are also **over 10,000 radio stations in the US,** and you can easily find which stations service your targeted market by going to www.radio-locator.com and searching by your city, state, or zip code. When looking for local TV stations, you can find them listed by defined media market (city) at: www.stationindex.com/tv/tv-markets.

A new evolution in TV advertising is also unfolding based on highly targeted user demographics AND behaviors. Unlike more traditional TV advertising based on a program or mass audience alone, new set-top technology and other online behavior patterns are now being analyzed on a per-household basis to provide more targeted TV marketing down to the household level; creating a whole new dynamic to TV advertising in the coming years ahead. Now considerations such as user viewing history, preferences, and demographics both online and offline can be analyzed to provide highly targeted advertising through this historically mass-media-only model.

The core benefits of effective TV and radio advertising are many. First, they **provide a means to rapidly build reach.** What you can potentially receive in total reach in a few months of TV and radio could take years to achieve in other forms of advertising. Second, **TV allows users to "visualize" your brand, product, and services** in a way that print and other forms of advertising cannot convey. Remember, people think in pictures, not text, so the visual aspect alone can be both compelling and memorable to your target audience. Finally, **TV advertising can be entertaining and captivating** and can grab and hold your audience's attention like no other—especially if you feel your service is better sold by people seeing as opposed to hearing about it. For those customers who can receive equal or greater value in hearing about your service, than radio could be a good option as well.

Pros:
- Large and rapid market reach-building potential.
- Excellent for brand and awareness building.

Cons:
- o Relatively high costs of production, distribution, and repetition.
- o Historically harder to target customers by narrow demographics (mass marketing).
- o Historically has been too expensive for many small business professionals to consistently afford.

Best Practices:

1. **Understand your production costs.** Production costs can get very expensive, and fast; especially when it comes to TV advertising. Most TV slots are produced and sold on ten, fifteen, thirty, and sixty–second time increments. Some may think that anything less than thirty to sixty seconds sounds very short, but you need to remember that **most sales on TV are made or lost within the first three to four seconds of the commercial.**[14] You can expect to spend around $3,000 and up for TV production; the higher the quality, the higher the cost. When it comes to radio, many radio stations may offer to produce the spot for free, and they will typically run in thirty- and sixty-second slots. When radio stations offer free creation, they will also frequently limit the use of your ads to their station. Other options include using a professional radio commercial company who can create radio ads that you can then own and use in multiple places at a production cost of around $1,000 per ad. If you have some advertisements you like as a comparison, then ask what the costs of production were for these similar advertisements to get a basis for a more accurate production budget.

2. **Consider timing and seasonality.** Depending on your target client profile, your advertising should always include considerations for timing and seasonality. For example, most people consider preparing their taxes after the first of the year through April 15, so if you are a CPA, running ads from May through October may not

be the best timing for you. If you are an auto-accident lawyer or run an automotive collision repair service in the northern United States, then your business is likely to pick up around the winter months—when you should be advertising the most. Timing can also be based on audience demographics such as what days and times certain people will watch TV or listen to radio based on age, income, location, interests, etc. It is also a good idea to avoid advertising during industry spending spikes such as contested election weeks, busy holidays, and other events that can help drive up advertising costs based on spikes in demand. Finally, it is also important to understand that pricing and rates frequently change every quarter. During certain seasons you can expect higher prices, such as during the fall time frame when viewership and new shows commonly increase. When it comes to radio, remember that **the largest radio audiences tend to come at times when people are commuting**—between 6 a.m.–10 a.m. and 3 p.m.–7 p.m. during weekdays.

3. **Make sure to factor in frequency.** As previously discussed in this book, the biggest mistake many small-business professionals make when starting out in TV and radio advertising is expecting immediate results and **not creating a long-term media strategy.** If you run one or two ads and simply give up because it "didn't work," then I am certainly talking to you. TV and radio advertising will both generate new business AND brand awareness for your business; both of

which are valuable. Over time, as you continue to advertise to the same audience, you are building brand awareness and brand equity, which leads to higher sales conversions down the road. If you give up after one or two ads, you are in effect throwing away any brand equity you started to create. For this reason, **make sure your media buys are no less than three months in duration.** If this becomes too cost-prohibitive, simply narrow your target (reach) so you can create a good balance with your frequency. It is also important to note that **radio listeners tend to be more passive than TV watchers** since many times they are doing other things while listening such as driving a car or working. Because of this, the lower levels of overall reach on radio means you typically have to run more radio advertisements (frequency) to achieve the same level of reach as TV.

4. **Negotiate to help keep your costs down.** There are a number of ways you can help keep control of your costs when buying TV and radio advertising. First, **pay up front when possible.** This will indicate that you are a serious buyer and the salesperson you are working with will have an added reason to help you. Second, **commit to buying a longer-term ad schedule of ten to fifteen weeks in advance.** The stations want to have their schedules filled in advance and this can make your business much more value to the station. Third, look for special advertising sales and options, including TV remainder (or remnant) advertising,

which can allow you to pick up unsold timeslots on the cheap. In radio, you can also buy based on a "run of the station," which again allows you to buy cheap based on open time slots when they come up. Just keep in mind that any random slots to fill for cheap may be cheap for a reason, so make sure the benefits outweigh the costs. Finally, negotiate for added value from the stations as part of the overall deal. For example, do they have a website? Great—ask for a website link and free advertising on the site. Do they have other events, shows, and media outlets? Why not ask for exposure there as well? What you can ask for ultimately depends on the station, but the bigger the station and network, the more options you have to work with.

5. **Utilize the help of an advertising agent.** If you are new to TV and radio advertising and all of this seems a little overwhelming to you, you may want to start out by using an advertising agent to help you. A good advertising agent can help you with the creation, production, stations, target markets, frequency, etc. The more complex and targeted your market, the more value a good advertising agent who specializes in your industry can become. When it comes to buying media times with stations, advertising agents can also utilize their own connections and experience to help you here as well. **Advertising agents are frequently paid a 15 percent agency fee from the stations** they will buy from on your behalf so, absent any other

arrangements, they are paid by the station to help you with your buy. Additional services are commonly negotiated on a per-diem or flat-rate basis, so make sure you ask about these costs in advance so they don't creep up on you later.

PRINT

Print advertising and marketing refers to ads created and placed in physical distribution vehicles such as newspapers, magazines, newsletters, mailers, posters, banners, etc. The birth of print advertising started in France around the mid 1800s when ads were first sold in newspapers to help lower the price of the newspaper to the consumers. Today, it is not uncommon to see newspapers and magazines chock-full of endless advertising. And for good reason; demand for print media is declining due to the rapid growth of the Internet, meaning they have to find ways to pay for their publication while their readership continues to decline.

Many forms of print advertising **have a response rate of around 1–2 percent.** Because of this, most businesses would have to **reach an audience of between 5,000 to 10,000 people by print just to receive 100 responses (or leads).** To assist in this effort, most publishers will produce an Adverting Rate Card that should include all details about their advertising options, including the total circulation (or reach) of their audience as well as other demographic details about their customers and/or subscribers.

For most small-business professionals, the more common form of print advertising came through the publication of phone books, newspapers, and direct mailings. Since we cover direct mailing in more detail separately, it is important to then discuss phone books and newspapers here. Printed mediums are typically complex and expensive to produce, distribute, and, once created, they cannot be changed—only replaced. Once the Internet came along, all of this changed. As a result, it is not uncommon to find piles of phone books now sitting in landfills and to see newspaper circulations continue to decline. In short, **the once great advantage of massive local reach these marketing mediums once provided is rapidly slipping away.**

So is print advertising dead? Not yet, but it is quickly heading in that direction. As circulations continue to decline and more readers turn to the Internet for news and information, you can expect to see a continued lowering of print advertising rates to reflect this drop in readership.

Pros:

- Falling levels of competition, leading to lower prices.
- Longevity of certain print publications, such as phone books, that are typically used more than once.
- Relatively higher levels of utilization in rural areas where Internet access may still be limited.

Cons:

o Rapidly declining circulation and reach of print publications (phone books, newspapers, etc.).

o Relatively high cost of print production and distribution.

Best Practices:

1. **Print is still stronger where the Internet is less pervasive.** There are still areas of the United States that lack either good or any Internet access. Currently there are around 60 million Americans who still do not have Internet access based largely on factors such as accessibility, affordability, or simple utility.[15] Although this is changing, some more rural areas are still hard to reach online and certain demographics of older Americans who came of age long before the Internet have developed habits of reading in print. Various ethnic groups also have strong followings of their own local publications, and reading content on a small smartphone screen can still be a struggle for many people with poor eyesight.

2. **Move to a print-on-demand model for your business.** Along with the rapid adoption of the Internet has come professional-quality printers and production software that now allow even the average PC user to produce professional-quality printed materials. Many professionals today create printed product and service brochures that they place in mailings, offices, on their website as PDFs, etc. In order to lower your print costs, try moving your printing online and on-demand so you can help limit all of the wasted print materials that become outdated and expensive to continue to reproduce, store, and replace.

3. **Create a compelling headline for your print ads.** Far too many people spend way too much time on the

details of a print ad and not enough on the headline. What they fail to understand is that **75 percent of buying decisions with print ads are made at the headline alone.**[14] This is the point at which people will decide whether or not they even want to learn more about your products or services. What every reader is ultimately asking themselves when reading a headline is, **"What is in it for me?"** So make sure that each print advertisement you produce includes a strong and compelling headline that answers this question for your target customer audience.

EMAIL MARKETING

Most Americans today use email, and many now have more than one email address to their names. Nearly half of all American Internet users check or send emails in a typical day, and **58 percent of adults check email first thing in the morning.**[16] Because of these staggering numbers, marketers love email marketing, and for good reason: **Email marketing typically is second only to search marketing as the most effective online marketing tactic in use today.**

Other advantages of using email for marketing are that it is cheaper and faster than traditional direct mail and, unlike many other forms of marketing, **you can accurately track the return on investment (ROI)** of email marketing campaigns. Moreover, email can provide actionable tracking of multiple performance metrics such as bounces, emails opened, email click-throughs, and calls received.

Business Type	Open Rate	Bounce Rate	Clicks (Click-Through Rate)	Opt-out Rate
Accountant/ Financial Advisor	18.44%	7.98%	7.46%	0.78%
Business Products/ Services	20.13%	12.47%	8.74%	0.74%
Consultant	9.85%	6.32%	7.31%	0.81%
Franchise	20.88%	8.91%	6.57%	1.24%
Hotel, Inn, B&B	21.74%	8.80%	6.92%	1.28%
Legal Services	28.24%	12.27%	6.59%	0.71%
Marketing/ Advertising	15.24%	10.02%	6.86%	0.65%
Medical Services	24.87%	12.21%	7.24%	1.05%
Personal Services	14.92%	5.16%	6.80%	1.38%
Professional Services	24.46%	11.22%	7.90%	0.98%
Real Estate	26.01%	14.56%	6.85%	0.68%
Salon & Spa	21.22%	13.61%	4.35%	1.27%
Technology	16.24%	10.30%	5.95%	0.91%
Web Developer	15.16%	7.61%	8.58%	0.39%

Source: Constant contact Industry Chart, Feb 2015

With a **response rate of .12 percent, most businesses would have to send out around 8,333 emails just to receive 100 responses (or leads).** Variables to this response rate typically include: the quality and targets of the email lists, what day and time the emails were received, how well the emails converted by phone or email, the content and call to action of the email, etc. When analyzing email performance, you will see metrics like "Open Rate," which is the percentage of emails sent that were opened by the recipients; "Bounce Rate," which is the percentage of people you sent emails to who did not receive them; "Click-Through Rate" (CTR), which is the percentage of people who opened the email and clicked on one of the links in the email; and "Opt-Out Rate" (OOR), which is the percentage of people who indicated they did not want to receive any further emails from you or your business.

Email marketing is typically performed by first generating a list of email recipients, which can include your customers, prospects, etc., and then sending them emails on a consistent basis to help enhance brand awareness, build relationships, sell products and services, and keep them informed. The ultimate success of your email marketing has to do with four primary steps.

First, you must be able to **create compelling and useful emails.** If your goal is to sell more products or services to new and repeat customers, you need to provide compelling and actionable email content to accomplish this goal. For example, emails can include exclusive and time-sensitive coupons and promotions for users to act on without delay. If your goal is to build brand awareness and drip-marketing to previous prospects who have gone quiet, you may want to provide incentives and additional reasons for them to want to buy from you in your emails. Moreover, the mere presence of constant emails over time can also help "remind" buyers of you when they are ready to buy on their time.

Second, you need to be able to **create a large enough email list to reach enough potential people to meet your sales objectives.** What is the point of creating a regular stream of emails if they are not getting to all of the people you need to see them? Typically the larger the list of targeted clients the better, and keep in mind that not all emails will reach all of the people on your list. It is not uncommon for only around **56 percent of mass emails to actually make it to their intended recipients,** with the remaining getting rejected and filtered out.[17]

Third, you have to **create the right balance of frequency with your emails for them to be effective.** As previously discussed, marketing is about creating an effective balance of the total number of people you can contact (reach) and the total amount of times (frequency) you can reach them. By creating a steady flow of emails, you are both building your brand and nurturing prospects into more convertible leads. For example, how much more likely would you be to buy from a business that you receive emails from on a monthly basis over the course of a year versus a business that provides a similar service but you have only heard from once? **Most people buy from people and brands they are more familiar with, which is why your frequency is just as important as the reach of your emails.**

Fourth, you need to effectively **track your email performance and convert the responses in a timely manner.** You will never really know how effective your email marketing campaigns are over time unless you have a system that tracks the performance of each and can trend that data for you. Many email-marketing tools provide strategic insights for emails campaigns such as who opened emails, who clicked through them, etc.—all of which is actionable and real-time insight to your business. It is also important that any insight gained be acted on immediately and without delay. This means that emails that are opened and responded to receive attention measured in seconds and minutes—not hours and days. The longer you wait to respond, the lower your chance of converting these actions into real sales opportunities.

Pros:
- Relatively high levels of return on investment (ROI). **Email marketing has a 200 percent higher return on investment** than cold-calling, networking, and trade shows.[18]
- Relatively high level of reach. 58 percent of adults check email first thing in the morning.[19]
- Improved actionable tracking capabilities such as email opens, click-through rates, etc.

Cons:
o Recent Federal CAN-SPAM email compliance restrictions. Many major mass email providers will rigidly

enforce compliance based largely on the source of email lists provided.

o Relatively low response rates of .12 percent.

o Increased levels of email competition in people's overflowing inboxes. Business-related emails received per person are also expected to increase from an average of 108 per day in 2011 to 140 per day by 2018; a 30 percent increase.

o Most businesses still have poor email campaign coordination with their other forms of marketing.

Best Practices:

1. **Emails sent between 5 a.m. and 9 a.m. local time get the highest open and response rates.** Since most people start their days by reading their new emails, sending emails early in the morning tends to produce the highest open and response rates. High response times are between 8 a.m. and 3 p.m., with **peak times between 8–9 a.m. and 3 p.m. each day.**

2. **Make sure you stay CAN-SPAM compliant.** In 2003, the US federal government passed the CAN-SPAM Act to help limit the unwanted solicitation emails (or SPAM) people were receiving.[20] Unlike the National Do-Not-Call Registry, CAN-SPAM legislation has not been well enforced and **has more to do with removals requests** from receiving further emails than permission to send to people in the first place. In order to be CAN-SPAM compliant, your emails have

to contain seven elements. First, you cannot provide false or misleading header information. Second, you cannot use false or misleading subject lines. Third, you must disclose any advertising in an email as an ad. Fourth, you must indicate where you are located with a valid sender street address or PO box. Fifth, you must give recipients a way to opt-out of future emails from you or your company. Sixth, you must honor all opt-out requests within ten business days. Seventh, you must monitor what others are doing by email on your behalf. For more details on CAN-SPAM, please visit www.fcc.gov.

3. **Use third-party email services.** There are a lot of great email marketing services that businesses can use today. The most common vendors include ConstantContact.com, MailChimp.com, GetResponse.com, and many others. These larger vendors work to stay fully CAN-SPAM compliant and typically make the creation, management, and reporting of emails very easy for the average user. They also provide additional ways to help you build up your distribution lists by allowing you to create newsletter sign-up forms and other web forms that can be placed on your website. They also provide detailed reporting such as information about who opened your emails, who clicked through them, and who unsubscribed. Many of these services are very affordable for most people based on a monthly subscription rate starting at $10 and up. Just be careful where you get your email lists from and

the quality of the lists you provide to these services. If they find that you are in violation of laws and their own rules for email solicitation, they can suspend you and even refuse you service.

4. **Include videos in your email marketing.** If you are looking for ways to get the biggest bang for your buck out of emails, videos are typically the answer. **Videos in emails can increase the click-through rates by 200–300 percent.**[21] With people's inboxes getting increasingly flooded with content emails, videos are one of the best ways to help sell you and your services to others in a different and more preferable way.

5. **Focus on your email subject lines.** Most people are inundated with emails, and fully **64 percent of people have indicated that they decide whether to open an email based on the subject line alone.**[22] When it comes to subject lines, the best performing ones are typically personalized and very short, containing nine characters or less. As a general rule, **it is a good idea to not let your subject lines exceed six words in length and to have your most important words first.** This is especially important since an increasing number of people are now reading emails on smartphones, which can limit the display of subject lines even more. Depending on your industry, subject lines that include questions and/or provide some sense of urgency ("tomorrow") or a call to action ("download") and include citations can be more effective. For example, the word "appointment" for attorneys and dentists,

"follow-up" for recent clients and "please reply by Wednesday" can all be effective when used properly. Things to avoid in your subject line include words in all-caps, excessive punctuation, and words that can come across as too salesy. Words to avoid using in subject lines can include "quick," "free," "newsletter," "meeting," and anything that starts with "FW:" (for forwarded emails). In the end, there is no real silver bullet for the right words to use, so you will likely need to experiment over time and find the best one for your industry and business.

6. **Use your blog posts for email content.** One of the benefits of writing blog content on your website is that it can be repurposed for use in your emails as well. Unlike web content that can be penalized for duplicate content publishing, emails do not get indexed in the search engines and therefore allow you yet another place to use the content you have already written. In many cases, you may only need to include a small snippet of the content with a link back to the content source on your blog, website, etc.

7. **Send emails that are most relevant to each segment of your customer base.** Emails that are relevant **typically drive eighteen times more revenue than broadcast emails.**[23] Each one of your customers and prospects can have unique aspects about them. This could include where they live, their age, gender, purchasing history, services rendered in the past, buying behaviors, etc. All of this information is considered to

be "business intelligence" (BI) and if properly captured and utilized can help you focus your emails down to the most actionable and useful information for each person. For example, if your business has a predictable repeat customer re-buy, such as dental cleanings every six months, you can time the emails and content to focus on people around this objective. If your customer purchased products or services in the past that need to be checked or updated, this too should be utilized in a targeted emailing. The options are infinite and the more BI you capture about your customers, the more effective your emails can become as a result.

8. **Focus on the frequency of your emails.** Emails are great for both sales and nurturing leads. In order to follow the Rule of 12 as previously discussed in this book, your goal should be to **send out emails to your customers and prospects a minimum of once a month.** Since only 56 percent of emails will typically reach their intended recipients, you may need to coordinate with your other marketing mediums to make up for this gap in reach.[22] Absent any other forms of marketing, this would mean that you would typically have to email each customer once every 2.5 weeks to make up for the difference.

9. **Use emails to stay in front of your prospects and those people who went quiet on you. Nurtured leads make 47 percent larger purchases than non-nurtured leads.**[24] Not everybody is ready to buy

when you want to sell to them, so email is a great way to help keep you in front of the prospective customer in a less-threatening manner until they are ready to buy. For this reason, nurturing of these leads—versus a hard-sale approach, which could simply turn them off—is essential. Therefore, these nurturing emails should **include useful information to the prospects that also convey your level of skills and expertise, as well as results your services have provided to others.** These can also include special promotions and coupons to provide them with yet another possible compelling reason to buy now if they are ready. The goal with nurturing these contacts over time is to provide them with a higher level of credibility and trust in working with you, and, when they are ready, to have them potentially purchase at a higher rate than other non-nurtured customers.

10. **Coordinate your emails with your other marketing mediums.** Emails should be part of a coordinated marketing effort to produce maximum marketing effectiveness and results for your business. Emails should be timed to work with phone calls, texts, mailings, events, TV, radio, and other marketing mediums for maximum effect in your marketing plan. For example, say you send out an email to 2,000 people and notice that 400 people opened your email, 40 clicked through to your website, 50 watched a video on a new service, and 50 clicked a link to a service promotion

you are running. All of this information can be viewed real-time in the most popular emailing vendor systems and can provide you with actionable information that you can now follow up on by phone, email, text, and with mailings to a much greater effect.

11. **Personalize your emails.** Emails that are personalized **can improve click-through rates by 14 percent and conversion rates by 10 percent.**[25] The two most important words anybody will hear from you is **their first and last name.** When we receive emails that look canned and not addressed to us by name, we tend to quickly ignore them. Newer mail-merge and email services allow for personally addressing each email with the person's first name, but you have to first capture their name along with their email address in your contact database to make this happen.

12. **Create a monthly newsletter.** One of the best ways to build frequency is with a customer newsletter. Customers and prospects know that newsletters tend to be more about sharing information and updates and less about sales, so they tend to be more receptive to receiving them. When you create a newsletter, make sure to provide easy access and reminders to people on your website and other places to quickly and easily sign up for your newsletter. **In order to encourage sign-ups, it is helpful to provide some type of gift, download, or free report to users who do.** These

could include first service coupons/discounts, helpful guides, key studies, and information downloads—all things that are potentially useful and compelling for the customers and prospects. For ideas about incentives and topics for your business, think about the most frequently asked questions you receive from customers, problems they deal with, or look at your website data and see which web pages and content are the most active.

PAY-PER-CLICK ADVERTISING (PPC)

Search engines like Google make most of their money from the advertising by businesses within the search results and network of advertising sites associated with Google's Ad Network. To see an example of what these ads look like, just do a common search in Google for "San Diego DUI attorney" and you will see a number of paid advertisements (PPCs) running on the right side and top of Google's natural search results screen.

Most PPC ads are based on desired keywords and terms that you would like to target for your advertisements. In short, search engines like Google will then match together searches by keyword/s used in search to the desired keywords and phrases associated with PPC ads. The challenge here is being able to accurately guess all of the thousands of different words and phrases used in searches today to target your ads to. Moreover, more than 50 percent of searches are now considered long-tail and include a combination of specific words and phrases that are rarely repeated online with any real frequency. These long-tail searches, although infrequently repeated, typically convert at higher rates in many industries than the more common vanity searches we all would think of today.

Pay-Per-Click essentially allows advertisers to pay search engines like Google a fee each time somebody clicks on their ads. Since Google owns these ad positions on their own search engines and properties, you are in effect buying rank and visibility through these advertisements. In short, **it is a way to buy visibility and traffic to a website instead of earning it organically through Search Engine Optimization (SEO) tactics.** Each time a PPC advertisement is run, search engines will provide data on that campaign such as the total number of "impressions" (or views) received, your average "Cost-Per-Click" (what you paid on average for your clicks), and your click-through rate (total number of clicks per impressions by percentage).

With a **typical click-through-rate (CTR) of around 2–4 percent and a conversion rate of clicks to leads of 4–5 percent, most businesses would have to pay for around 2,000 to 2,500 clicks to receive 100 responses (or leads).** This is where the cost-per-click becomes so important to keep track of and manage; if your clicks become too expensive and your overall return on investment drops below a 3-to-1 return, then you have to make changes quickly. The challenge for most small business professionals, however, is keeping track of these costs because they can change all the time.

When Google first introduced PPC advertising in 2002, it was a revolution in the advertising world. PPC is designed to work when businesses bid-up prices for placement online in an open bidding system where the highest bids win. Since this bidding process continues indefinitely, the bids and positions can change along with them. As a result, Google allows users to set daily budgets, position adjustments, etc., to help automatically account for these constant gyrations. The problem is that when unchecked and unmanaged, these changes can end up costing a lot of money to the average business.

With the initial success of Google PPC in their search engine results pages, Google then expanded their advertising network in 2003 to include other high-traffic websites, videos, and web properties through their AdSense program. AdSense basically allows for Google ads to be placed on affiliated websites, thereby dramatically increasing the potential reach for their advertising beyond their own website/s and search engines. Companies and websites that actively participate in Google's AdSense program are then paid on a cost-per-click or per-impression basis for hosting these ads. AdSense is ideally designed for websites that have higher traffic levels that you can then serve your ads to.

In addition to Google, PPC is also run on sites such as Yahoo!, Bing, and others. Social media sites like Facebook, LinkedIn, and others also allow for paid advertising but are typically targeted around user demographics instead of keywords—giving you additional online advertising options.

Pros:

- Rapid marketing campaign creation and utilization versus more traditional organic advertising options like websites and active content strategies.
- Targeted marketing based on desired-keyword and geographic targeting.
- Expanded marketing content networks and website options and reach beyond just the search engines.

Cons:

o The ever-increasing costs of open bidding for clicks.

o Rapid adoption and utilization of mobile devices with smaller advertising footprints.

o Relatively lower return on investment (ROI).

o Brand hijacking by competitors running PPC around known names and brands.

Best Practices:

1. **Measure your costs based on conversion, not clicks.** Many small-business professionals today get PPC sticker shock the first time they look at the cost-per-click (CPC) for many popular terms, and rightfully so; many keywords have increased dramatically in costs over the past years. But you need to remember that all marketing should be ultimately measured by a return on investment (ROI), and CPC is simply an ancillary measurement to that objective. In order to calculate your ROI for PPC, you need to know three

numbers: your Revenue-Per-Customer (RPC), your Cost-Per-Click (CPC), and the most important aspect: **YOUR CONVERSION RATE.** Each of these numbers together will produce a Cost-Per-Conversion (CPCon), which is the basis for your ROI. The equation looks like this: ROI = [(Customer Value – PPC Spend) ÷ (CPC ÷ Conversion Rate)].

For example; if you have a CPC of $100 and are able to convert 100 percent of those clicks to a customer worth $400, then your ROI is 3 to 1 on a Cost-Per-Conversion (CPCon) of $100 per customer. You can also achieve the same ROI if you only convert 1 percent of your clicks with a CPC of $10 and a converted customer worth $4,000, giving you a Cost-Per-Conversion (CPCon) of $1,000 per customer. In each example, your Cost-Per-Conversion (CPCon) is different ($100 versus $1,000) but your ROI is the same (3 to 1). In each example, **the most important number is NOT the CPC but the conversion rate relative to the Cost-Per-Conversion (CPCon), which results in your ROI.** In the end, if you know the value of a new customer then you should only be measuring Cost-Per-Conversion (CPCon), not Cost-Per-Click (CPC) using this simple PPC formula: **CPCon = (Total Ad Costs ÷ # Conversions).** Once you determine the CPCon, you can then calculate your total maximum bid for a PPC term by dividing the CPCon by the total number of clicks needed to reach a conversion. This calculation looks like this: **Total Maximum PPC bid**

= (CPCon ÷ Total Clicks Needed to Reach 1 Conversion).

2. **Use Google Analytics to track your conversions.** One of the most valuable (and free) online marketing tools you have at your disposal is Google Analytics. This website-tracking tool not only allows you to measure the performance of your website but also allows you to track the performance and ROI of your PPC ads that convert on your website. In Google Analytics, you can easily define what you consider to be a conversion from your PPC ads, such as a visitor landing on a specific page, submitting a web form, etc. For each of your campaigns, you can then track the performance of each PPC ad relative to the desired conversion to help determine what is working and what is not. Since Google provides both PPC and Google Analytics, they are designed to work together in a very seamless and easy-to-use manner.

3. **Use Google's keyword tools.** When it comes to finding the proper keywords and phrases for your PPC ads, Google provides very helpful keyword tools (Search: "Google Keyword Tool") that can provide you with estimates for keywords and phrases by cost and expected click volumes. They can also suggest other keywords and terms based on your business type and location.

4. **Establish your goals, budgets, geography, dates, and times.** Before you begin your campaigns, make

sure to define your budget and how you want to target your ads based on factors such as geography, days, times of the day, displays on search engines or affiliated ad networks, etc. Google PPC will allow you to set a budget and even provide a budget estimator based on your desired options. The key is to make sure you have a defined budget in Google and to set up your campaign to not exceed it. Once a budget is reached, Google can then stop your campaign until your next budget period, typically defined by day. Because of this, **you need to pay close attention to when your budget limit is reached each day.** For example, if you would expect your best customers to come from searches made later in a day, you do not want your campaign to stop earlier each day when you hit your budget limit. Ideally you need to balance your budget with your campaign options to make sure your ads are never down during your ideal advertising times.

5. **Test your campaigns and test them again.** PPC advertising is more of a journey than a destination, so you need to start with the proper expectations. First, due to the constant changes in the bidding for prices, positions, etc., there is no one way to run a PPC campaign. Second, **most businesses need to test different campaign configurations before they can truly find what works best for them.** Third, there are many different ways to test your campaigns beyond just pricing, keywords, and geography. Other options

can include using site links, calls to action, pricing displays, display URLs, and remarketing to try to increase the click-through rates in your ads.

6. **Go vertical with your campaigns.** One of the biggest mistakes small-business owners make when running PPC campaigns happens when they try to become too broad in focus on a limited budget. Going broad with too many keywords and/or categories can quickly run up costs and also negatively impact your conversions by not having enough focused landing pages to convert for every term. Because of this, it is wise to **fight the temptation to go broad and instead focus your campaigns on a more narrow and vertical strategy.** For example, say a law firm has five practice areas, which can include thousands of potential keywords it can utilize in its PPC campaign. On a limited budget, it typically is better to start out with a higher level of focus on terms for one practice area or for only very specific aspects of those practice areas instead of going after everything all at once.

7. **Know your competitors' ads, and design yours to stand out.** In case you haven't noticed, you have a lot of potential competitors for most PPC advertising positions online. Because of this, you have to find ways to **"stand out" among all of the other ads** that are competing with yours for attention. Simply doing what everybody else is doing does not help create differentiation and will commonly lead to poor results. So make sure to take time to study what others who

are competing against your ads are doing, and find ways to be different and better.

8. **Use landing pages to improve your conversions.** Most businesses today will run PPC ads and have their clicks go directly to their standard website pages, which is a huge mistake. If you are going to pay the kind of money PPC requires to drive traffic to your website, you need to do everything possible to most effectively convert them when they arrive. Standard website pages are not designed for optimal PPC conversion because they either lack focus and/or they give users who arrive on those pages from a PPC ad too many choices and navigation options, potentially leading them away from your desired conversion. Because of this, you should ideally have a highly targeted landing page on your website to uniquely convert these users when they arrive.

A landing page is nothing more than a targeted content page with a dead end for further site navigation. When a user arrives on landing pages, they should only have a very limited course of action: to call or submit a web form or navigate back out, and that's it. **Good landing pages do not allow for the opportunity to navigate away from the page to somewhere else on your website, and focus purely on the desired conversion of the PPC ad.** When creating landing pages, make sure to only create and use landing pages that are relevant to your keywords and targeted customers. In many cases, using good landing pages **can increase** your PPC conversions by 100 percent or more, so the time and cost needed to use these pages with your PPC ads should yield excellent returns. You should never run PPC campaigns without landing pages to support them.

9. **Always include a call to action in each advertisement.** Businesses run PPC ads for a reason, and that reason almost always requires the target audience to take some form of action. Because of this, every PPC ad you run should include a clear call to action so people can fully understand what the next steps are in response to your advertising. Simple call to actions include terms like **"Learn More," "Buy Here,"** and can also include special pricing offers and promotions. Without a call to action, how do you expect to get your desired results? Remember: If you never ask for something, the answer is always "No."

COLD-CALLING

Most seasoned sales professionals are familiar with cold-calling and will honestly tell you it is their least favorite task in sales. Cold-calling is a form of interruption marketing when you reach out and touch someone by phone. The problem is that over the years these calls have increased to the point that B2B people now hire gatekeepers to help manage these calls, and the National Do Not Call Registry was recently created to help prevent unwanted B2C calls into our homes. People are also getting very busy during their days and the attempts to reach them are growing along with it. **The** number of cold calls attempted to reach the average person has increased from 3.68 attempts in 2007 to 8 in 2013; nearly a 100 percent increase in 6 years.[18] Despite these limitations, cold-calling is still a commonly used form of prospecting, and the people who are most effective at it understand that it is **largely a numbers game resulting in far more objections than success.** With a **typical response rate of 8–12 percent, most businesses would have to call between 833 to 1,250 people just to receive 100 responses (or leads).**

Since most people don't take rejection well, the process of slugging through the disproportionately large number of rejections is a mental battle for many small-business professionals to consistently handle over time. For this reason, many professionals and small businesses will hire external cold-calling resources and/or services to perform these tasks for them. As you would suspect, this is not glamorous work for most people in any organization, so the turnover rate of these resources tends to be high, which can lead to higher levels of fluctuations in quality and results. Additionally, hiring people to call and/or making the calls yourself can be time consuming and therefore costly to you; especially if you are making the calls yourself. **The higher your expected earnings per hour, the more costly this can become and the more leverage you can receive by delegating this service to others.**

There are also strict federal laws about cold-calling in the United States and who you can cold-call as a result. In 2007, the federal government officially opened the National Do Not Call Registry, which allows consumers to register their own phone numbers in order to limit the solicitation calls they receive in their homes. The website for this registry is www.DoNotCall.gov. The registry was designed to register residential numbers, not business numbers, but as our society increasingly moves to smartphones, these numbers and devices are increasingly one in the same for many people.

One of the potential **workarounds to the US laws** dealing with cold-calling and the National Do Not Call Registry is the time frame you have to call a customer after an initial customer relationship existed, such as when they last **made a purchase, delivery, or payment**. In this scenario, **you have up to 18 months to continue to contact that individual**. For customers who **submit an application or place an inquiry with your company, you have up to 3 months** to contact them as well.[26] These provisions currently apply unless the person specifically asks the company not to contact them again, in which case you cannot. For more information and up-to-date rules governing cold calling, make sure to visit www.ftc.gov.

Pros:
- Relatively high response rates of 8–12 percent.
- Allows for more reactive responses and follow-up since a caller can immediately respond to their initial responses.

Cons:
o Relatively low return on investment (ROI).

o High levels of competitive callers and trained gatekeepers to help keep you out.

o National Do Not Call Registry (US).

o Relatively inconsistent results and fragmented service providers.

o Time consuming for most professionals and requires discipline (it is a numbers game).

o Typically poorly coordinated with other marketing activities by most small-business professionals today.

o Relatively high levels of call-resource turnover rates.

Best Practices:

1. **Only cold-call with a professional and positive attitude.** Studies involving phone-based communication have shown that only 16 percent of your impact comes from your words while **84 percent comes from your voice.**[27] The tone of your voice can have a lot to do with your success over the phone. Most people tend to **associate a strong voice with confidence and passion** and a weak voice with a lack of both.

2. **Record your phone calls for training and improvement.** How do you plan to improve your effectiveness and that of your resources on the phone with prospects and customers unless you can record and review them? You can learn a lot by reviewing recorded phone calls, but make sure that you have the proper consent to record them first. US federal and state wiretapping laws exist to make sure recordings

are consensual and legal, so make sure to check both before you start this process. At the time of this book, US federal law prohibits recording of telephone calls and in-person conversations without the consent of at least one of the parties (one-party consent).[28] In this case, you or one of the people calling on behalf of your business could count as the "one-party" to this consent. Some **states such as California, Connecticut, Florida, Illinois, Maryland, Massachusetts, Montana, New Hampshire, Pennsylvania, and Washington have passed "two-party consent" laws,** which require the consent of EVERY PARTY on a phone call or conversation to agree to a recording in order to make it legal.

3. **Strategically time your cold-calling efforts.** As previously discussed, **the best times to cold-call are between 8–10 a.m. and 4–5 p.m.,** and the best days to call are typically **Thursdays** and **Wednesdays,** with Tuesdays being the worst. It is also important to coordinate your cold-calling efforts with your other marketing functions such as immediately after sending out a mailing, when receiving new leads, after sending out emails, and when giving a speech at a major event. For example, following up on leads you have received with a "coordinated" follow-up schedule of emails and phone calls can typically result in a 16 percent increase in the chance of reaching the lead by phone. Most prospecting efforts are far more effective

when they are run in an interrelated marketing system than independently and on their own.

4. **Whenever possible, research your prospects online before calling them.** People receive a lot of solicitations each day and the number of distractions they receive are constantly growing. Because of this, people are making split-second decisions when they receive your calls **by asking themselves, "What is in it for me?"** You need to be able to address this quickly, and one of the best ways to do this is to **Google the person's name and review their information online.** Websites like LinkedIn, Yelp, Google, Facebook, and others can provide you with critical personal information about your prospect before you call. With this unique information, you can start asking the right questions and ultimately get them to "what is in it for them" as quickly as possible.

5. **Find ways to quickly establish credibility and trust with your prospects.** Many cold callers sound like robots when they call and rigidly stick to a script. This can immediately send a signal to your prospects that this is all about the caller and not about them. For most people, this type of delivery is disrespectful and leads to immediate hang-ups. In order to make this work to your advantage, always try to come across as respectful, personable, and as somebody who wants to help the prospect first in order to help **gain their attention and trust.** It is also a good idea to ask intelligent questions about their needs and

problems, which will help you gain credibility with the **prospect.** Finally, it is always a good idea to start out each call with a **personalized touch** such as "I just saw your website" or "I see you drive a Ford F150" or "Congratulations on your daughter's graduation."

6. **When possible, do your cold-calling with an automated dialer.** Cold-calling is largely a numbers game and that means a LOT of potential dialing and actions. For those people who make a lot of cold calls, an automated dialer will make the process much more efficient for you when it comes to dialing, leaving messages, taking notes, sending emails, etc. Auto dialers can be utilized as both a device as well as a software system, and with the growth of cost-effective VOIP calling services, a simple PC with the proper software can become a very powerful and effective auto dialer.

LEAD GENERATION

Most small businesses are not good at all of the functions and processes needed to fully market and advertise for new business. Limitations in resources, time, and expertise will often lead many small-business owners to struggle with the successful and consistent generation of new leads. As a result, a growing industry of professional lead-generation companies have emerged that now specialize in generating new leads for other businesses that need them.

Lead-generation companies will commonly source their leads from multiple lead channels and then sell those leads at a profit to businesses that need them. Leads are commonly purchased by businesses so they can build newsletter lists, prospect lists, and generate new sales. The sources for these leads can range from Pay-Per-Click (PPC) advertising, telephone calls, content marketing, advertisements, emails, events, TV and radio ads, online and offline affiliates and websites, purchasing-customer lists, etc. Many companies with high-trafficked websites will also allow people to run ads on their site and then get paid for each lead received from them; commonly referred to as affiliate lead generation. Of all the lead sources, **email, events, and the Internet are still the primary sources for many industry leads today.**

When buying many of these leads in bulk from affiliates, lead-generation companies can potentially achieve better economies of scale with their purchases than a typical small business can do on their own. They can also potentially buy larger media spots on TV and radio and then distribute those leads to more than one source, allowing for greater advertising reach than many small companies can achieve independently.

Leads can be purchased in literally hundreds of different industry verticals. Some of the more popular verticals today include: home and auto insurance, financial services, home services, legal, secondary education, credit cards, mortgages and real estate, online dating, elder care, etc.

Unlike the other leads you may generate on your own, leads purchased from lead-generation companies **typically lack any branding equity,** which can create some complexities when converting these leads. In short, many of the leads you buy may never have heard of your company and will typically

require a high level of conversion activity to successfully contact and convert into new customers. If you have strong brand awareness in your target market it can help with conversion upon initial contact, but most small businesses and professionals will lack this in the larger markets where most leads are purchased.

A lack of branding when generating leads can also act as an advantage for some businesses. For example, what if you have a law firm that is branded for insurance defense work yet you want to start generating new plaintiffs' cases as well? By buying plaintiffs' leads you can then generate new cases without creating a branding problem both on and offline with the insurance companies you may already represent and cater to. You can also benefit by buying leads quickly in a market that you don't currently service and/or have no brand equity in. Or what if you only want to test selling to new customers in a new market that is dissimilar to your own? These are all examples of when buying leads without brand value can actually help you.

Another issue with leads has to do with their latency from the point of need to the point of conversion. In certain instances, such as with personal injuries, plumbing problems, dental emergencies, etc., people may already be shopping around due to an immediate need. This can create challenges in reaching and effectively converting these leads on time. Other leads dealing with less time-sensitive matters such as routine home repair, filing claims, and buying non-essential products and services may be better suited for latent lead conversion.

To learn more about the lead generation industry, visit www.LeadsCon.com.

Pros:
- Quick way to scale and generate leads through third-party marketing.
- Allows for potential diversification of new-business-generation sources.
- Allows for ways to generate business that could otherwise conflict with your own brand.

Cons:
o The lead generation industry is still largely fragmented, producing an inconsistent quality of leads and results.

o Most leads require competitive and timely follow-up.

o Most professionals **DO NOT properly convert leads,** leading to lower lead conversion rates than most professionals are accustomed to.

o Leads typically have little/no branding citations when received.

Best Practices:
1. **Be prepared to set up a defined lead-conversion process for your leads.** Don't expect non-branded leads to convert in the same way branded leads do; they commonly won't. Purchased leads typically require extensive and timely follow-up. In short, if you only plan to call a lead once or twice on your schedule and

then give up on them, then don't buy leads for your business. Most leads today require many follow-ups using multiple mediums on a defined schedule. So what are some best practices for following up on leads by both phone and email? For phone follow-ups, you should try three attempts on the first day (one minute, thirty minutes, and two hours after receiving) and one additional attempt on days five, fourteen, and fifteen after receiving the lead. For cold-call follow-ups, the best times to call are between 8–10 a.m. and 4–5 p.m., and the best days to call are Thursdays and Wednesdays, with Tuesdays being the worst. For emails, you should send an email each day starting with day one (within thirty minutes) and again on days four, eight, fifteen, and twenty-two. When sending email follow-ups, to best times for responses are between 8 a.m. to 3 p.m. with peak times between 8–9 a.m. and 3 p.m. each day. The benefit of following this **"coordinated" follow-up schedule typically results in a 16 percent increase** in the chance of reaching the lead by phone, in addition to the overall conversion rate increases gained by the timing and frequency of the attempts. If you have a prospect's mobile phone number, you can also drive up your conversion rates further on this schedule by texting at the same intervals as your emails. (See Resources for an example of a Lead-Conversion Schedule.)

2. **For lawyers, it is important to understand that *a lead is NOT a case.*** You are not buying a case when

you buy a lead. Rather, you are buying what could become a case (buying a case, especially from a non-attorney, could be a violation of ethics rules). Following this logic, it is also important to note that all leads will not become a case. Most attorneys historically have received leads via referral, which are almost always the best and highest-converting leads. Because of this, many attorneys are used to receiving and converting referral leads that convert well above 50 percent, while many attorneys struggle with converting purchased leads that can commonly convert down to the lower single digits in many cases. In short, **you should expect the work needed to convert purchased leads will well exceed that of a referral lead in order to get enough cases out of the leads you receive.** And in both cases, you should also remember that until it is converted into a case by you, what you are receiving and paying for is a lead first, not a case.

3. **Know the difference between lead generation versus Pay-Per-Click (PPC) based on return on investment (ROI).** A growing number of businesses use or have used Pay-Per-Click (PPC) advertising in the past, yet many are still unfamiliar with buying leads and the economic comparison between the two. If you are considering both options, always make your comparisons based on results measured in return on investment (ROI). Let's look at attorneys as an example here, since they are frequently some of the largest PPC spenders online. In many instances, the conversion

rate of a purchased sales lead to a legal case can be well under 50 percent and even in the single digits depending on the quality of leads you are buying. For many businesses, this may be an alarmingly low number until you consider the PPC alternative.

For example, in my experience **most Google Pay-Per-Click (PPC) leads for attorneys will case-convert at between 1–1.5 percent.** That means for every 100 clicks you pay for on PPC, you can commonly expect to receive 1 to 1.5 cases from a PPC advertising campaign. To take this a step further, say you run a PPC campaign for motor vehicle accident leads in Los Angeles and are paying around $125 per click (yes – these are accurate numbers as of this writing). Following this example you can expect to pay between $8,333 to $12,500 per new case generated from PPC advertising. That new case would then need to be worth between $33,332 to $50,000 in fees for you to achieve a 3 to 1 Return on Investment (ROI). This is why a growing number of professionals like attorneys are looking for additional and more economical lead source alternatives to PPC.

Continuing with this example, let's say you decided to buy motor-vehicle-accident leads from a lead provider at a cost of $300 per lead. To buy 50 leads, you would then be paying $15,000 for those 50 leads with the hope of achieving a lower cost-per-case then you would have paid in the above mentioned PPC example ($8,333 to $12,500 per case). By converting two of these leads into a case (a 4 percent conversion rate), you would already be achieving a superior ROI to PPC ($7,500 per case for a purchased converted lead versus $8,333-$12,500 per case for a PPC converted lead). So as you can see, the real focus here should be on the **lead conversion rate, which will tell you what your ROI is as a basis of comparison between PPC and all other lead providers.**

4. **Know how the leads you are buying are distributed.** When businesses buy leads from lead providers, they are *distributed in differing manners.* For example, some lead providers will send out one lead to multiple customers simultaneously thereby spreading out the costs and selling their leads for a lower cost per lead to each client. The result is early bird gets the worm and, as you can imagine, it is not uncommon for each lead to get inundated with contacts from multiple businesses with the best and most diligent at converting the lead being the key benefactor. This form of mass distribution can be problematic since we know from recent studies that around **50–72 percent of consumers will retain the first attorney, real estate agent, etc. that contacts them.**[29]

Conversely, some lead providers will provide leads exclusively whereby a lead is designated to a specific customer until rejected. This helps to prevent the early-bird effect but also results in a higher cost-per-lead since only one customer is now paying for the lead. Finally, some lead providers will cherry-pick through leads and sell them based on the perceived quality of the lead. As you can imagine, the lead providers in this instance may want to retain the best possible leads and/or sell them at a much higher cost. When it comes to lead distribution, it is important to ask questions dealing with the lead exclusivity or the lack thereof and your ability to manage the early-bird processes of mass lead distribution. If good lead conversion is not your cup of tea, then buying exclusive leads may be a better fit for you. It is also important to determine how the leads are initially distributed to make sure you have a fair chance at receiving good quality leads before somebody else has removed them from a fair distribution. The ideal way of managing this is if each lead is automatically assigned to a customer before any human sifting can possibly take place.

5. **Know that leads are priced based on a number of factors.** Lead costs are typically based on factors such as: *lead type, lead sources, lead qualities, lead quantities, and lead distribution* (exclusive vs. mass-distribution). For example, if you are an attorney and buy a motor-vehicle-accident lead exclusively, you can expect to pay more for it compared to a slip-and-fall lead that is sent out to multiple attorneys. You could also help drive down lead costs by buying a much larger quantity of leads, leading to better economies of scale. Finally, you could also pay less for

Internet-generated leads as opposed to leads generated from more traditional marketing sources such as TV and radio, which typically cost more to produce.

6. **Know where the sources of your leads are coming from.** Not all lead providers are the same, and in most cases you get what you pay for. Some lead providers are nothing more than Pay-Per-Click (PPC) advertising companies that intake their leads from their own advertisements on PPC and then sell you the results. If you run your own PPC today, they can in effect be competing with your advertising and then selling you the results at a markup. Worse yet, many will send out the leads to multiple customers, creating further competition. Typically the smaller the lead provider, the more likely that some or nearly all of their leads will come from PPC. On the other hand, there are lead providers who will utilize different markets and/or affiliates to generate their leads, typically at a lower cost. These affiliates can commonly include their own Internet properties and/or high-traffic websites that commonly fit the demographic of the prospective leads they want to buy. In these instances, advertisements and/or solicitations are run on these web properties, leading to client intakes via an online web form.

One of the primary challenges with web-form generated leads is the latency of time between when the form is submitted and when you receive the lead; **if your leads are typically time sensitive, then this delay** can become a huge conversion problem for you. Finally, some larger lead providers will generate leads from more expensive and traditional means of mass-media advertising such as TV and radio. These forms of advertising are frequently not economical for any one small business to utilize on their own due to the relatively high costs of production and distribution. Some lead providers can overcome this problem by **buying mass media for multiple customers simultaneously, thereby spreading the cost among multiple buyers.** These economies of scale can work, but it also means that any individual branding cache must be removed from the advertising to accommodate all of the lead buyers—not just one.

DIRECT MAIL

Most people know what direct mail is; it's all that "stuff" you have to sift through in your mail to find your bills and other important items. This means that your attention and decisions about what to do with each of these unsolicited mailings is often measured in seconds or less. So why do businesses still send them out despite the fact that their most likely path from your mailbox is directly to your garbage can?

The reason people still use direct mail is because it still works for many businesses based largely on a numbers game. With a **response rate of .05–4 percent, most businesses will have to mail out between 2,500 and 20,000 pieces of mail just to receive 100 responses (or leads).** Variables to this response rate typically include: who the mailers are mailed to, the design and calls to action of the mailer, when the mailings were received, the conversion of the contacts received, etc. That may not strike you as a high response rate, but if a real estate agent were to get 1 to 3 new home listings out of a $500 mailing, they would likely consider it a success despite the added landfill donations.

Pros:
- Relatively high levels of reach since most people have a fixed residence
- Good brand creation and awareness
- Good for personalization and for current-customer targeting

Cons:
o Relatively low response rates of .05–4 percent
o Relatively high costs of production and distribution
o Requires higher levels of frequency and discipline (since most people will give up too quickly)

Best Practices:
1. **Follow the Rule of 3 when direct mailing.** Most professionals will give up after only one or two mailings since they didn't see the results they expected (more instant results). In these cases, **most mailings fail based on poor expectations alone and not based on performance.** The most successful professionals I know who successfully utilize direct mail realize that the most consistent results will come from the third

mailings on. In short, it takes most professionals at least three mailings to the same target market before the market fully responds to it. This is what I refer to as the Rule of 3. When you create your direct marketing campaign, **plan on at least three mailings to the same target audience** before you assess and potentially give up. Also make sure to schedule and coordinate these mailings as part of your overall marketing plan.

2. **Take time to target your mailings.** Most business-people spend far too little time in creating their targeted mailing list, leading to potential failure right from the start. List companies have become very sophisticated in allowing you to segment your list of recipients by different criteria, ranging from zip codes, age, income, gender, profession, religion, special interests, etc. Once you have created your target client profile, try to match the demographics to what a list company can provide you with and then narrow it down as much as possible. Targeting also allows you to budget for additional mailings and apply the Rule of 3 to each mailing campaign. Another way to help you target is to analyze your current customers by geography to see where you are really pulling most of your best customers from. From that information, you might find clusters of clients in certain pockets or areas that you should be concentrating your efforts on. Many industries also highly value new movers' lists since many of these people need to reestablish services. Professionals like dentists will also commonly buy lists

based on a radius of 5 miles, give or take, depending on their location and competition. Moreover, we have also seen from recent studies that when it comes to hiring professionals like attorneys and real estate agents, **around 70 percent of people think it is important to hire a professional within a 25 mile radius of where they are located.**[29] This can also help you narrow down your list to a potentially "serviceable" area as well.

3. **Make your mailings personal.** The best mailings for conversions are always personalized mailings. The only problem is that most people do not have enough of their own time to write handwritten notes each month and instead will send out canned copies to the masses. But that doesn't mean ALL of your mailings should be that way. One of my favorite stories about handwritten mailings is from Joe Girard, the world's greatest car salesman. Every month Joe's former customers would receive a handwritten note from Joe. After many years of record-setting sales, thousands of handwritten notes continued to go out on a monthly basis to his former customers. What was the result? Nearly 70 percent of Joe's business came from repeat customers or people they knew. Not only that, Joe eventually hired people to write the letters for him; providing him with even greater leverage.[30] The moral of this story is that **sending handwritten notes to your most important people (i.e., former customers, promoters, and referrals) is a great way to**

help you get a huge return on your direct mailings. Think about it: when was the last time you received a handwritten letter from a company you have previously done business with? Since most mailings today are mass-produced, they are highly impersonal and garner little attention. This all starts from the envelope to the content. But **how much more likely are you to open a letter or view a mailing that is fully written by hand?** It may take you and your resources more time to write these by hand but if the results are potentially so much greater, why wouldn't you do it? If you are a doctor, attorney, real estate agent, dentist, insurance agent, etc., writing handwritten letters each month can be one of the most effective forms of marketing you have at your disposal. The good news is that most of your competition doesn't do this, so you already have an advantage if you do.

4. **Create timing and a sense of urgency in your mailings.** To maximize the effectiveness of each of your mailings you should ideally include a call to action and/or a time-sensitive offer. If you are offering a promotion, make sure that it is **unique, compelling,** and has a **clearly defined expiration date** so the people receiving your mailing have a reason not to wait but rather to act now. Remember, you have a very short amount of time to capture a reader's attention and to get them to act, so make sure each mailing can clearly and quickly define the **"What is in it for me?"** question

every potential customer will be asking themselves when they receive your mailings.

5. **Coordinate your mailings with your other marketing initiatives.** Mailings should be part of a larger converged marketing strategy so that the impact of all of your marketing efforts produces greater results together than when done separately. For example, when you send out a mailing, what happens both before and after the mailing? Did you also run a radio or TV spot prior to the mailing for greater awareness? Or are you planning to send a follow-up email to your prospects and customers after the mailing to remind them of any promotion and deadline to act? Or how much "warmer" would a cold call be if you called around the same time the mailing is received? These are just a few examples of how you can get better results from your mailings by timing and coordinating them with your other marketing efforts. Ideally, this should be defined chronologically in your business's marketing plan (see example in the Resources section).

6. **Follow up on your leads ASAP!** Most leads received are highly time sensitive and we also know that around **50–72 percent of people will retain the first professional who contacts them.**[29] Because of this, any contact and/or lead received from a mailing should be acted on within a matter of seconds and minutes, not hours and days. If you cannot reach the prospect, don't give up, and make sure to follow a

defined lead-conversion system and/or drip-marketing system to make the most of each lead you receive.

7. **Target your demographics to younger professionals and older people.** When sending direct mailings, recent studies have shown that **the highest response rates come from the 18–34 and 65-and-up age groups.**[31] With the younger segment, especially those who are 22–24 years old, response rates are typically higher largely due to the fact that mail is different from the typical information overload younger people receive today, which is mostly digital. As for the 65 and up crowd, these people tend to open their mail more often and live longer in one place, so they are easier to keep track of by mail.

8. **Don't be afraid to use mailings as a "loss leader."** When setting goals for your mailings, remember that the return on investment (ROI) may not be immediate but based on larger and more long-term business objectives. In some cases, you may want to use a promotion or incentive in your mailing that may initially be unprofitable in order to lead them into future profitable services with your business. These "losses" are referred to as "loss leaders" because the business is taking an initial loss in order to lead the customer "in the door" with the goal of selling them additional services that will be profitable either now or in the future. For example, the vast majority of people who choose a new dentist will do so for a cleaning or an exam. In order to incent them to choose a particular

dentist, a promotion that may be initially unprofitable for the dentist may be provided to get them in the door. However, when you factor in the value of future services and possible referrals they can provide, the lifetime value of the new customer should typically far outweigh the initial loss needed to secure their business. Attorneys commonly do this as well by offering a "free initial consultation" to new prospective clients at the cost of their own time. And finally, perhaps the most famous example of a loss leader comes every year when businesses in the US advertise "door buster" deals on Black Friday in order to entice shoppers into their stores to hopefully buy more. Ironically, many of these Black Friday deals now arrive by mail.

PERSONAL BRAND AND REPUTATION MANAGEMENT

Every day more than **one billion names** are searched in Google alone.[32] We call these "branded searches" since they are looking for information about a specific business, product, service, or individual. These searches take place in nearly all aspects of business today. For example, nearly half of all job recruiters are required to Google potential employees by name to learn more about them. And not all of this branded data is flattering, either. Recent studies have shown that around 45 percent of people have indicated that they have found something in a Google search that made them **NOT do business with somebody.**[32] Moreover, nearly one-third of all customer reviews on the various customer review websites online are negative. This is the kind of negative brand information that cannot only turn away potential new customers but also referral customers who are sent to you as well.

Most professionals and small businesses get their best clients by referral. Referrals are typically the warmest leads that convert the highest into paying customers. The problem with receiving referrals today has to do with the advent of the Internet, where potential customers can now get far more information and citations about you than what was historically only provided by the referrer. Moreover, the majority of consumers now trust the opinions provided about you by third parties online over the opinions you provide about yourself; including on your website.

Most people today have an online (or digital) footprint, and it is growing exponentially every day. Just Google your name and see what comes up on the first page for your own search results. In some instances you have direct control over parts of your digital footprint through tools like your website/s, blogs, and to a lesser degree the social media that you control. However, the largest part of your footprint, the one typically controlled by third-party sources, is the fastest-growing component of your footprint and the one consumers are placing a greater amount of trust in than ever before. This is why proactive brand management is becoming so important.

Most small-business professionals have a similar problem: They start out with little or no established branding in their target market. When small-business professionals operate as solos and/or in smaller businesses they have a distinct disad-vantage. Namely, they have less brand awareness, recognition, and equity compared to their larger and more well-known competitors. For example, if I receive an attorney referral to a lawyer who works for Jacoby & Meyers, how does that referral initially compare to an attorney I have never heard of named Jim Smith who owns a private practice? Or how about a tax accountant referral to somebody at H&R Block versus a new contact named Jan Smith who is a solo CPA? The list by industry can go on and on and the same principle applies; consumers trust industry brands even if we as business professionals who know these brands better than most don't. Why? Because **when faced with too many unknown choices, consumers trend to familiarity, trust, and the promise that a well-established brand conveys to them.**

A good example of the power of branding comes from the story of McDonald's. One of the questions I frequently ask groups I speak to is, "Who sells the best hamburger in the world?" Names of all types of burger chains and even home chefs will fly around, but the one name always missing just so happens to be the name of the company that has sold more hamburgers than any other company in the world: McDonald's. Why? Simple; you may hate the product, but you understand the brand. You know what the name McDonald's promises to provide to you each and every time in any of their locations throughout the world, and you and your children—along with nearly person in the United States—are familiar with the name. What this also illustrates is that **the most important element of branding is consistency;** something you need to focus heavily on with your brand as well.

Since concepts like brand management are so new to most small-business professionals, I am frequently asked what the difference is between brand management and reputation management. The difference is simple: Your brand is what you define and control about yourself while your reputation is what other people think about your brand credibility. Therefore the way the two interrelate is based on **how well you take control of your brand—for your reputation is a direct result of your brand management.**

Creating an effective brand-management strategy involves a process of taking control of your brand footprint and staying in control of it over time. Due to the ever-changing climate of online information management, effective brand management is more of a journey than a destination.

Now that you understand what brand management is, let's discuss three areas you should always be focused on in measuring the effectiveness of your brand strategy.

1.) **Brand Value:** What is your brand worth now and what do you want it to be worth in the future? This is a very important aspect of your business since it has a direct impact on the income and equity value of your business. For example, what is the equity value of a CPA firm that does one million dollars in annual income that nobody has ever heard of versus one that has the same income but is named H&R Block? If the owners of each firm were to sell their business and step away from it, what is left of value? **Absent a strong business brand, all you have left are personal** brands that, once removed, leave the business with no brand value and transferable worth. For example, how many people walk into H&R Block expecting to work directly with Henry or Richard Bloch? Clearly nobody does this yet they confidently walk into this business based on the branding value it conveys. **A strong brand also allows for lower marketing costs** because you have less of a branding gap to fill, better trade referral leverage and you can more easily attract new customers and have a better ability to deal with competitive threats when they surface.

2.) **Brand Opportunity Cost:** What are your brand management efforts—or more important a lack thereof—costing your business in lost sales, growth, and equity value? I remember meeting with a famous attorney on the anniversary of a landmark trial he was involved in 20 years prior to that date. The attorney, who was previously made famous as a public prosecutor, was now a private practice attorney and struggling to grow. Upon Googling his name, I noticed a number of very negative articles written about him by third-party sources. When I asked why he let this happen his response was sadly not unfamiliar to me. He told me people will say whatever they want about him and there was nothing he could do about it. This lack of proactive brand management was costing him dearly both professionally and personally, and it doesn't have to be this way. Ignoring your brand and failing to take control of it is an opportunity cost of doing business. The simple truth is that **unless you take control of your brand, others will control it for you.**

3.) **Brand Hijacking:** Brand hijacking is a relatively newer development thanks largely to the Internet and online advertising. Brand hijacking, as the name denotes, is the process of improperly using the brand value of others for your own gain. A famous Hollywood example of brand hijacking was seen in the movie *Coming to America* when the McDowell family created a brand and restaurant that closely resembled McDonald's, thereby hijacking the brand value of McDonald's for the benefit of their new restaurant named "McDowells." Most brand hijacking of business professionals in the real world takes place today online. Brands we know and trust are frequently searched daily and in volume in search engines like Google. In many cases, these businesses may have brand equity in multiple places including names of their companies, products, services, and people. What many of these businesses fail to do is protect that brand value from others who can hijack the search results accompanying it through paid advertising and other accompanying tactics to pull customers away from their intended search targets. This has recently become particularly pervasive in search engines that display very limited search results in mobile devices, thereby prominently placing advertisements and potential brand hijackers above organic search results when not properly protected.

Now that you understand the basics and fundamentals of brand management, the next step is to create a proactive brand management strategy for your business by following these steps:

First, **identify all of your brands and/or the brand names** you want to establish over time. These can include your business name, professionals and people within your business, names of your services, etc. You then need to Google each of those brand names and keep tabs on the page-one results of those searches. The idea is to clearly define these brands and include them in your marketing plan so they are not forgotten in your overall marketing efforts.

Second, **identify your top 3–5 competitors** in your target market by brand name/s and Google them to see their page-one results as well. Once you can see their results, compare them to your own and see how you stack up to them. Remember, referrals to business professionals are typically given out in multiples, and people will tend to shop around and not sole-source for services. If you can identify who these potential competitors are you can then see **how their branded results in Google compare to yours** and get a clear picture of which branded results will better compete and convert to new clients.

Third, **identify all of the key branding points** within your industry that typically have the most authority and display the highest in Google. For example, prominent branding points for law firms today typically include a website, LinkedIn profiles and pages, the Better Business Bureau, Google Plus pages, Facebook pages, AVVO, FindLaw, Lawyers.com, YouTube, Yelp, and Super Lawyers. These will vary by industry, so keep tabs on them over time and look for the ones that tend to show up the highest for other successful brand players in your industry. Make note of these resources and, when appropriate, utilize them for yourself. Many of these resources are free, while some are paid services. Most successful brand managers will have a combination of both.

Fourth, **create and promote your brand awareness everywhere.** Create and promote links to all of your branding properties such as your LinkedIn profiles and pages, Facebook pages, Twitter page, etc., on places like your email signatures, business cards, stationery, newsletters, advertising, website and blogs, content, speeches, etc. Many of these social media properties allow you to create custom URL links to these properties as well as "follow" and "like" buttons to these resources that can be prominently placed nearly anywhere on the web.

Fifth, **create a proactive online-customer-review strategy** so you can better take control of the reviews people provide about you and your business online. Depending on your industry, there are currently up to thirty-two customer review sites online where people can share opinions about you and your business. There are a few more prominent and ubiquitous review sites like Google, Yelp, Angie's List, etc., that display prominently in the search engines and should receive the primary focus of your efforts. Due to the constant changes in search results, the idea is to keep tabs on these review sites and make note of the ones that tend to display most often on page-one searches. Once you have identified these review sites, create a proactive customer review system with an email you can send out to all of your happy clients that includes simple instructions and hot links to your most prominent two or three customer review sites. It is typically best to **send these review requests out right after a successful customer engagement when they feel the highest level of engagement and sense of obligation to write a positive review for you.** Finally, make sure to diligently but tactfully follow up with them on these requests, reminding them to complete a review and providing any help in order to get them to complete this task. The highest success rates in doing this typically come right after a happy interaction and last a very short time, so make sure you and/or your staff act on these immediately. Time is not your ally here.

Sixth, **monitor your results and be proactive.** The best way to monitor branding results is to track them over time and trend the results. One of the first resources you should use to help you is Google Alerts, which can be accessed at Google.com/alerts. Google alerts is free and allows you to create an alert for each brand name so you can receive regular updates from Google any time your brand names are mentioned on the Internet, including blogs, media, video, books, etc. You can also set the frequency with which you receive these alerts. The default I always recommend to start with is weekly. It is also a good idea to check your major online review sites at least once a week to make sure you are on top of and can respond to any negative reviews in case they pop up. Finally, you can also track your progress in brand measurement based on key indicators such as new "likes" and "follows" on your social media sites, connections and followers on LinkedIn, website traffic to your biography and information pages on your website and other third-party business/professional biography sites, etc.

If you have reached this point and all of this seems over-whelming to take on your own, well, you are not alone. Brand management is a developing industry, and a growing number of companies and consultants are emerging that can handle any and all of these components for you. Just understand that at some point in your growth cycle you will likely need to have some or all of these tasks handled either by your own support resources or through an outside service. If you do decide to keep these tasks in-house, it is best to create a clearly defined process that includes each of these items step-by-step so they can be consistently completed, monitored, and adjusted over time.

CONTENT MARKETING

Content marketing is nothing more than the creation of **"useful" content** with the sole purpose of publishing that content to generate and/or support new and existing cus-tomers. Noticed I used the word "useful" here, because that is the key element to successful content marketing that most people miss. The Internet is filled with both useless and useful content, all of which was published for various reasons. Ulti-mately "useful" content is content that clearly addresses the

"What is in it for me?" question for your current and future customers. In the end, your reasons for creating new content should be simple: Content marketing should help you grow your business, period.

Content marketing is not only written content but also includes other mediums such as video, print, etc., all of which are discussed in separate parts of this book. For our purposes here, we are going to largely limit content marketing to written online content.

Most online content is published in various places including websites, blogs, social media, trade publications, industry-specific directories, news engines, online media sites, etc. For small businesses and professionals, most content is published on their websites and blogs. The primary difference between the two is how that content gets published and indexed. Publishing content to a website typically involves some level of technical expertise to add the content to the site that the average businessperson does not have. Moreover, the search engines who send out spiders to index a website will not typically know when there is new content to index, which means weeks and even months may pass before it may be read and indexed in the search engines. As a result, blogs were created.

Most blogs today are deployed within a website and now allow practically anybody to quickly and easily publish information to the blog without technical expertise. Content posted to a blog also gets treated differently by the search engines since they know that content written to a blog is typically new or fresh content and therefore requires new and rapid indexing. The problem with most blogs, however, has nothing to do with the blog and everything to do with the writer.

If you look at many small-business websites today you will likely see 2–3 blog entries and then nothing else. If you want to know when somebody built or last updated their website, this will give you a pretty good guess. The problem we have in today's society is that most people want instant gratification and results; something not commonly provided by most **content marketing today. Because of this, I frequently remind people that content marketing is both a business and a brand-building process and requires both time and discipline to be successful.** If you have ever watered a plant and then expected to see it grow right in front of you then you will know that your expectations were wrong. The same principle applies to most content marketing.

Another dirty little secret with content marketing is that the majority of the content you read that was written "by" a small business or professional was really written "for" a small business or professional. For various reasons, most business-people and professionals cannot produce the steady flow of content needed to be successful at content marketing. Therefore, many people will utilize third-party writers and/or industry vendors to write on their behalf. The content quality produced by many professionals today is typically superior to what the typical third-party writer will produce for you, so writing yourself should always be your first option. If that fails, just know that there are plenty of people out there who can help make this happen for you.

Finally, content marketing is not only beneficial in customer development and support but also in building your brand/s. A good, steady flow of content means more mention of you and/or your business's name in front of all of your customers, prospects, and referral partners. Just because they may not read your content doesn't mean they didn't see your name putting out that content on a consistent basis. **When it comes to brand marketing, you need both reach and frequency, and content marketing is a great way to help support both.**

Pros:

- **Content is the number one source of lead generation online for most businesses today.** Recent studies have shown that fully 83 percent of B2B marketers use content for lead generation and 77 percent of B2Cs use content marketing.[10] The search engines love fresh content and your customers love "useful" content. The marriage of these two elements is a winning proposition.

- **Google loves active content creation and distribution.** The search engines love content, especially fresh content. Remember, the goal of search engines like Google is to provide a superior search experience and results for their users. Nobody wants a whole page of old information when looking for answers to current questions and the search engines know this.

- **Good brand creation and awareness capabilities.** Content marketing can create reach for your business beyond the more traditional forms of marketing. When searching for professionals, most prospects want skilled experts, and content marketing is a great way for you to convey that skill and expertise for others to see.

- **There are a growing number of places to publish unique content (blogs, LinkedIn, PR, guest posts).** With the rapid growth of the Internet and social media, the places to publish unique content are quickly becoming infinite. Because of this, your ability to build reach with your content is becoming much more effective and profitable.

- **Allows for multi-source distribution by repurposing content in emails and newsletters.** Content marketing allows for multiple use of your content that is already created. For example, what you write once for your blog can be used more than once in your off-line email newsletters, print, etc.

Cons:

o **Content can be very time consuming and cost intensive to consistently produce.** Most business professionals are severely limited in time and resources, both of which are necessary for successful content marketing.

o **Relatively hard to directly track a return on investment (ROI) around.** Content marketing is frequently one piece of a larger marketing puzzle and therefore it can be hard to directly track a measurable ROI to each marketing medium. Moreover, content can have a long and useful lifecycle ranging from months to even years in some cases, making tracking ROI around the full lifecycle of the content difficult.

o **Most professionals don't have the skills and discipline to consistently produce active content.** Not everybody is a good writer. Otherwise we could all be authors instead of professionals in other fields. Even many of the best books written today are written by ghostwriters since the well-known author of the book is not an experienced writer. Moreover, business professionals have to prioritize their days and time—many won't see writing as a priority when the rubber meets the road.

o **Duplicate content penalties in Google.** Writing content now means having to be careful about re-publishing anything you didn't write. Google has introduced penalties to websites and blogs that republish duplicate content that can severely damage their authority and search engine results. In short, the content you create and publish online should be unique and your own.

Best Practices:

1. **Produce new content on a fixed and recurring schedule.** Most people fail at creating an active content strategy because they do not discipline themselves to stick with it over the long term. Active content creation and distribution should be clearly defined in your marketing plan and your time to complete it should

be prescheduled and inflexible. For example, I commonly advise

2. **Publish time-sensitive content to your blog and connect your blog to your social media.** Most "static" website content (i.e. standard web pages) on an average small-business's website will get indexed by the search engines once every month or two. If you have important and time-sensitive information, publish it on your blog. Recent studies have shown that blogs are the most effective platform for content with 54 percent of B2C respondents and 31 percent of B2Cs indicating that they publish new content multiple times per week.[10] Your blog differs from your website since it will **produce a special ping notification to the search engines each time new content is added, which will then "call the crawl" of the search engine spiders to index the new content rapidly**—oftentimes in a matter of seconds. It is also important to have your blog content directly feed your posts to your social media sites for maximum reach. This is commonly done automatically through a Real Simple Syndication (RSS) feed from your blog to your social media properties.

3. **Use Google alerts for content ideas.** Most businesspeople will run into writers block and simply run out of ideas to write about. There are two ways to help solve this problem. First, set up Google alerts (Google.com/alerts) to provide you with a constant

feed of information to write about. This could be information that mentions you, your business, your industry, competitors, products, etc., from multiple sources ranging from the web, blogs, news, social media, etc. Second, **use the notes tool on your smartphone and create a notes page for "writing topics" so when you think of things to write about throughout the course of your week, you will always have a place to quickly jot them down for future use during your scheduled writing blocks.**

4. **Do not utilize duplicate content on your online properties.** The search engines like Google do not like duplicate content, especially when republished without the author's permission. Because of these duplicate content penalties, make sure that the content you produce and publish is your own. You can reference sources and snippets of information in your work but make sure the vast majority of your work is your own and not published elsewhere online. When in doubt, run your content through copyscape.com to check for duplicates.

5. **Distribute your content to multiple content publication tools.** Do not just publish all of your content in one place. There are a growing number of places that want to publish your unique content, which means better reach and distribution options. Typical places include your blog, LinkedIn posts, industry-specific directories, news engines, online media sites, trade publications, etc. These sources can help to both

extend your audience and create more traffic and in-bound links to your website as well.

6. **Utilize your online content in your newsletters.** One of the benefits of publishing content online is that you can use it again offline. If you have a newsletter and emails you send out, your online content can be just as useful there without worrying about having it penalized for duplication use online.

7. **Add video to support your content conversions.** Content is great for indexing, but video is even better for conversions. Whenever possible, **include a video in the content topic** you produce to better convert prospects to customers. Remember, people love to watch videos and prefer watching over reading.

8. **Utilize your content to help support your web authority online.** One of the key backbones to authority-building for websites in the Google search algorithm is based on the inbound links your website receives from other relevant, high-authority sources. When you publish content on separate websites, always try to include a link back to your website and/or other important web properties. This can help not only with your conversions but your authority and rankings within the search engines as well.

9. **Only write content that is "useful" to your target audience.** Writing is a way to provide something useful to somebody else and that is the only reason anybody else would want to read it. The best way to

do this is to identify the problems your customers frequently deal with and what they are trying to gain the most. Remember, 70 percent of people buy to solve a problem and 30 percent buy to gain something. Your writing should have a similar distribution and provide useful ways that your prospects and customers can help address their needs. Be sure to include a call to action that can lead them to you for answers and services.

VIDEO MARKETING

Videos are one of the most effective marketing mediums in use today. The problem is that most small businesses and professionals are not using them to their full potential or at all. **Videos can provide significantly higher conversion** rates when included in websites, newsletters, products pages, services pages, emails, social media, etc. In recent studies around 70 percent of marketing professionals have indicated that video converts better than any other marketing medium.[33] Video is also an **excellent brand management tool** that allows you to position and sell yourself and your services in one of the most effective manners today.

Perhaps the greatest single value you can receive from videos is increased conversion from your existing online marketing efforts. For example, the average visitor's time-on-site for many small-business professionals' websites is only around two minutes. That means that the average person will read only about a paragraph's worth of content before they move on—if they read at all. **When video is present, it**

dramatically stops the shopping-around process and can in effect convey up to 1.8 million worth of words in only one minute of video.[18] The preference for watching videos over reading content is pervasive with nearly all ages, not just younger people. For example, we know that **more than 50 percent of senior executives have indicated that they prefer to watch a video over reading content online.** In professions like real estate they have also seen around a 400 percent increase in responses to listings that include video over those that do not.[34]

When it comes to video websites, the 10,000-pound gorilla is still YouTube.com, which if it were its own search engine would be the second largest search engine in the world behind Google—who just so happens to own YouTube. YouTube has made the process of uploading, hosting, and streaming videos very easy for the average user. Beyond YouTube, there are other smaller video websites like Vimeo, Metacafe, Hulu, and others. Many social media properties like Facebook, Pinterest, Instagram, LinkedIn, and others also allow for easy uploading and distribution of videos as well.

Video production has also become very cost effective over the past few years for most small-business professionals. There are a growing number of professional-quality video production companies including those that even focus on videos in niche verticals like legal, dental, and accounting. With new smartphone technologies, people are now even able to produce high-quality videos from their own smartphones and then edit them for little or no cost using a number of popular video-editing tools, including Microsoft's free Movie

Maker software system. Due to the growing number of video services, the cost differential between your time and the cost of hiring a professional to shoot and produce videos is rapidly declining, leading more businesspeople to choose the professional video-production route.

Videos aren't just for your website, either. When Google introduced universal search in 2007, they included a number of different information sources into its search results pages, including videos. It is not uncommon now to see properly optimized videos displayed in search results; especially when it comes to a branded search. **When people look up professionals and their companies by name, videos can have a huge impact on the results they see.** When a video thumbnail is displayed along with all the other content sources about you or your business, people tend to gravitate to the videos due to their own preferences for watching over reading. If you get referrals from other professionals and customers, most of them will now look you up online before they ever contact you. This is where having a video can help you better sell yourself and convert those prospects into customers.

Pros:
- **Videos provide the highest level of conversion compared to all other social media advertising.** The more advertising you do from all sources (web, TV, radio, print, etc.), the more important web conversion using video can become.

- **Excellent brand-building and awareness capabilities.** Short of being there yourself, video provides the best mechanism online to help build up your brands and sell them to others.

- **Universal search integration (thumbnails in search).** Videos can show up anywhere online today from social media to search engine results pages.

- **Relatively easy to optimize and distribute.** Video production, editing, and distribution has never been easier. If my nine-year-old son can do it on his phone, so can you.

- **Multi-source utilization (websites, YouTube, emails, etc.).** Videos are not just for websites anymore. A good video can now be utilized to support multiple marketing channels, making it an even better bang for the buck.

- **Relatively easy to produce moderate-to-higher-quality videos on most smartphones or mobile devices.** Most people have smartphones today and with most smartphones comes a relatively high-quality video production camera. Smartphone quality has become so good now that a recent film at the Sundance Film Festival was filmed entirely with an iPhone.[35]

Cons:

o **Relatively high initial production costs for "professional-quality" videos requiring production skill and professional editing.** If you are new to video production, editing, and distribution, you have a learning curve ahead of you if you want to produce professional-quality work yourself.

o **Can become expensive to reproduce in businesses with high turnover rates.** Videos take time and resources to produce, and if you are in a rapidly changing business where your people and services are constantly changing, you might find it harder to produce videos that can keep up with your changes.

Best Practices:

1. **Keep your videos short and topically related.** Ideally each video you produce should be no longer than 60 seconds with 90 seconds being the maximum length. Remember, **the typical attention span of an adult is only 15–30 seconds,** and with video you have up to 10 seconds to grab their attention before they decide to click away—the longer the video, the higher percentage of click-aways. Ideally, it is preferable to produce a lot of smaller topical videos over one lengthy one. Shorter topical videos will better hold your users attention, allow for better optimization, and be more relevant to the web pages and specific information they are supporting.

2. **Make sure you fully optimize your videos.** Video optimization is critical if you want to maximize the effectiveness and visibility of your videos online. This includes proper titling and descriptions using keywords, authority building, hosting on YouTube and embedding players on your website, creating a video sitemap, uploading your video transcript into YouTube, etc.

3. **Include videos in your email marketing.** If you are looking for ways to get the biggest bang for your buck with emails, videos are typically the answer. **Videos in emails can increase the click-through rates by 200–300 percent.**[21] With people's inboxes getting increasingly flooded with content-only emails, videos are one of the best ways to help sell you and your services to others in a different and more preferable manner.

4. **Include videos on your website and web pages.** People love to watch and hate to read so the only things that really want to read website pages are the search engine spiders—which is why there is so much content out on the web today. When people get to your website pages, the goal should then be conversion. The best way to do that is to **have a video on that page that speaks to the topic of that page.** In the perfect world you would have a 30–60 second topical video on each of your services pages on your website.

5. **Create a channel for your business on YouTube.** Creating a business channel allows you to easily publish, manage, and report on all of your videos in one place. A YouTube channel also allows you to customize the channel to use your own images, graphics, and messaging for your videos as well. Finally, a YouTube channel allows you to track the performance of your videos, monitor user comments and discussions, manage subscribers, and much more.

6. **Load your videos to your YouTube Channel and use their video player on your website.** Once you upload and optimize a video to YouTube, they will provide you with the code needed to install the video and video players on your website and other web properties. This will allow people to watch your videos while on your website and still allow YouTube to track all activity for your videos in one place.

7. **Add annotations to your videos.** The YouTube video editor allows you to edit your videos and add annotations (or notes) to your videos as they run. The most common annotation to add is a **"subscribe"** message to get people to subscribe to your channel. This means they will then be following your channel moving forward. The more subscribers you get, the more people will receive updates of any new videos you add to your YouTube channel.

8. **Create a video production schedule in your marketing plan.** Video production should be like content production; it should be steady and constant over time. Most professionals will create a new website and shoot all their videos at once, post them up, and then stop. This is a mistake you should not be making. The frequency of your new video production does not need to mirror your content frequency, but on average, you should try at a minimum to produce a new video at least once every three months. Remember, people and search engines love new content and they love new videos as well. Since both allow users to filter

information by date, the newer your videos are the more up-to-date and relevant it will appear to viewers.

PUBLIC RELATIONS

Many people get public relations companies confused with advertising agencies, so it is important to start out by indicating what public relations IS NOT. Public relations companies typically DO NOT buy advertising and do not do creative design for you. Public relations companies DO **help promote your businesses and brands in the marketplace** by commonly leveraging their skills, connections, and expertise with other media providers to your benefit.

In today's mass media world of TV, print, news services, radio, speeches, events, and public relations, most small-business owners and professionals do not have the time, expertise, connections, or strategy needed to utilize these highly leveraged assets to their benefit. This is why they rely on public relations experts to help guide them through it. Most public relations professionals are former journalists and media insiders, and the good ones will commonly **have key connections to current media contacts that most people will never have.** Moreover, because of their relationships, they can bring a much higher level of credibility and trust on your behalf to their contacts.

In addition to being potential "connectors," public relations professionals can also help businesses and professionals create press kits, strategically coordinate and conduct press conferences and special events, write and distribute press releases, conduct market research, write to and support social media, and deal with negative information both online and offline.

Small business and professionals primarily use public relations professionals to **help build their brand awareness by using more traditional forms of mass media.** Despite the proliferation of websites and blogs, many people still get their news from major media sources, and these people can be the key to utilizing them to your advantage.

Pros:
- Skilled at providing quick **access to major media contacts** and resources.
- Can help you strategically reach a much larger potential audience compared to more conventional online forms of advertising.
- Can help you professionally time events and press releases, and develop press kits.
- Can bring key strategic industry insight and consultation to a business.

Cons:
o Many PR firms can be relatively **expensive to work with**—especially if you are a smaller business with limited resources.
o Many PR firms are limited in scope and should not be confused with an advertising agency.

Best Practices:

1. **Select a firm based on their expertise, chemistry, and experience.** When you hire a public relations expert, you are in effect **hiring a strategic consultant.** Because of this working relationship you will have to form with the PR firm or person, you have to feel comfortable in working with them. You also need to know their experience in working with businesses like yours and preferably in your same industry. Ask for success stories and make sure they have the right level of experience to meet your expectations and business goals, which should be clearly defined before your start your work with them.

2. **Clearly understand the value exchange in choosing a PR firm.** Most good public relations experts do not come cheap, and **the more experience and key media contacts they have, the more expensive they can become.** But don't let the cost alone dissuade you from considering a higher-priced PR professional. If they can clearly articulate the value THEY can provide to you, they may be worth the costs. The good news here is that public relations experts typically out-earn their media-industry contacts. With all of the recent downsizing in the media world, there will likely be an even greater supply of media refugees coming into the public relations space, creating further competition and supply, which can lead to lower costs.

3. **Use your public relations work to generate authority offline and online.** In the world of Search Engine Optimization (SEO), the authority-building process of inbound link building and citations has become increasingly difficult and complex for many small businesses over the past few years. But many of the major media outlets still have high-value domain authority on their news websites and some even have a large reach with many of the various websites in their news distribution networks. Because of this, **a proper PR strategy that includes these valuable inbound links and citations can be one of the most effective authority-building strategies on the web today.** In short, a strategic media strategy can help execute on these two key marketing efforts at once.

WEB ANALYTICS, CRM, AND CONVERSION TOOLS

There is an old saying in business that you cannot manage what you cannot measure. When it comes to sales and marketing today, far too many businesses do not measure either effectively. For example, we know from recent studies that:[36]

- 44 percent of Chief Marketing Officers (CMOs) say they lack quantitative metrics to demonstrate the impact of marketing spend.
- Approximately 20 percent of CMOs use the manager's "judgment" to measure marketing ROI.

- 67 percent of companies do not formally evaluate the quality of their marketing analytics and despite all the previous stats, spend on marketing analytics is set to increase by 73 percent in three years.
- Only 65 percent of companies surveyed indicated that they have a defined sales process. Of those, 15 percent use a sales process provided by their CRM vendor.

As previously discussed in this book, all businesses are on one of two trajectories; they are either innovating and growing or they are dying. The problem with innovation is knowing when true progress is being made through your innovations. In short, **how do you know innovation is leading to progress without the ability to measure any incremental gains?** This is where many small businesses and professionals have failed in the past.

All progress in business can only be measured "by the numbers." Any other forms of measurement beyond numbers are simply not fully quantifiable and leave too much room for interpretation. When it comes to sales and marketing, running your business "by the numbers" ideally includes every aspect of your operations, ranging from prospecting activity, sales conversions, sales follow-ups, lead follow-ups, sales meetings, close rates, customer retention rates, customer referral rates, average rings to answer incoming phone calls, best days and times for each marketing activity, etc. The list is nearly endless for most businesses, so the goal should be to **start by prioritizing what metrics are most important first** and getting deeper into the numbers as you grow.

Another reason to run your business "by the numbers" is that no one person instinctively "knows" how to manage all aspects of a business all the time. In most cases, **far more of your business will be out of sight than in sight,** so you need to keep your eyes on the numbers at all times. For example, think about how aircraft pilots deal with similar situations today. Pilots typically start out by getting a Visual Flight Rating (VFR), which allows them to fly by sight, and then receive their Instrument Flight Rating (IFR) so they can fly by instruments alone in situations such as nighttime and inclement weather conditions, which can render visibility to zero. IFR-rated pilots will commonly tell you that rule number one for flying by IFR is to **never take your eyes off your instruments. As a business professional, this should be your rule as well.**

The good news for most business professionals is that the tools needed to better measure your business today are far more plentiful and affordable than in the past, thanks largely to web-based technologies. The bad news is that the industry is still relatively fragmented, and even though many systems are designed to interoperate together, the interconnectivity is still cumbersome for most small-business professionals to understand and keep up with. When it comes to measurement tools, most professionals should have at least three systems in operation.

The first is a **sales opportunity management system,** commonly referred to today as a **"CRM"** or Customer Relationship Management system. The primary benefit of CRM systems are that they allow you to manage and track all leads and opportunities within your company; **the more sales activity**

you have, the greater the value of a CRM system. CRM systems also provide detailed sales analytics to help you break down all phases of your sales activity so you can track things like your sales pipelines, sales velocity, opportunities created and closed, new leads, etc., all in one system. For companies with a sales force, the activities of all of your salespeople can be rolled up at the company level as well in one CRM system. Some of the more popular CRM systems in use today by small business professionals include Salesforce.com, NetSuite, Infusionsoft, Bullhorn CRM, ProsperWorks CRM, and others.

The second measurement system is a **website analytics tool.** Website analytics allow you to track key data and activity on your website and web properties. In these tools you can analyze key data points such as unique visitors, conversion rates for both organic and paid (PPC) advertising, time-on-site data, referring-website data, webpage activity, bounce rates, etc. If you have a website today (which every business owner should have), you absolutely should have a website analytics tool measuring your website activity. Some of the more commonly used web analytics tools in use today by small-business professionals include Google Analytics, Clicky, CrazyEgg, ClickTale, and many others. By far the most widely used web analytics system today is **Google Analytics,** and for good reason: it is easy to set up, works well, and is free to use.

The third measurement system is for **conversion management.** Of all three systems, these are by far the most fragmented today but are also the fastest-growing in use. The challenge with conversion measurement today is that most reporting is unique to the tools in use. For example, phone systems will provide their own phone interaction data, videos will provide video activity data, chat will provide chat-session data, social media will provide their own data, and so forth. As many of these systems move to a cloud-based architecture, the ability to share this information through open APIs and RSS feeds will increase. For social media, we are also seeing the emergence of centralized social media systems managers like Hootsuite, which have the ability to report on many of your most important social media tools in one place. For larger organizations with greater resources, many will build custom web dashboards that can integrate data from many of these disparate systems. However, this is not something that is typically an option for most small-business owners and professionals due to the high costs to develop and maintain.

Pros:

- Systematic ways to measure what you manage in your business.

- Can provide key metrics to support and measure sales and marketing performance and innovation efforts.

- Many conversion systems today are web-based, easy to use, and very affordable.

Cons:

o The web-based-measurement-tools market is still relatively fragmented and involves a number of different systems and vendors, especially for conversion management.

o Initial setup and integration of even the most widely adopted web-based measurement tools today still requires some level of technical expertise to set up and run.

o Many business owners will not initially know what data is the most important to look at in these systems and why. Nor will they discipline themselves to effectively help run their business by them.

Best Practices:

1. **Start with Google Analytics for your website, especially if you plan on running Google Pay-Per-Click (PPC) advertising.** Google Analytics is by far the most widely adopted web analytics tool in use today. Setup is relatively easy, the interface and use is fairly intuitive for the average user, and best of all, it's free. Also, if you ever plan to run Google Pay-Per-Click (PPC) advertising, you will find the conversion and campaign traffic reporting for both your PPC and organic results to be invaluable. Google Analytics also has a great app that you can download that allows you to quickly access key data anywhere from your phone, including real-time site activity, which can be very helpful when on the move.

2. **Try to utilize cloud-based or software-as-a-service (SAAS) systems.** One of the greatest innovations to software was the movement of software systems to the web. This allowed companies to significantly scale their systems and drive down their costs, all of which

is to your benefit. Because of this, it is a good idea to run as many of your systems as possible, including Internet, phone, CRM, conversion management, business management, etc., through these web-based offerings. More important, web-based systems can now allow you to quickly scale your business for rapid and virtual growth if needed. This **can be a HUGE consideration for potential investors and buyers** who will frequently look at the growth potential of your business and how your systems can scale to support it.

3. **Follow the Keep-It-Simple-Stupid (KISS) principle when it comes to data analysis.** Most measurement systems today are designed to work for both large and small businesses, which means a great deal of the initial data reporting provided in these systems is simply "not critical" to most small-business owners and professionals. Because of this, you need to **define in advance what the Key Performance Indicators (KPIs) are for your business** before you look at all the system measurement data that may or may not be relevant to support it. Once you have your defined KPIs, you can look to the data provided to see what impacts each has on those numbers. In the end, focus the majority of your time on the key data that supports your KPIs. Otherwise it can and will get lost in the sea of data and systems in front of you.

4. **Track and trend your key measurement numbers over time.** Running a small-business can be over-whelming at times and far too often small-business

owners and professionals will be trending in a wrong direction long before they finally realize it, if they ever do. Because of this, you need to not only track your key numbers but trend them over time as well. For example, let's say you noticed over the past quarter that you had a 20 percent drop in new client sales—long after the quarter was over. You then start asking your sales manager what happened, and they don't know. You then ask your office staff, and they don't know. Now what? The potential answers can be many, but without the data to support it, you may never know until it is too late. Following this example, what if you were to look back in your phone and web analytics tools and noticed that during the same three months last year you had a similar drop in sales? And what if you noticed that the drop in calls started the first week of the quarter and just so happened to coincide with a similar seasonal drop in website traffic? By tracking and trending this type of information, you can see not only patterns develop but it can help you make adjustments when needed to better your business results.

PUBLIC SPEAKING

Most people have an innate fear of public speaking, **a fear that almost any one of us can overcome with experience and discipline**. Some people come to public speaking naturally while most do not. Because of this, good speakers are typically in high demand and therefore have a unique advantage in most industries in building up their own brand awareness and selling services.

One of the greatest advantages public speaking can provide you with is **leverage.** Leverage is the ability to multiply your sales efforts in a way that scales and maximizes your limited time and resources to its maximum effect. In sales, speaking is the difference between spending thirty minutes selling to one person versus selling to twenty, fifty, and even hundreds of people in the same time frame by speaking to them all at once.

One of the biggest mistakes many professionals make when speaking is not understanding what they are truly trying to accomplish when they speak. In most instances **you are directly selling your thoughts, insights, ideas, and yourself AND NOT your products and services when you are public speaking.** The ideas of what you are speaking about should typically lead your audience to the services you provide without overtly selling them in your speech. Most people don't want to listen to a thirty-minute selling infomercial, nor will they—this is not why people want to listen to public speakers. What people are looking for is unique insight from experts in their respective fields. That is where your true opportunity is with speaking. Most professional organizations will provide and help facilitate speakers at their meetings, conferences, seminars, and continuing-education programs to add value to their meetings and their members. Your goal as a professional should be to speak at these events to help establish yourself as an authority and help build your brand in your industry.

Most great speeches provide useful, unique, and entertaining information that is of value to both the audience and you. Remember, when you speak, **your audience is in effect paying you with their time.** In order for them to want to listen to you speak, you have to make that exchange of time mutually beneficial. The benefit for you is to help build up the awareness of the value of what your services can provide to your customers and how you are uniquely qualified to provide it to them. The goal is to get your audience to understand the "why" of your presentation and services, which will ultimately lead them to you as the provider of that service. This is important because **people will not buy what you do, but rather why you do it.**

Pros:
- **Great sales-time leveraging tool.** The multiplier effect of reaching a large audience in a short period of time is one of the greatest advantages to selling through speaking. Most people would tell you that 50 to 1 is a much better multiplier than 1 to 1.

- **Great brand building and exposure.** Advertising can provide you with exposure at a price but good public speaking can help define your brand and reputation with others and increase your exposure **at little or no cost at all.** If you are largely the brand of your service, then speaking allows you to establish your brand identity and potential referral exposure to other industry experts.

- **Typically provides a high return on investment (ROI) to speakers and their organizations.** Many good speakers will speak for free, but the elite among them will be paid relatively lucrative speaking fees to speak to select groups and organizations. Unlike other forms of advertising, the only real investment made by speakers is their time. Since speaking opportunities are a great way to help sell books and promote your business and services, there are few, if any, other forms of marketing that can provide this level of ROI potential.

Cons:

o **Requires experience to speak publicly effectively.** Most people don't come to public speaking naturally and many have fears they need to overcome before doing so. Like anything else, speaking requires learning, experience, and practice to master.

o **Requires some level of expertise in your field.** In order to get speaking roles, you need to have a reason people will want to listen to you. The value you can provide in speaking will come from the expertise and unique insights you can provide, which is why most people will seek out experts in their respective subjects to be the best sources for speaking. If you have not yet reached this level of authority, it can take time to develop it.

o **Requires access and exposure to people who coordinate speaking engagements.** Most public speakers get asked to speak over and over again because they have developed both a reputation as a valued speaker and have also developed connections with the people who coordinate speaking engagements. Initially developing this reputation and connections can take time and patience.

Best Practices:

1. When possible, **work the room before your speech.** Try to arrive early to introduce yourself, get names, shake hands, and set the mood for your room. Nothing is more impressive than **interjecting the names of people in your audience and your conversations with them into your speech.** To make this even more effective, look for Promoters in the room; they are typically the people who others congregate around and come up to. Get their names, have a brief conversation and ask them what they would like to get out of your speech, and then use it in your speech.

2. **Start out your speech with a bang.** Make a provocative statement that will get everybody thinking and more important will get their attention. Tell a powerful and personal story, add humor, or simply ask a question that gets people to think and challenges their conventional line of thinking. For example, one of my favorite introductions is, "I know what you're probably thinking: 'Oh great, I have to listen to this asshole for the next sixty minutes. But when you think about what a proctologist has to do every day it kind of makes the next sixty minutes of your life sound a lot better, now doesn't it?"

3. **The most important part of a presentation is the last five minutes,** so make it memorable and make sure it leads to a desired call to action.

4. **What you say is not as important as how you say it.** When you speak, only 7 percent of your impact will come from your words while 38 percent will come from your voice and **55 percent from your non-verbal communication.** So make sure your voice is confident and commanding and focus in on your non-verbal cues such as your appearance, eye contact, facial expressions, attitude, posture, gestures, and movement. If fully 93 percent of our communication comes from "how" you speak, why do people spend so much more time on the content of the speech and so little on the delivery?

5. **Use stories and parables in your speeches** to help solidify the points you most want your audience to remember. Stories are powerful because they give the audience a point of reference and association, which is why **63 percent of attendees will remember a story while only 5 percent will remember statistics.**[18] It also helps to keep them engaged in your speech and not wandering off in thought. Remember, **the typical attention span of an adult is only 15–30 seconds,** and stories will help keep their attention on you.

6. When utilizing references and PowerPoints in a presentation, **maximize your visuals and minimize your text.** People process visuals 60,000 times faster than

text, so give your audience something to look at and not something they need to read. Moreover, don't use slides that you have to read from—this is not a bedtime story.

7. **Practice, practice, practice,** and don't forget to practice. Remember, fortune favors the prepared mind, and you can never get enough practice in making a great speech. One of the keys of your speech should be to talk through the slides and not read from them. Know how to **make smooth and effective transitions** between slides and know how to incorporate stories within your slides. Know how to manage questions and your audience while giving your presentation and anticipate questions before you receive them. Most important, **practice how to remain cool, confident, and in control in any situation.** Trust me; after speaking for many years now I have learned through experience that you can always expect the unexpected when speaking.

8. When possible, try to **avoid speaking in the few hours after lunch** and late in the evening at the end of a series of speakers. These are the times when people are more physically exhausted, **making it harder for you to capture and keep their attention.**

9. **Limit the information in your speech.** Most people pack far too much information into a speech and then find themselves rushing through it just to finish on time. This rushing commonly results in fewer memorable stories, fewer questions, faster talking, and

fewer key points that you want your audience to take away from your speech.

10. **Always be respectful of time limitations.** Even if your time is unexpectedly shortened by somebody other than you, be respectful of other people's time. Be prepared where to cut your speech short if needed and always treat the time and limitations of the audience with a higher regard then your own. If they want you to speak longer they will ask you. If not, stick to the deadlines.

11. **Always have a good attitude no matter what.** Attitudes are contagious. Therefore, your attitude sets the tone for the entire audience. If you stay cool, relaxed, and seem happy to be there, your audience will reciprocate and respond the same way.

TRADE SHOWS AND CONVENTIONS

In a world where every product and service provider increasingly gravitates to going online and into the ether, trade shows provide centralization to an increasingly decentralized business world. Trade shows allow customers and businesses to congregate in a centralized marketplace to better network and learn about products, services, and best practices in a focused environment. Trade shows have been around since the dark ages, but with the adoption of the Internet and a world of information online, they are changing.

Most industries have their own trade shows and conventions that tend to meet annually, semi-annually, or even quarterly. Trade shows are typically a giant circus of vendors and prospective customers all in one place at one time. Over the years, many shows have moved to destination locations like Las Vegas, Orlando, and other exciting places to provide added personal incentives to attend. Others have brought in marquee celebrities and speakers. Even annual shareholder meetings like Berkshire Hathaway's and Salesforce.com's have grown to resemble traditional trade shows in structure, draw, and even include associated vendor participation.

Pros:

- **Good way to get industry exposure and brand awareness.** Many smaller businesses fight for exposure and advertising that can match their larger rivals. Trade shows, although infrequent, can be effective ways to place your business alongside your major competitors for more equal consideration and exposure.

- **Relatively easy to track direct return on investment (ROI) from leads produced from a trade show.** Unlike many marketing mediums today, most sales made at trade shows tend to be easy to track to the source and therefore easier to quantify an ROI around. This might be one reason marketing departments continue to throw money at them despite some dubious historical results.

Cons:

o **Typically involves a high level of cost, time, and resources to participate and facilitate.** Trade shows commonly require a booth that must be created, packed, shipped, unpacked, set up, taken down, and then shipped back again. All of this takes a lot of time and money in addition to the fees to exhibit and advertise at the show. Then you have your people who must travel in, be housed, fed, entertained, compensated, and taken away from their normal duties—including your own. Finally, what do all your giveaways and materials cost? It all adds up, and fast.

o **Higher levels of competition require more uniqueness to stand out.** Just because you may now be side-by-side with other major vendors and competitors doesn't mean you will stand out to your potential customers. Larger businesses that are frequent trade show participants will commonly have more experience, time, and resources to better stand out at future shows—especially if they are well attended and therefore more expensive. Moreover, many of these larger vendors will also pre-pay for premium trade show floor spaces years in advance just to get the best visibility.

Best Practices:

1. **Only attend well-known trade shows, not new ones.** Well-known trade shows already have a brand, reputation, and following, versus new shows, which do not. Don't run the risk with your valuable time and money to attend an unknown event. If you were wrong, you can always attend next year.

2. **Promote your participation in the show.** If you plan to use the show to promote and sell your services, make sure that all of your customers and prospects know you will be there in advance. More important, make sure your promoters and potential promoters know you will be there as well and have a reason to stop by. Whenever possible, try to get a copy of the show's attendee list prior to the event and send them an invitation to your booth—with an added incentive, of course.

3. **Create new buzz at the show.** Do you have any new exciting services or breaking news you want to release? Why not time it to release at the show? Most event promoters want to talk about what is unique and great about their shows and this is your chance to help them do it—with your unique and exciting news.

4. **Get a speaking or panel appearance at the show.** Most shows have special breakouts and featured speakers that are the focus of the shows. Your goal either now or at future shows is to be a part of both. Find out who the event coordinators are long before the agenda is set for the next show and ask them what they need and how you can become a speaker and be on panels for their upcoming shows.

5. **Prepare and incent your trade show team.** Most people dread standing in trade show booths for countless hours, so why not incent them to be more engaged? If the goal of exhibiting is to generate new sales, how about a sales contest where the person

with the most sales closed at the show wins a $500 gift card? If the goal is building awareness, how about a gift card for the person who is able to collect the most business cards or potential sales prospects at the show? Give your people a real reason to want to be engaged at the show, not to just arrive and imitate a statue.

6. **Find unique ways to draw traffic to your booth.** Your goal at a trade show should be to stand out from the crowd. A trade show should not be a lemming convention, but that is exactly what most vendors let it become. You need to find ways to be different. **Figure out what pains attendees and prospective customers feel the most at each show and find unique ways to address it.** If people are thirsty, offer free drinks and bottles of water. If they are hungry, offer free popcorn or snacks. If you decide to give away tchotchkes, make them unique and something they will likely use over and over again—with your name on it. Remember, the best tchotchkes are the ones people will see and use the most every day. If your customers work in an office, provide them with items that will sit on their desks. If they work out of their cars, give them something they can use there. Bottom line: Get creative, think useful, and don't give out free candy bars at a dental convention and throwing knives to personal-injury attorneys.

7. **Follow up on trade show leads ASAP.** Most people at shows will meet a lot of people—and I mean *a lot.*

If they meet you, they will soon forget you if you forget about following up with them first. Their first measure of your level of service is your follow-up with potential customers, so start showing your prospects why they should work with you now by being the first to follow up after a show. In order to effectively do this, it is a good idea **to have your trade show team meet at the end of each day and review all leads received for next steps and notes.** As a rule of thumb, **no trade show lead should sit without action for longer than three days.**

8. **Create professional name tags and take them with you everywhere.** Most people who do networking and trade shows will fill out a less-than-professional-looking name tag that is often written by hand and only includes your name. Conversely, a professional name tag can be created once and can include your name, your business's name, business branding and colors, a QR code, and will make you stand out from the crowd. Once created, **keep your name tag in your bag, purse, or whatever you have with you most when working,** and always use your professional name tag when you have the option.

PRINTED SALES COLLATERAL

Here is something most marketing managers don't want you to hear: **Salespeople consider between 80 and 90 percent of the sales collateral and marketing material provided to them today to be useless.**[37] To add further insult to injury, other studies have shown that 86 percent of executives say that a salesperson's message has no commercial impact on them.[38] What all of this helps illustrate is how sales and marketing are NOT commonly aligned in most companies. Steve Jobs spoke to the core of this problem when he stated that, "You've got to start with the customer experience and work back toward the technology—not the other way around." Unfortunately for most marketing and salespeople today, we train and operate the other way around. But you should not fall prey to this trap.

Your sales collateral should always speak to one key point; **the value (or the "why") your services provides to your target customers.** Instead of focusing in on this key point, most product and marketing people will spew out all the great features and capabilities of their services; something that typically has nothing to do with generating **curiosity, obligation, and urgency**—the three most important aspects of effective prospecting. If your sales collateral speaks to "why" the customer needs your services and the benefits they can receive from its utilization, then you will be able to talk about all the great features of your services after the sales process has begun; if it is even comes up at that point. Remember, **most services are invisible during a sales process and are nothing more than a promise of a benefit and gain delivered through a relationship with the customer**—which is what people are really buying from you in the end.

Sales collateral is also expensive to produce and today ends up in far more landfills than sales processes. So don't waste much time here. Ideally, any useful collateral you create should be in PDF format for easy updating, downloading, and printing from your website. This will also allow you to print on demand as needed for those times when you need something for people to temporarily hold on to until it ends up in the trash.

Pros:

- **Good way to outline and introduce new services and capabilities provided.** There will be times when people cannot access your website for information about your services. This might be in waiting areas, trade shows, and with documentation folders/mailers that include forms and bills. Collateral in waiting rooms can also help introduce new services to the customer during their "idle time" when they may be waiting for other services instead.

Cons:

o **Relatively high cost to produce.** Printing high-quality sales collateral is not cheap. Many times small-business professionals don't know how much to produce so they go for the big-volume discounts and end up with a whole bunch of colorful kindling instead.

o **Collateral can quickly become outdated and obsolete once produced.** Once you change any aspect of your services, what you had previously printed about it has now become obsolete. The more your services change, the worse this problem can become.

o **Collateral typically finds its way into a landfill faster than a sales process.** Most people have enough clutter in their lives, and when it comes to sales collateral, most people have only one file folder for it and that is their trash can.

Best Practices:

1. **Place your sales collateral online, preferably in PDF documents.** Use something simple and easy like a Microsoft Word document as the source of your file and convert it to a PDF for easy publishing. That way when you need to make quick updates, you can easily do so at the source, reconvert to PDF, and replace the old one online with no new printing costs, no updating your shelves, and no needless delays. Remember, most things in the world today are moving to an on-demand model and so should your collateral.

2. If you have to print collateral, focus on printing to **support newer services and complementary offerings** to your more standard-known services. Put these printed materials in areas like **waiting rooms** and **in bills that are mailed out to your customers**—anywhere you have a more captive audience.

3. **Don't go crazy with the amount of collateral you produce.** Most small-business professionals will tell you that more of what they have printed ended up in the trash than with customers and prospects. Use moderation and not emotion when ordering; you can always print more later if needed.

NEWSLETTERS

Newsletters are one of the most effect tools to enable a customer-reselling process. Historically, newsletters were costly and time consuming to produce and distribute by mail, but with email and the Internet, emailed newsletters have become much more cost effective and beneficial. The greatest benefit most businesses receive from newsletters is **being kept consistently in front of their clients, prospects, and referrals.** Emailed newsletters can be managed both internally and externally, and based on the results, there is no reason why any business—no matter how small—should not have a newsletter.

Pros:

- **Can provide a very good return on investment (ROI),** especially when reselling to existing customers.
- **Great way to build branding and frequency.** One of the biggest benefits of newsletters is that they nurture leads and opportunities and make them more convertible. The Direct Mail Association has shown that for every month you don't communicate with your customers, the value of that customer diminishes by 10 percent.[39] So if you haven't communicated with your customers in ten months, that customer is about as cold as a new sales prospect.
- **Good way to establish yourself as a potential thought leader and trusted advisor.**

- Great way to produce boomerang sales from stalled sales opportunities.

- **Acts as another source to republish active content used on the web.** Duplicate-content penalties for the republishing of content only apply to the web, not emails and print. This is why many CPA newsletters are canned and used countless times over. If you are publishing information on your blogs, press releases, etc., make sure to repurpose that content in your newsletters as well so you can maximize their effectiveness in your marketing.

- **Can provide actionable sales insight based on recipients' actions.** Most commonly used email newsletter providers can now supply you with real-time reports of when specific people have either opened or clicked on a newsletter you have sent.

Cons:

o **Requires time and discipline to consistently produce and publish monthly.** Somebody has to write the content, create the newsletter formats, import and update your email list, send it out, and follow up on the actions. This can take a lot of work, so you need to be prepared to handle it. Otherwise, use a third-party service to do most of this for you.

o **Can require some basic computer skills in creating a newsletter.** Most email newsletter systems today are pretty easy to use, but only to the average-to-more-advanced computer user. For example, if you are not comfortable with using images and layouts, you may want to consider a third party to help you if you want truly professional-looking newsletters.

Best Practices:

1. As a general rule of thumb, try to **send out your email newsletter once a month** to all of your customers, prospects, and referral contacts. If you want to send out a physical newsletter, try to send them out once every six months in addition to your regular monthly email newsletters.

2. When sending out emailed newsletters, ideally you should see **open rates in the range of 20–40 percent and a click-through rate (CTR) of at least 2 percent.** The higher the CTR the better you are doing.

3. There are **a lot of great email newsletter systems online you can use today.** To find them, simply Google "email newsletter service" and you will see the results. At the time of this book, common choices include MailChimp, Constant Contact, and GetResponse. These services are great because they help you stay compliant with CAN-SPAM laws and allow people to automatically unsubscribe through their service. Many of these services also provide newsletter sign-up forms that you can easily add to your website, blogs, etc., to help build your subscriber base over time.

4. When sending out newsletters using the most common email newsletter providers, **keep track of email "opens" and "clicks" from their reports and act on**

them. These are typically "warmer" leads and, depending on the email, can trigger follow-up actions that can help lead to a sale.

5.   When using newsletter service providers, **be careful of the lists you provide them with to use.** If the list is of poor quality, they could notify you or even suspend your account.

6.   If you are trying to activate inactive customers, **include a special offer** in the newsletter that **expires 7–10 days** from the date of receiving your newsletter.

7.   Make sure that the majority of the content in your newsletter is **NOT SALESY, but rather useful information to your customers** and prospects so they will want to read your newsletters instead of feeling like they are being sold to.

WRITING A BOOK

Somebody once told me that if you want to really get noticed, write a book. And they were right! After I published my first book, I was amazed at the responses I received from people; many of which treated me like I had just run a four-minute mile. Not only was the book a success, it opened countless doors to people and new opportunities that I never would have imagined before becoming a published author. What this goes to illustrate is that few if any marketing tools can provide such returns as what you can receive from publishing a successful book.

Another potential benefit to publishing a book is the ability to **help solidify your credentials as an expert in your chosen**

specialized field. For example, there are plenty of books on being a lawyer and even being an estate-planning lawyer, but how many books are written on a breach of fiduciary duty surrounding estates? When Paul Rheingold wrote the first book on mass tort litigation, what do you think it did for his reputation and business as a mass tort lawyer? Or what do you suppose having Howard Farran's *Dentaltown* magazine mailed to over 120,000 dentists each month is doing for his brand and notoriety?

Finally, you don't have to have a great agent or publisher to get your book published today. Thanks to the Internet and new printing on demand (POD) technologies, **literally anybody can now produce professional books online** and have them printed on demand at the time of their order. For example, CreateSpace and Lulu are well-known self-publishing websites, with CreateSpace having the added advantage of currently being owned by the largest online bookstore in the world: Amazon.com. Self-publishing also allows you to potentially earn more money from your book by retaining any royalties you would have to pay to a big-house publisher.

However, the advantage of using a more well-known traditional publishing house is the added credibility and exposure it can provide to you and your book. The challenge is that breaking into the traditional publishing world can be very difficult, time consuming, and frustrating for first-time publishers. The larger publishing houses also have **access to physical bookstores and can help you scale and sell more books fast, which is the business goal for most publishers.** Remember, they are in the business to make money, so they will want to buy your book as low as possible and try to sell it to as large a market as possible—while using you and your resources to help them sell it.

If you are insistent on having a major publishing house review your book proposal, you will most likely need to use a literary agent to get their attention and help to get you in the door. Most publishing houses receive a lot of proposals every day and your chance of getting their attention unsolicited is very small. If, on the other hand, you use a literary agent who knows these people and can get you in the door, then you just became a warmer lead for them. But this will come at a cost. Most literary agents work on commission, commonly 15 percent of your take, which means they have skin in the game as well, and they don't get paid until you get paid. Agents also add value as an advisor in both the publishing process as well as in any subsequent speaking engagements that could come after it.

Pros:
- **Unique way to establish yourself as an authority and expert in your field.** To many people, writing a book is a rite of passage that most will never achieve in their careers, despite their stated desires to the contrary.

- **Can provide better access to speaking and publishing outlets.** A speaker who is a published author typically has more credibility than someone who is not. A book also allows you to turn speaking engagements into another potential revenue source by giving you another venue to sell your book/s.

- **Can provide an additional revenue source for your current work.** Successful books sell, which means added income for you. This requires that you actively promote the book in order to help make this happen.

- **It is much easier to publish today through self-publishing.** Most major publishers will say "no" many times over, but most self-publishing services will not. So you will always have an option.

Cons:

o **Requires a great amount of time, discipline, and resources to complete.** Most people either don't start writing a book or simply give up when they realize how large of a time commitment it really is. And believe me—it is! If you are writing a book, it can greatly take away from your personal time, so you need to make sure that you and your dependents know this and expect it before it happens.

o **Most new authors have to "learn the ropes" of the publishing process.** Most new writers get excited about writing a book until they get to the endless editing, proofing, copyright registration, ISBN designations, cover designing, promotion, and all the other fun stuff that will commonly take more of your time to initially complete than the time it took to write your book.

Best Practices:

1. **Create a plan and stick to it.** Whatever time you initially think it will take to publish your first book,

triple it so you and your loved ones really know what to expect. There are a lot of great books and websites on the steps to publishing a book; far more information than I can provide here. To help motivate yourself, create a simple cover of what you think your book cover could look like, print it out, and place it prominently above your desk so you never forget that your goal is to complete that book, period.

2. **Try for publishers and plan for self-publishing.** Wouldn't it be great to get published by the big publishers? Well, what if you don't? Just because you may receive rejections from the publishers shouldn't mean you can't get self-published instead. Always have a backup plan so no matter what happens, the book WILL go to print. Many great authors and books were both initially rejected and started as self-published works before they made it big, so DON'T GIVE UP!

3. **Get plenty of good endorsements.** Most people will read endorsements on a book for a reason—they want to know the credibility and potential value of the book. After all, **you are asking people to not only pay you for your book but to continue to pay with their time to read it.** So it better be worth it to them, right? Since most first-time authors are relative unknowns outside of their circles, it is a good idea to leverage other people who are well known to help give credibility to your book. Create a list of well-known people relative to the book

subject and ask them to review your work and provide a quote for it. If your book is good enough and you reach enough people, you might be surprised at who responds—I certainly was.

4. **Promotion of your book is key!** Publishers will ask you the same thing you should ask yourself: **How do you plan to promote and sell your book?** Plan on promoting and pre-promoting your new book to make a splash. Build a website to support it. Speak to promote it. Send advance copies to key promoters to have them help you promote it. There is nearly nothing you can do to promote your book too much, so start planning now and get out the word.

5. **Sell your book on the world's largest online bookstore: Amazon.com.** It is not hard to create an account on Amazon.com to sell your book. Since they also own CreateSpace, users of this Print-on-Demand (POD) service may find the integration with Amazon even more effective and compelling. Once your book is listed for sale, get as many reader reviews as possible for your book listing on Amazon.com. The more good things people have to say about your book, the better the chances you will have of other people wanting to buy it when they see it listed there.

6. **Don't think this will be your last book.** After I published my first book, I had lunch with a well-known bestselling author who had endorsed my book and he informed me that it took his fourth book to hit it big

as a published author. And even that book initially started out slow. His advice was to enjoy the journey and not the destination. The fact that you are now reading my second book speaks to this truth.

MY RECOMMENDED BOOKS
AND READING LIST

• • •

"Leaders are readers."—Harry S. Truman

Learning should never stop. The minute you stop learning is the minute you stop innovating. If you are not innovating, you are not growing—in business and in life. It is commonly said that people use only 10 percent of their brains, and based on many of the top "entertainment" TV programs we waste our time watching for hours on end each day, I believe it. If you want to become successful, you need to **learn how to become successful.**

When I endeavored to build my first race cars in my early teens, I was constantly asked by others how I knew how to build high-performance engines and race cars. The fact is I initially didn't know much at all and therefore needed to learn. But what allowed me to learn how to do it were all of the books and publications I read and questions I asked of others who did know. As a result, I quickly learned at a very early age that all of the knowledge I needed to accomplish nearly anything I wanted in life was already out there; most of which is published and freely available. Absent the ability to read, **there is no excuse why anybody cannot learn nearly anything they need to learn based on the published learnings of others.**

I have established a personal goal to read at least two books a month. I do not read fiction, and my goals in reading each book are to learn and grow. I have countless boxes of books in my garage to attest to this goal. I believe that it is just as important to exercise the mind as we do the body, and reading is the best way to exercise my mind on a constant basis.

Since I am frequently asked what business books I would recommend to others, I have created a list below of some of my favorite books that I have read over recent years based on various business-related categories:

Sales

- *Sell Yourself First: The Most Critical Element in Every Sales Effort*. Thomas A. Freese, 2010.

- *How To Sell Anything To Anybody*. Joe Girard with Stanley H. Brown, 2005

- *The Challenger Sale: How to Take Control of the Customer Conversation*. Matthew Dixon and Brent Adamson, 2011

- *How to Win Customers and Keep Them for Life*. Michael LeBoeuf, Ph.D., 1987

- *Real Leaders Don't Do Power Point: How to Sell Yourself and Your Ideas*. Christopher Witt with Dale Fetherling, 2009

- *Endless Referrals: Network Your Everyday Contacts into Sales*, Third Edition. Bob Burg, 2006
- *Winning With Integrity: Getting What You're Worth Without Selling Your Soul.* Leigh Steinberg and Michael D'Orso, 1998

Communications / Productivity

- *How To Win Friends & Influence People: The Only Book You Need to Lead You to Success.* Dale Carnegie, 1981.
- *The Power of Habit: Why We Do What We Do in Life and Business.* Charles Duhigg, 2012
- *The 4-Hour Workweek: Escape 9–5, Live Anywhere, and Join the New Rich.* Timothy Ferriss, 2007.

Hiring

- *Never Hire a Bad Salesperson Again—Selecting Candidates Who Are Absolutely Driven to Succeed.* Dr. Christopher Croner and Richard Abraham, 2006
- *The Successful Sales Manager: A Sales Manager's Handbook for Building Great Sales Performance.* Dustin W. Ruge, 2014

Business

- *The E-Myth Revisited: Why Most Small Businesses Don't Work and What to Do About It.* Michael E. Gerber, 1995
- *The Loyalty Effect: The Hidden Force Behind Growth, Profits, and Lasting Value.* Frederick F. Reichheld and Thomas Teal, 1996

- *The Google Story: Inside the Hottest Business, Media and Technology Success of Our Time*. David A. Vise and Mark Malseed, 2005, 2008.

- *NUTS!: Southwest Airlines' Crazy Recipe for Business and Personal Success*. Kevin & Jackie Freiberg, 1996

- *Grinding It Out: The Making of McDonald's*. Ray Kroc with Robert Anderson, 1977

- *Sam Walton: Made in America*. Sam Walton and John Huey, 1992

- *Leadership Secrets of Attila the Hun*. Wess Roberts, Ph.D., 1985

NOTES AND REFERENCES

• • •

Introduction

1.) Eric T. Wagner, 2013. "Five Reasons 8 Out of 10 Businesses Fail." *Forbes*. http://www.forbes.com/sites/ericwagner/2013/09/12/five-reasons-8-out-of-10-businesses-fail (accessed June 6, 2015)

2.) "Pareto Principle." *Wikipedia*, 2014. http://en.wikipedia.org/wiki/Pareto_principle (accessed July 21, 2014)

Chapter 1: Sales Planning: The Roadmap to Sales Success

1.) David A. Peoples, 1993. *Selling to the Top*. New York: John Wiley & Sons 10:217

2.) Dan Perry, 2011. "Sales Management: 3 Ways Sales Management Can Stop Obsessing Over the Forecast." *Sales Benchmark Index*.

www.salesbenchmarkindex.com/bid/72183/3-Ways-Sales-Management-Can-Stop-Obsessing-Over-the-Forecast (accessed April 2, 2014)

3.) Mark H. McCormack, 1984. *What They Don't Teach You at Harvard Business School.* New York: Bantam Books

4.) Greg McKeown, 2012. "The Disciplined Pursuit of Less." *Harvard Business Review: HBR Blog Network.* blogs.hbr.org/2012/08/the-disciplined-pursuit-of-less/ (accessed April 2, 2014)

5.) Frederick F. Reichheld and Thomas Teal, 1996. *The Loyalty Effect: The Hidden Force Behind Growth, Profits, and Lasting Value.* Boston: Harvard Business School Press

Chapter 2: Prospecting: Creating Awareness and Prospects for Your Business

1. BuzzBuilder Lead Generation Software, 2013. "20 Shocking Sales Stats That Will Change How You Sell." *Slideshare.* www.slideshare.net/JakeAtwood1/20-shocking-sales-stats (accessed March 8, 2014)

2. Pamela Vaughan, 2012. "30 Thought-Provoking Lead Nurturing Stats You Can't Ignore." *HubSpot Blogs.* http://blog.hubspot.com/blog/tabid/6307/bid/30901/30-Thought-Provoking-Lead-Nurturing-Stats-You-Can-t-Ig-nore.aspx (accessed June 6, 2015)

3. Frederick F. Reichheld and Thomas Teal, 1996. *The Loyalty Effect: The Hidden Force Behind Growth, Profits, and Lasting Value.* Boston: Harvard Business School Press 8:327

4. "The Net Promoter Score and System." *Satmetrix Net Promoter Community*, 2015. http://www.netpromoter.com/why-net-promoter/know (accessed June 6, 2015)

5. "From Promotion to Emotion: Connecting B2B Customers to Brands." CEB Marketing Leadership Council, 2013. http://www.executiveboard.com/exbd-resources/content/b2b-emotion/pdf/promotion-emotion-whitepaper-full.pdf (accessed June 6, 2015)

6. Lonny Cocina, 2006. "The Average American Is Exposed To . . ." *Media Relations Inc.* http://www.publicity.com/ad-vicetips/the-average-american-is-exposed-to (accessed June 6, 2015)

7. BuzzBuilder Lead Generation Software, 2013. "20 Shocking Sales Stats That Will Change How You Sell." *Slideshare.* www.slideshare.net/JakeAtwood1/20-shocking-sales-stats (accessed March 8, 2014)

8. "Emails expected to rise to 140 a day by 2018." News.com.au, 2014. http://www.news.com.au/finance/work/emails-expected-to-rise-to-140-a-day-in-2018/story-e6frfm9r-1226904239876 (accessed June 6, 2015)

9. Allison Schiff, 2012. "DMA: Direct mail response rates beat digital." *Direct Marketing News*. http://www.dmnews.com/direct-mail/dma-direct-mail-response-rates-beat-digital/article/245780/ (accessed June 6, 2015)

Chapter 3: Sales Process: Create and Follow a Standard Sales Process

1.) Michael E. Gerber, 1995. *The E-Myth Revisited: Why Most Small Businesses Don't Work and What to Do About It*. New York: Harper Business 16:221

2.) "Conversations That Win Executive Insights." *Slideshare*. Corporate Visions, 2013. . http://www.slideshare.net/CorporateVisions/conversations-that-win-executive-insights (accessed June 6, 2015)

3.) BuzzBuilder Lead Generation Software, 2013. "20 Shocking Sales Stats That Will Change How You Sell." *Slideshare*. www.slideshare.net/JakeAtwood1/20-shocking-sales-stats (accessed March 8, 2014)

4.) Michael LeBoeuf, Ph.D., 1988. *How to Win Customers & Keep Them for Life*. New York: Berkley Business 15:130

Chapter 4: Selling Effectiveness: Turning Your Prospects into Customers

1.) "The Golden Circle Clip." TED: Simon Sinek—The "Golden Circle" Clip. *YouTube*, 2012.

www.youtube.com/watch?v=l5Tw0PGcyN0
(accessed January 28, 2014)

2.) BuzzBuilder Lead Generation Software, 2013. "20 Shocking Sales Stats That Will Change How You Sell." *Slideshare*. www.slideshare.net/JakeAtwood1/20-shocking-sales-stats (accessed March 8, 2014)

3.) Joe Girard with Stanley H. Brown, 2005. *How to Sell Anything to Anybody*. New York: FIRESIDE

4.) Janine Willis and Alexander Todorov, 2005. "First Impression: Making Up Your Mind After a 100-Ms Exposure to a Face." Princeton University. http://psych.princeton.edu/psychology/research/todorov/pdf/Willis%26Todorov-Psych-Science.pdf (accessed June 6, 2015)

5.) Pon Staff, 2011. "How facial expressions affect trust." *Harvard Law School Daily Blog*. http://www.pon.harvard.edu/daily/negotiation-skills-daily/how-facial-expressions-affect-trust/ (accessed June 6, 2015)

6.) "Would I Lie to You? (Engineering Trust with your Face)." *Social Capital Blog*, 2008. https://socialcapital.wordpress.com/2008/08/20/would-i-lie-to-you-engineering-trust-with-your-face/ (accessed June 6, 2015)

7.) Matthew Dixon and Brent Adamson, 2011. *The Challenger Sale: How to Take Control of the Customer Conversation*. New York: Penguin Group 6:101-118

8.) Tom Riley, 2008. "First Impression: When You Can't Compete on Price." *NAHAD News*. http://www.nahad.org/aws/nahad/asset_manager/get_file /36375 (accessed January 21, 2015)

9.) Amanda Sibley, 2012. "19 Reasons You Should Include Visual Content in Your Marketing." *HubSpot Blogs*. http://blog.hubspot.com/blog/tabid/6307/bid/33423/19-Reasons-You-Should-Include-Visual-Content-in-Your-Marketing-Data.aspx (accessed June 6, 2015)

Chapter 5: Closing the Sale: Where It All Pays You

1.) BuzzBuilder Lead Generation Software, 2013. "20 Shocking Sales Stats That Will Change How You Sell." *Slideshare*. www.slideshare.net/JakeAtwood1/20-shocking-sales-stats (accessed March 8, 2014)

2.) Ken Krogue, 2012. "Why Companies Waste 71% Of Internet Leads." *Forbes*. http://www.forbes.com/sites/kenkrogue/2012/07/12/the-black-hole-that-executives-dont-know-about (accessed June 6, 2015)

3.) "The Ultimate Contact Strategy: How to Use Phone and Email for Contact and Conversion Success." *Velocify*, 2015. http://pages.velocify.com/rs/leads360/images/Ultimate-Contact-Strategy.pdf (accessed June 6, 2015)

Chapter 6: Marketing Success: How to Make It Rain

1.) Frederick F. Reichheld and Thomas Teal, 1996. *The Loyalty Effect: The Hidden Force Behind Growth, Profits, and Lasting Value.* Boston: Harvard Business School Press 1:4

2.) Jake Sorofman, 2014. "Gartner Surveys Confirm Customer Experience Is the New Battlefield." *Gartner.*
http://blogs.gartner.com/jake-sorofman/gartner-surveys-confirm-customer-experience-new-battlefield
(accessed June 6, 2015)

3.) Pamela Vaughan, 2012. "30 Thought-Provoking Lead Nurturing Stats You Can't Ignore." *HubSpot Blogs.*
http://blog.hubspot.com/blog/tabid/6307/bid/30901/30-Thought-Provoking-Lead-Nurturing-Stats-You-Can-t-Ignore.aspx (accessed June 6, 2015)

4.) BuzzBuilder Lead Generation Software, 2013. "20 Shocking Sales Stats That Will Change How You Sell." *Slideshare.*
www.slideshare.net/JakeAtwood1/20-shocking-sales-stats
(accessed March 8, 2014)

Chapter 7: Marketing Resources: So Many Choices!

1.) Melissa Miller, 2012. "Inbound Leads Cost 61% Less Than Outbound." *HubSpot Blogs.*
http://blog.hubspot.com/blog/tabid/6307/bid/31555/Inbound-Leads-Cost-61-Less-Than-Outbound-New-Data.aspx
(accessed June 6, 2015)

2.) "Keep Them Coming Back to Your Website." *Mompreneur Magazine*, 2015. Blog, http://themompreneur.com/blog/2015/05/27/keep-them-coming-back-to-your-website (accessed June 6, 2015)

3.) *Maxymiser*, 2013. "Maxymiser Study Reveals Customer Experience Is Critical for Mobile Engagement." *Marketwired*. http://www.marketwired.com/press-release/maxymiser-study-reveals-customer-experience-is-critical-for-mobile-en-gagement-1825233.htm (accessed June 6, 2015)

4.) Eric Siu, 2012. "24 Eye-Popping SEO Statistics." *Search Engine Journal*. http://www.searchenginejournal.com/24-eye-popping-seo-statistics/42665 (accessed June 6, 2015)

5.) Modulates.com, 2012. "A Minute of Video Is Worth 1.8 Million Words, According to Forrester Research." *Yahoo! Finance News*. http://finance.yahoo.com/news/minute-video-worth-1-8-130000033.html (accessed June 6, 2015)

6.) Jennifer Dunphy, 2012. "How Video Marketing Powers SEO." *Econsultancy Blog*. https://econsultancy.com/blog/9583-how-video-market-ing-powers-seo/html (accessed June 6, 2015)

7.) Dan Zarella, 2010. "Which Types of Form Fields Lower Landing Page Conversions?" *HubSpot Blogs*. http://blog.hub-spot.com/blog/tabid/6307/bid/6746/Which-Types-of-Form-Fields-Lower-Landing-Page-Conversions.aspx (accessed June 6, 2015)

8.) "Limelight Networks Research Identifies Mobile Commerce Features That Will Drive Conversions This Holiday Season and Beyond." *Limelight Networks*, 2011. http://investors.limelightnetworks.com/press-release/lime-light-networksr-research-identifies-mobile-commerce-fea-tures-will-drive-conversion (accessed June 6, 2015)

9.) Doug Aamoth, 2013. "Study Says We Unlock Our Phones a LOT Each Day." *Time*. http://techland.time.com/2013/10/08/study-says-we-un-lock-our-phones-a-lot-each-day (accessed June 6, 2015)

10.) "The Ultimate List of Marketing Statistics." *HubSpot.com*. http://www.hubspot.com/marketing-statistics (accessed June 6, 2015)

11.) Nathania Johnson, 2008. "93% of Americans Expect Companies to Have Social Media Presence." *Search Engine Watch*. http://searchenginewatch.com/sew/study/2053421/93-americans-expect-companies-have-social-media-presence# (accessed June 6, 2015)

12.) "Fun Facts." *IACP Center For Social Media*, 2013. http://www.iacpsocialmedia.org/Resources/FunFacts.aspx (accessed June 6, 2015)

13.) Craig Smith, 2015. "By the Numbers: 80+ Amazing YouTube Statistics." *DMR* http://expandedramblings.com/index.php/youtube-statis-tics (accessed June 6, 2015)

14.) Michael E. Gerber, 1995. *The E-Myth Revisited: Why Most Small Businesses Don't Work and What to Do About It.* New York: Harper Business 16:221

15.) Caitlin Dewey, 2013. "The 60 million Americans who don't use the Internet, in six charts." *The Washington Post Blogs,* http://www.washingtonpost.com/blogs/the-switch/wp/2013/08/19/the-60-million-americans-who-dont-use-the-internet-in-six-charts (accessed June 6, 2015)

16.) Dayna Rothman, 2013. "Email: Wanted Dead or Alive [infographic]." *Marketo Blog,* http://blog.marketo.com/2013/07/email-wanted-dead-or-alive-infographic.html (accessed June 6, 2015)

17.) "Email Marketing." *Wikipedia.* http://en.wikipedia.org/wiki/Email_marketing#cite_note-7 (accessed June 6, 2015)

18.) BuzzBuilder Lead Generation Software, 2013. "20 Shocking Sales Stats That Will Change How You Sell." *Slideshare.* www.slideshare.net/JakeAtwood1/20-shocking-sales-stats (accessed March 8, 2014)

19.) Christopher Lester, 2014. "7 Stats That Prove Email Is Here To Stay (And Power Your Business)." *HuffPost Business, The Blog.* http://www.huffingtonpost.com/christopher-lester/7-stats-that-prove-email-_b_5614903.html (accessed June 6, 2015)

20.) "CAN-SPAM Act of 2003." *Wikipedia.* http://en.wikipedia.org/wiki/CAN-SPAM_Act_of_2003 (accessed June 6, 2015)

21.) Katie Franklin, 2014. "Believe It: Video Email Marketing Will Increase Click-Through Rates." *Envision Creative Group*. http://www.envision-creative.com/video-email-marketing-will-increase-click-through-rates (accessed June 6, 2015)

22.) Amanda Nelson, 2013. "25 Mind Blowing Email Marketing Stats." *Salesforce blog*. https://www.salesforce.com/blog/2013/07/email-marketing-stats.html (accessed June 6, 2015)

23.) Etix, 2015. "8 Ways To Drive ROI With Email Marketing Automation." *Slideshare*. http://www.slideshare.net/etixworld/8-ways-to-drive-roi-with-email-marketing-automation (accessed June 6, 2015)

24.) The Annuitas Group, 2011. "The Lead Management Framework." *Slideshare*. http://www.slideshare.net/CAnnuitas/the-annuitas-group-lead-management-framework-sm (accessed June 6, 2015)

25.) Aberdeen Group, 2015. "Email Marketing: Get Personal With Your Customers." http://www.aberdeen.com/research/4904/ra-email-marketing/content.aspx (accessed June 6, 2015)

26.) "Q&A For Telemarketers & Sellers about DNC Provisions in TSR." Federal Trade Commission. https://www.ftc.gov/tips-advice/business-center/guidance/qa-telemarketers-sellers-about-dnc-provisions-tsr (accessed June 6, 2015)

27.) "Presenting 4 Success" *iSpeak*.
http://ispeak.com/tools/Presenting4Success%20Booklet%20v1.3.pdf (accessed June 6, 2015)

28.) "Recording Phone Calls and Conversations." *Digital Media Law Project*, 2015. http://www.dmlp.org/legal-guide/recording-phone-calls-and-conversations (accessed June 6, 2015)

29.) FindLaw, 2014. "Understanding Today's Legal Consumer." *Slideshare*. http://www.slideshare.net/Find-LawLawyerMarketing/findlaw-2014-us-consumer-legal-needs-survey-37061283 (accessed June 6, 2015)

30.) Joe Girard with Stanley H. Brown, 2005. *How to Sell Anything to Anybody*. New York: FIRESIDE

31.) "Facts & Stats: Mobile Marketing." *CMO Council*.
https://www.cmocouncil.org/facts-stats-categories.php?view=all&category=mobile-marketing (accessed June 6, 2015)

32.) "Why It Matters: Bad Results Hurt and Good Results Help." *BrandYourself*.
https://brandyourself.com/info/about/whyCare (accessed June 6, 2015)

33.) Tyler Lessard, 2014. "2015 Will Be the Year of Video Marketing." *Marketing Profs*.
http://www.marketingprofs.com/articles/2014/26719/2015-will-be-the-year-of-video-marketingrates (accessed June 6, 2015)

34.) Jess Maria. "45 Video Marketing Statistics." *Virtuets*. http://www.virtuets.com/45-video-marketing-statistics/ (accessed June 6, 2015)

35.) Jess Denham. "Tangerine: The Sundance Film Festival Trans Movie Shot Entirely on an iPhone 5s." *The Independent*. http://www.independent.co.uk/arts-entertainment/films/news/tangerine-the-sundance-film-festival-trans-movie-shot-entirely-on-an-iphone-5s-10013900.html (accessed June 6, 2015)

36.) The CMO Survey, 2014. "CMO Survey Report: Highlights and Insights." *Slideshare*. http://www.slideshare.net/christinemoorman/the-cmo-survey-report-febraury-2014-highlights-and-insights (accessed June 6, 2015)

37.) Ben Reed, 2015. "When sales thinks marketing is useless—and what to do about it." *Pitchmaps*. http://pitchmaps.com/when-sales-thinks-marketing-is-useless/ (accessed June 6, 2015)

38.) Barbara Giamanco, 2014. "Is Your Message Targeted?" *Barbara Giamanco*. http://barbaragiamanco.com/is-your-message-targeted/ (accessed June 6, 2015)

39.) Dental News, 2005. "They Didn't Teach This In Dental School." *Dentaltown*. http://www.1800dentist.com/they-didnt-teach-this-in-dental-school (accessed June 6, 2015)

NOTES

NOTES

NOTES

RESOURCES

. . .

The following resources are mentioned throughout the book. These resources along with the tables and charts found in the print version of this book can be downloaded at
www.TheSuccessfulSalesManager.com
(from the "Tools" menu).

ABC COMPANY MARKETING PLAN (EXAMPLE)

The goal of this marketing plan is to firmly establish (Your business name here) as the industry leader in providing _____ services to the _____ area. We plan to accomplish this objective by establishing, growing, and positioning our business into the recognized industry expert within the _____ area by helping our customers achieve the following key benefits: _____from our services.

ABC Company will target _____(Target Client Profile here)_____ who are located in the following geographic markets: _____. Our company's specialty (or niche) is to provide our target customers with: _____.

ABC Company Marketing Mix (Example)

	Advertising Medium	Frequency	Reach	Resources Needed
1.)	Pay-Per-Click (PPC)	Daily	Based on prospective customer demographics based on targeted keywords, GEO, etc.	Vendor/s (name here) or Internal administrator who can provide weekly performance reports.
2.)	Online Advertising	Daily	Based on targeted industry directories, social media, etc.	Internal / external administrator to target, fulfill, and track all online advertising on a weekly basis with status reports provided.
3.)	Website	Daily	Based on SEO for maximum targeted visibility and maximum conversion	Vendor/s (name here)
4.)	Blog & Social Media	Weekly (M,T,TH)	Based on current and former clients / leads and social media audience.	Vendor/s (name here)
5.)	Content Marketing	Weekly	Based on current and former clients / leads, trade publications and social media audience.	Internal / external content writers and administrator assistant to handle all content syndication processes.
6.)	TV Advertising	Daily	Based on targeted and measured in Cost-Per-Thousand People reached (CPM)	Vendor/s (name here) and internal administrator who can receive / produce recurring performance reports.
7.)	Radio Advertising	Daily	Based on targeted and measured in Cost-Per-Thousand People reached (CPM)	Vendor/s (name here) and internal administrator who can receive / produce recurring performance reports.
8.)	Billboards	Monthly	Based on targeted GEO / location	Vendor/s (name here) and internal administrator who can receive / produce recurring performance reports
9.)	Lead Generation	Daily	Based on all leads received by sales, phone, email, etc.	Vendor/s (name here) and internal administrator who can receive / produce recurring performance reports
10.)	Cold Calling	Daily	Based on all / targeted prospects, new leads based on lead conversion schedule, pre and post event follow-ups	Internal / external callers along with a sales/CRM system to manage all customer interactions.
11.)	Email Marketing	Weekly / Monthly (newsletter)	Based on current leads and customers, former leads and customers, prospects with email addresses	e-newsletter system / production vendor (name here), internal emailing resources based on leads and event schedules, etc.
12.)	Direct Mail	Bi-Weekly / Daily (Leads)	Based on each new lead received (following a lead conversion schedule), targeted prospect lists and event driven mailings	Vendor/s (name here) for production and distribution. Also internal resources to mail based on lead conversion schedule.
13.)	Trade Shows	Monthly (based on shows)	Based on targeted Trade Shows (Prospective customers and referrals)	Internal trade show administrative assistant and resources / people to schedule for shows.
14.)	Public Speaking	Monthly	Based on targeted Trade Groups (Prospective customers and referrals)	Internal speech writing and administrative scheduling assistant for events.
15.)	Conversion	Daily	Based on each new lead received (following a lead conversion schedule)	Internal Lead Conversion Schedule and administrator to carry out hourly/daily steps, CRM systems and/or a lead management automation system.

Download Spreadsheet: TheSuccessfulSalesManager.com ("Tools" Section) ©TheSuccessfulSalesManager.com

We plan to use the following marketing tools and mediums to support these objectives:

(Your company name here) will have a reputation for providing

_____. The initial marketing budget will be

___(X) ___ percent of our budgeted annual billings, which works out

to a marketing budget of $_____ per month and $_____ for

the year. All marketing functions will fall under the responsibility of

_____ and results will be reported to

_____ on a _____ basis. Other necessary

resources needed to fully execute on this marketing strategy will include_____.

Key Performance Indicators (KPIs) for marketing will include:

- At least a **3 to 1 (300 percent)** Return on Investment (ROI).
- A Lead-Conversion-Rate (LCR) of at least **20 percent.**
- A Cost-Per-Lead (CPL) of **$100 or less.**
- A Customer-Acquisition-Cost (CAC) of no more than **$450 per customer.**
- At least a **25 percent** Return on Marketing Investment (ROMI).
- Monthly and annual new sales objectives: $_____/ _____.
- Targeted annual customer retention rate of at least: _____percent.
- Targeted customer referrals of at least ___percent of sales.
- . . .

Services Provided and Pricing to our customers will include:

- ...
- ...
- Etc.

Key Messages about our services provided will include:

- ...
- ...
- Etc.

SWOT Analysis:

- Strengths:
- Weaknesses:
- Opportunities:
- Threats:

MARKETING BUDGET AND TOOLS
(SEE FOLLOWING PERFORMANCE REPORT)

ABC Company Marketing Performance Report (Example)

	Advertising Medium	Spend (Cost)	New Leads	New Customers	Total New Customer Revenue	Average Revenue Per Customer	New Sales Profit Margin	Net New Gross Profit (Margin)	Lead-Conversion-Rate (LCR)	Cost-Per-Lead (CPL)	Customer-Acquisition-Cost (CAC)	Return-On-Investment (ROI)	Return-On-Marketing Investment (ROMI)
1.)	Pay-Per-Click (PPC)	$1,500	9	2	$4,500	$2,250	33%	$1,485	22.22%	$166.67	$750.00	200.0%	1.0%
2.)	Online Advertising	$1,200	14	4	$6,500	$1,625	33%	$2,145	28.57%	$85.71	$300.00	441.7%	78.8%
3.)	Website	$900	32	8	$7,500	$938	33%	$2,475	25.00%	$28.13	$112.50	733.3%	175.0%
4.)	Blog & Social Media	$300	2	1	$2,800	$2,800	33%	$924	50.00%	$150.00	$300.00	833.3%	208.0%
5.)	Content Marketing	$800	2	1	$9,200	$9,200	33%	$3,036	25.00%	$200.00	$800.00	1050.0%	279.5%
6.)	TV Advertising	$3,000	4	1	$4,200	$4,200	33%	$1,386	33.33%	$1,000.00	$3,000.00	40.0%	-53.8%
7.)	Radio Advertising	$800	0	0	$0	$0	33%	$0	0.00%	NA	NA	-100.0%	-100.0%
8.)	Billboards	$1,000	4	1	$6,000	$6,000	33%	$1,980	25.00%	$250.00	$1,000.00	500.0%	98.0%
9.)	Lead Generation	$1,200	12	2	$9,200	$4,600	33%	$3,036	16.67%	$100.00	$600.00	666.7%	153.0%
10.)	Cold Calling	$1,200	4	2	$3,800	$1,900	33%	$1,254	50.00%	$300.00	$600.00	216.7%	4.5%
11.)	Email Marketing	$400	22	11	$3,300	$300	33%	$1,089	50.00%	$18.18	$36.36	725.0%	172.3%
12.)	Direct Mail	$1,400	23	2	$4,500	$2,250	33%	$1,485	8.70%	$60.87	$700.00	221.4%	6.1%
13.)	Trade Shows	$4,500	42	2	$8,200	$4,100	33%	$2,706	4.76%	$107.14	$2,250.00	82.2%	-39.9%
14.)	Public Speaking	$240	35	6	$7,800	$1,300	33%	$2,574	17.14%	$6.86	$40.00	3150.0%	972.5%
	Totals (All):	$18,440	206	43	$77,500	$2,962	33%	$25,575	20.87%	$89.51	$428.84	320.3%	38.7%

Download Spreadsheet: TheSuccessfulSalesManager.com ("Tools" Section)

©TheSuccessfulSalesManager.com

MARKETING TIMELINE (BY MONTH):

Monthly Marketing Calender (Example)

Sunday	Monday	Tuesday	Wednesday	Thursday	Friday	Saturday
1	2	3 Publish Article - To Trade Journal	4 Make Cold Calls - 8am-10am & 4pm-5pm Blog Post 9am	5 Publish Monthly Email Newsletter 8am-10am Make Cold Calls - 8am-10am & 4pm-5pm Blog Post 9am	6 Shoot Two 30 Second Marketing Videos	7
8 Blog Post 9am	9 Send Out Mailing (for Wednesday Arrival) Blog Post 9am	10 Blog Post 9am	11 Make Cold Calls On Newsletter Email Data: Clicks, Opens, Video 8am-10am & 4pm-5pm	12 Place Follow-Up Calls, Emails, And/Or Texts To Mailing Recipients 8am-10am & 4pm-5pm Blog Post 9am	13	14
15 Blog Post 9am	16 Email Upcoming Trade Show Attendees 10am Blog Post 9am	17 Publish Press Release Blog Post 9am	18 Make Cold Calls - 8am-10am & 4pm-5pm	19 Attend Trade Show Blog Post 9am	20 Follow-Up On Trade Show Attendees by Calls / Emails / Texts 8am-10am	21
22 Blog Post 9am	23 Send Direct Mail Blog Post 9am	24 Email Customer RSVP About Friday's Event At 9am Blog Post 9am	25 Email Customer RSVP About Friday's Event At 3pm Make Cold Calls - 8am-10am & 4pm-5pm	26 Place Follow-Up Calls To Mailing Recipients 8am-10am & 4pm-5pm Blog Post 9am	27 Host Customer Event	28
29	30	31	1 10am Email Upcoming Speech Attendees Make Cold Calls - 8am-10am & 4pm-5pm	2 Publish Monthly Email Newsletter 8am-10am Blog Post 9am Make Cold Calls - 8am-10am & 4pm-5pm	3	4 Speak At Conference
5 Blog Post 9am	6 Send Out Mailing (for Wednesday Arrival) Blog Post 9am	7 Publish Article - To Trade Journal Blog Post 9am	8 Make Cold Calls On Newsletter Email Data: Clicks, Opens, Video 8am-10am & 4pm-5pm	9 Place Follow-Up Calls, Emails, And/Or Texts To Mailing Recipients 8am-10am & 4pm-5pm Blog Post 9am	10	11

NEW LEAD CONVERSION PROCESS:

New Lead Conversion Schedule

Days from Receipt of new lead:	Day 1	Day 4	Day 5	Day 6	Day 8	Day 14	Day 15	Day 22	Total Attempts
Actions									
Phone Call	1.) Immediately 2.) 30-60 Minutes 3.) 1-2 Hours		4.) Between 4pm-5pm			5.) Between 4pm-5pm	6.) Between 8am-10am		6
Email	1.) 0-15 Minutes	2.) Between 8am-10am			3.) Between 5am-8am		4.) Between 8am-10am	5.) at 3pm	5
Text	1.) 15-30 Minutes	2.) Between 4pm-5pm			3.) Between 5am-8am		4.) Between 8am-10am	5.) at 3pm	5
Mailing	1.) 3+ Hours if no contact is made			2.) Again if no contact is made					2

Total Combined Attempts To Contact: __18__

©TheSuccessfulSalesManager.com

Notes:
Actions in the process continue until contact is made and qualified upon which time the process can stop
The best time to **call** is commonly between 8am-10am, and 4pm-5pm each day
The best time to **email** is early in the morning before people start their work
The **best days** to reach somebody are Thursday & Wednesdays with Tuesday being the worst
If no response received after all attempts, add to monthly **drip-marketing** email/mail list
Make sure your messages include a **reason for your contact** and a **sense of urgency (deadline)** to call you back
This schedule is just a starting point and can be modified to best fit the business, market, and leads

SALES CLIENT MEETING GUIDE

(EXAMPLE)

(Use/take with you during sales appointments)

Date:

Company Name:

Meeting Contact Names *(Get Biz Card*

_____   _____

_____   _____

_____   _____

OPENING (ASK QUESTIONS ABOUT THEIR BUSINESS AND GOALS):

"Before we begin, I would like to learn more about your business, goals, needs, etc."

➢ Number of employees: _____

➢ Where (GEOs) do you sell?: _____

➢ Who are your Target Clients?: _____

➢ Out of 100 percent, what capacity is your business running at today?: _____ percent

WHEN CONSIDERING OUR PRODUCTS/SERVICES...

➢ **What problems are you trying to solve?**

o _____ *Impacts:* _____

o _____ *Impacts:* _____

o _____ *Impacts:* _____

o _____ *Impacts:* _____

o _____ *Impacts:* _____

➤ What are you trying to gain/achieve?

o _____ *Impacts:* _____

o _____ *Impacts:* _____

o _____ *Impacts:* _____

o _____ *Impacts:* _____

o _____ *Impacts:* _____

How and/or what do you currently use to manage this problem/opportunity today? What do you spend on it?

o_____ $ _____

o_____ $ _____

o_____ $ _____

Total $ (Monthly): _____

➤ Goals for the business ("If I were to come back here three years from now and you had everything you needed, how would things be different?")

o _____

o _____

o   _____

o   _____

➢ How are purchasing decisions like this typically made in your business?

_____

KEY QUESTION: HOW ARE YOUR CURRENT SYSTEMS AND PROCESSES SUPPORTING YOUR GOALS?

➢ Proposed products/services needed (Initial estimate for proposal):

o   _____

•   _____

•   _____

•   _____

•   _____

•   _____

➢ Next steps / Action items in process:

o   _____

o   _____

o   _____

SALES DAILY CHECKLIST

(EXAMPLE)

Date: _____

Sales Activities:

❏ **2–3 sales meetings** (existing and new clients)

❏ **Cold Call** 40–60 new sales prospects

❏ **Drop in** 6–8 new sales prospects (in area of daily appointments)

❏ **Email** 20–30 new sales prospects

Prospecting Activities:

❏ Schedule lunch/breakfast referral meetings (with customers) for the next day

❏ **Follow-up** call on the previous day's emails sent & drop ins

❏ Schedule at least 3–4 **additional appointments**

❏ **Map out** your sales meetings and drop-in locations for next day

Weekly Close Targets: 1–3 sales (list targets below):

❏ _____Mtg Date:_____

❏ _____Mtg Date:_____

❏ _____Mtg Date:_____

ABOUT THE AUTHOR

. . .

Dustin Ruge is a published author and an award-winning sales and marketing professional with over twenty years of successful sales and sales management experience. Dustin's experience in sales, marketing, and business strategy ranges from technology startups to Fortune 500 companies. Dustin has been referenced in such publications as *Inc.* magazine and is a frequent speaker at professional conferences across the nation.

Working in sales and marketing from startups to many corporate industry giants has provided Dustin with unique insight into the opportunities and challenges faced by sales and marketing organizations today.

How to follow and/or connect with Dustin:

Book Website: http://www.TheTop20Percent.com

Website:
http://www.TheSuccessfulSalesManager.com

Facebook: https://www.facebook.com/thesuccessfulsales-manager

LinkedIn Page: https://www.linkedin.com/company/the-successful-sales-manager

Google+: https://plus.google.com/+Thesuccessfulsales-manager/

Twitter: https://twitter.com/TopSalesResults